BEATING THE
COLLEGE BLUES
SECOND EDITION

Paul A. Grayson, Ph.D.
Philip W. Meilman, Ph.D.

Checkmark Books™
An imprint of Facts On File, Inc.

Beating the College Blues, Second Edition

Copyright © 1992, 1999 by Paul A. Grayson, Ph.D. and Philip W. Meilman, Ph.D.

Checkmark Books
An Imprint of Facts On File, Inc.
11 Penn Plaza
New York NY 10001

Library of Congress Cataloging-in-Publication Data
Grayson, Paul A.
Beating the college blues / Paul A. Grayson and Philip W. Meilman. — 2nd ed.
p. cm
Includes bibliographical references (p.) and index.
ISBN 0-8160-3985-2. — ISBN 0-8160-3986-0 (alk. paper)
1. College students—United States—Psychology. 2. Stress (Psychology) 3. Adjustment (Psychology) I. Title.
LA229.G74 1999
378.1'98—dc21 99-13230

Checkmark Books are available at special discounts when purchased in bulk quantities for businesses, associations, institutions or sales promotions. Please call our Special Sales Department in New York at (212) 967-8800 or (800) 322-8755.

You can find Facts On File on the World Wide Web at http://www.factsonfile.com

Text design by Donna Sinisgalli

Printed in the United States of America

MP SW 10 9 8 7 6 5 4 3 2 1
(PBK) 10 9 8 7 6 5 4 3 2 1

This book is printed on acid-free paper.

CONTENTS

Note to Readers iv

Acknowledgments iv

Introduction v

1. Getting Started and Fitting In 1

2. Your Studies 22

3. Feeling Down and Getting Back Up 46

4. Dealing with Anxiety, Indecision, Anger and Stress 68

5. Coping with Your Family 86

6. How to Survive Falling in Love 106

7. Sex 126

8. Sexual Harassment and Rape 156

9. Alcohol and Other Temptations 164

10. Eating Issues 180

11. Is Counseling for You? 193

12. Is There Life after College? 203

Appendix 1: Sources of Help on Campus 213

Appendix 2: National Sources of Help 216

References 221

Index 228

NOTE TO READERS

This book is intended as a general guide. While every effort has been made to ensure the accuracy of the information included here, the reader should consult qualified professionals for answers regarding specific situations. Neither the publisher nor the authors are engaged in rendering psychological, psychiatric, medical or legal services to the reader. If such expert assistance is required, the services of a competent professional, with knowledge of the reader's situation, should be sought.

ACKNOWLEDGMENTS

We are most grateful to our editor, Jim Chambers, for inviting us to revise this book. As always, Bob Silverstein, our agent, has offered supportive and wise counsel.

A number of persons read early drafts of chapters and made suggestions that considerably strengthened the manuscript. On the NYU side, our thanks go to Jane Bogart (but lose that red pencil), Mary Commerford, Keith Jepsen, Phil Johnson, Julie Lichtstein, Reji Mathew-Benjamin and Trudy Steinfeld. Cornell readers were Roz Kenworthy, Kate McCann and Bob Mendola. We also wish to thank the many people who made contributions to the first edition and whose influence is still reflected in these pages.

Finally, once again we especially wish to express our appreciation to our college student clients. After 20 years for each of us in the college counseling business, we feel no less privileged to be college counselors, no less fascinated and gratified by our work, than when we first started.

INTRODUCTION

If you are a college student or are about to become one, some problems are troubling you. How do we know? Student life is far too challenging and complex for it to be otherwise. Possibly you haven't voiced your concerns to anyone, because you think they sound silly or are embarrassing. The concerns may be about shyness, a failed relationship, procrastination, sexual feelings, a drinking problem or your parents' divorce. In *Beating the College Blues*, you will find discussions about hundreds of problems that privately trouble college students.

The questions in this book have been culled from our combined professional experience counseling more than 6,000 students at a half-dozen colleges and universities. As you will see, the topics range over many categories. Not only are students diverse, so are their problems. So you are not the only one to experience certain fears or doubts, to have certain self-defeating habits, to harbor certain painful memories. Whatever is troubling you—even if it doesn't appear in these pages—rest assured that other college students are secretly struggling along with you.

In the responses to the questions, you will find three main features. First, there is basic information about the problem—definitions, distinguishing features and signs of difficulty. For example, you will learn the difference between depression and sadness, the different types of depression and the signs of being depressed. Such information can help you view your concerns with perspective, cutting exaggerated fears down to size while opening your eyes to problems you may have underestimated.

Second, you will read suggestions for coping with problems. In some cases we suggest actions to take; in others we propose fresh ways of thinking about problems. Of course, these are not in-depth solutions, they're not tailored to your personality or circumstances, and they're no substitute for personal counseling. These are quick "self-help" remedies, which can't possibly do justice to the complexity of you and your problems. Still, our experience is that sometimes a tip or two can show the way out when someone feels stuck on a problem. These suggestions, though not panaceas, are reasonable first steps to take if you want to try to solve problems on your own.

What if you follow the suggestions and they don't work, or if trying them seems easier said than done? In that case, professional assistance may be required. The third feature of this volume is information about counseling (see especially Chapter 11). The general commonsense advice running like a refrain throughout these pages is to seek professional help for a problem whenever your own efforts aren't achieving results.

This book is about problems, but it's not written in a pessimistic spirit. We know from experience that college students' problems are not trivial, but we have also learned that college students are blessed with resources to work on problems. Consider your assets. Unlike earlier years, you've matured to the point where you can reflect on problems, discover motives and recognize patterns of behavior. Your family also doesn't control your life as it did before. You're freer now to try out new ways of thinking and relating, to become your own person. Yet while you're old enough to think and act for yourself, you are also still young, with a future rich in possibilities. Unlike later years, you are a work in progress, your personality still developing, your life choices still waiting to be made. In a nutshell, you can change.

With these advantages, you are at an ideal age while at college to tackle personal concerns. The progress you make now will carry over for the rest of your life. We hope this book is a guide that helps point you in the right direction.

GETTING STARTED
AND FITTING IN

So now you've arrived at college and you just love it, right? Well, not necessarily. As exciting and liberating as college can be, the initial adjustment isn't always smooth. The first few days in particular can be a dizzy blur of new faces, strange buildings and waiting on endless lines; don't be surprised if you daydream about packing up and hopping the first plane or bus back home. Then there's the roommate issue. Perhaps you lucked out and are matched with a kindred spirit. But if you're not so lucky, even if you're paired with someone you normally wouldn't speak to, you still have to work out living with this person, as if in an arranged marriage. Meanwhile, another task is to find your niche in the college community and adapt to the bustling social scene. Other students are everywhere, yet it can be hard to make friends and develop a sense of belonging. If you're from a minority group, the social challenges are that much greater.

Going off to college is one of the major transitions of a lifetime. In later chapters we discuss academics, families and other aspects of this transition. Here we focus on what it's like to get started at school and how you can find your way socially.

FIRST DAYS

Q: I just got here and I'm afraid I'm going to lose it. What can I do to make this easier?

A: For starters, be patient with yourself. If you're scared now and in the first days after arrival, so are half your classmates. Feelings of anxiety, loneliness and disorientation are typical for new students—that's why colleges conduct orientation programs. So expect these feelings, and comfort yourself when you have them. Don't be self-critical if in the beginning, life at college feels difficult.

1

Here are suggestions for making the first few days easier:

- **Think back to previous major transitions.** Remember when your family moved or you started high school? Remind yourself that at first the going was bumpy then too. You made it, though, and you can make it now.
- **Use familiar coping devices.** What works for you during times of stress? Long walks? Music? Writing in your journal? Working out? Phone calls to old friends? Employ your usual coping methods to make it through these trying times.
- **Organize your room (or your half of it) the way you like it—** arrange your desk, put up posters, display photographs, buy a plant. This will give you a reassuring feeling of being in control, of bringing order and familiarity into your new home.
- **Familiarize yourself with the campus and the neighboring community.** Stop in at the library, bookstore, gym, student center and major classroom buildings, as well as banks, drugstores, movie theaters and pizza parlors. The sooner you know your way around, the sooner you'll feel at home.
- **Make social connections right from the start.** Make sure to join your roommate or the people next door for dinner, and visit the students you met during orientation. An early sense of belonging, of knowing people, will make the transition much easier.

Q: After three weeks here, I'm still miserable and I want to go home. Is this a bad decision?

A: At this point, it probably is. If you still feel this way weeks and months from now, then by all means consider leaving school. There's no point banging your head against the wall and subjecting yourself to prolonged suffering. But homesickness and unhappiness often ease up after a while. It would be a pity to give up during the predictably rough beginning when it's quite possible your outlook will brighten before very long.

Q: Why do I feel so unhappy?

A: There are many reasons. You may feel shy around your classmates and despair of making friends. New classes, academic requirements and the sheer size of the college may seem intimidating, and you may feel lost with the relative lack of structure, unsure how to manage being on your own so much of the time. You may miss your family, your high school friends, your dog, your own bedroom, your car, your hometown. Your family may likewise miss you and subtly signal for you to return—or, equally bad, they may seem to have forgotten about you.

As if any of these reasons weren't enough, you may feel embarrassed and ashamed of your feelings, as if homesickness were only for children (it isn't). Embarrassment and shame only make matters worse and reinforce your urge to go home.

Q: What should I do if I'm so unhappy?

A: Very often all you have to do is hang on, because the roughest part may end within a few weeks. By then you may have made a friend, survived your first test or become excited about an extracurricular activity, and you'd hate the thought of leaving college. In the meantime, get as much support from home as you need. Going to college needn't be a radical break from family and friends. It's okay to call, exchange letters and plan weekend visits. With backing from home you may feel encouraged to throw yourself into college.

On the other hand, not everyone is ready to go away to college or chooses the right college to attend. So if your spirits don't brighten by, say, the midpoint of the term, discuss options with your family and perhaps a counselor. Next term it may make sense to go on leave or transfer to another college, possibly one where you can live at home. There's nothing shameful about taking one of these steps. The important thing is to do what's best for you.

If your reaction to college is extreme—if you are feeling suicidal or are unable to study or carry out other responsibilities—this decision shouldn't wait. Speak to your parents and a counselor about the pros and cons of leaving college right away.

Q: How do I get a good night's sleep around here?

A: It isn't easy. For one thing, dormitory life is remarkably noisy. If you're lucky enough to go to bed without an electric guitar wailing

or a fire alarm going off, then expect to be awakened at dawn by an alarm clock or your roommate doing exercises.

But noise is only one factor. You also may lie awake at night because of stress and worry, depression, poor sleep habits or physical problems. Fortunately, losing sleep isn't dangerous, and for a short while it shouldn't hurt you in class or on tests. While prolonged sleep loss does dull performance (and too many all-nighters are a bad idea), you can probably work up to capacity after a night or two of tossing and turning.

Here are suggestions to help you sleep:

- **Don't panic about losing sleep.** Worrying about sleep loss only keeps you awake. Instead of thinking "this is terrible" and "I must get to sleep!" and frantically checking the clock every 10 minutes, remind yourself that you can perform fine tomorrow even if you don't sleep a wink tonight.
- **Keep regular sleep habits.** Wake up at roughly the same time each morning, and go to bed at roughly the same time each night. Avoid oversleeping the next day after a poor night's sleep. This way you train yourself to fall asleep at a set time each night.
- **Avoid taking afternoon naps**—unless for some reason they help you sleep at night.
- **Drugs:** Stay away from sleeping pills (after a few days they make insomnia worse) and don't do street drugs. In the afternoon or evening, abstain from alcohol, coffee, caffeinated soft drinks, chocolate and smoking.
- **Exercise:** Stay active and exercise during the day, but don't exercise at night.
- **Eating:** Try not to eat heavily before bedtime. A light snack may help you fall asleep, however.
- **Use your bed for sleeping**—not for reading, watching TV or writing. The bed is then associated with falling asleep rather than wakeful activity.
- **Worry time:** Make time early in the evening to think about worries and plans rather than saving heavy thinking for bedtime.
- **Don't force yourself to sleep.** If you can't fall asleep, get up, do something relaxing and try again later when you're drowsy.
- **Mask noise:** Buy earplugs, or use a white noise machine.
- **And if these methods don't work:** If after a week you still can't sleep well, perhaps the cause is psychological or medical. Consider making appointments at your college's counseling center and health center.

Q: At home I never had to do the laundry or make the bed. How do I learn things like this now?

A: Well, we're not talking about organic chemistry here. If you're smart enough to get into college, you should be able to decipher the mysteries of the washing machine and the hospital corner. The biggest hurdle to overcome will be your embarrassment at having to ask. See if your roommate, RA (resident assistant) or a friend can give you a crash course on laundry and such, or go home for a weekend and have your parents teach you. If you need to, have them also explain the basics of ironing, dry cleaning, cooking, shopping, balancing a checkbook and cleaning up in the kitchen and bathroom.

ROOMMATES

Q: I've never shared a room with anyone before.

A: Then you're in for an adjustment. You and your roommate will have to work out when the lights go out, when music plays, how to clean up common areas and who gets to make the next phone call. Compromise is the watchword. Everything you're accustomed to deciding for yourself is now a matter for mutual concessions and agreement. Prepare also for a loss of privacy. No longer can you retreat to your room and escape the entire world.

Lest all this sounds too discouraging, consider that living with a roommate is good practice for sharing a life with other people in the future. And if you're at all lucky, having a roommate provides a ready-made companion and a friend.

Q: My roommate borrowed my CDs without asking and always leaves dirty dishes in the sink. How do I approach him about this?

A: The best way is the direct way. Mention the CDs and the dirty dishes, and ask that he get your permission before borrowing your things and clean up after himself in the kitchen.

Your effectiveness with this message will depend on how assertively you deliver it. Try not to sound meek and apologetic, because then he may dismiss your concerns. But try not to sound blaming and angry either, as if he's a horrible person; that will make him defensive. In both your choice of words and tone of voice, strive to come across as one friendly, reasonable adult talking to another friendly, reasonable adult. You have something important you want to say, and you assume he'll listen.

While stating your case, make sure also to listen to your roommate and respect his point of view. Maybe you've been doing some pretty irritating things yourself that have been driving him crazy. By listening nondefensively as well as talking assertively, you create a climate for resolving conflicts.

Some colleges encourage roommates to write up a contract at the beginning of the term spelling out living arrangements. Agreements are drawn up about sharing things, cleaning up, the use of drugs, alcohol and tobacco and having overnight guests. Even if your college doesn't have this policy, you and your roommate may want to draft your own written agreement, or at least discuss ground rules.

Q: But shouldn't my roommate know to be considerate? Why do I have to tell him or put it into a contract?

A: You can't take for granted that your roommate, or anyone else, will know what you want or do what you think he should. People aren't mind readers. To get results, you have to communicate assertively, expressing your wishes, feelings and needs and exercising your rights. And to be really successful, you should also consider other people's wishes, feelings and needs and respect their rights, because doing so inclines them to respond favorably.

Consider the alternatives to assertive communications. You could take the passive approach by complaining to your friends about your roommate but not saying a word to him, or by dropping little hints around him, giving him the cold shoulder, rolling your eyes or flashing dirty looks. You might wash his dishes yourself while muttering under your breath. These passive, indirect tactics all have one thing in common: They won't get you very far. Afterward you'll still have missing CDs, a cluttered sink and pent-up frustration.

Another strategy is to go on the attack, acting aggressively. You might call him names ("You're selfish and a slob."), threaten ("Don't do that again or else . . .") or toss in loaded side issues ("You're really a jerk with women too."). You could "borrow" something of his without telling him. You could break his dishes. These aggressive tactics might feel good for 10 minutes—you're letting out your frustration. But afterward you may feel guilty, and you'll probably have a bigger problem on your hands than just CDs and dishes, since now it'll be his turn to attack. Aggression begets aggression. Soon your room may turn into a war zone.

Remaining passive when you're upset doesn't work. Reacting aggressively is even worse. Your best bet is the assertive middle course of expressing yourself calmly, directly and reasonably while also listening to your roommate with an open mind.

Q: But when I tried talking to my roommate before about the dishes, he screamed at me. How can I stop him from yelling?

A: Possibly you can't. Friendly, calm, reasonable language usually invites a like response, but not always. Your roommate may be someone who can't stand to be confronted and automatically goes on the attack. Some people are like that.

We still think you should express your concerns. Aggressiveness shouldn't bully you into silence. But if he does attack you, it's important to know how to protect yourself. These two techniques[1] may come in handy (but use them only as a last resort):

- **Broken record technique:** Keep repeating your main point no matter what your roommate says or how loudly he says it. Don't get sidetracked by unfair criticisms, irrelevant points or baiting questions. So again and again you might say, "I want you to return my CDs and clean your dishes." There's little the attacker can do—at least verbally—against this airtight defense.
- **Strategically retreat:** Refuse to deal with your roommate while he's attacking you. Say, "We can talk about this later, when you've calmed down," or "I won't talk about this until you stop yelling at me."

Q: My roommate has this New York accent that drives me crazy. How can I let her know it bothers me?

A: We're not sure you should. While we encourage you to speak up assertively when basic needs and rights are at issue, often little annoyances are best overlooked. This is especially true when the problem is beyond your roommate's ability to change, such as the way she talks. You can't make your roommate be just what you'd like her to be. You're probably not perfect in her eyes either.

When your roommate gets on your nerves, sometimes the best medicine is to visit a friend, study in the library or spend a weekend off campus. Afterward you may be glad to see her, the annoyance forgotten. It also may help to remind yourself of the good times you've had and the interests and activities you share. Now may be the time to suggest a game of cards or to go out together to a movie.

Q: Why doesn't my roommate like me?

A: Her feelings may have less to do with you personally than with your situation. Dormitory rooms are a breeding ground for annoyances. You and your roommate are cooped up in a small living space, both of you are under considerable pressure, and under these conditions little irritations and even animosity can surface. If the two of you didn't live together, you might get along fine.

Q: But what should I do about my roommate? She never includes me when she goes out with her friends, and when she talks to me it's always in a sarcastic, condescending tone of voice.

A: Certainly speak to her about this problem, if you haven't already done so. Maybe she's upset over solvable issues—the personal questions you ask, or your smoking in the room. Once the issues are out in the open and solutions are discussed, she may soften toward you.

But if her dislike isn't based on a specific complaint—if she's made up her mind against you—then there's not much you can do. You can't force her to invite you along when she goes out. You can't write up a contract mandating her to be your friend.

What you can do, though, is insist on civil treatment. You have a right to be treated with respect, especially in your own room. If your roommate is sarcastic and condescending, speak to her about it. Point out what she's doing, and ask her to change: "Please don't make comments about my clothes. If you don't like what I wear, I'd rather not hear about it."

Sometimes roommates get along fine even though they're not friends. They work out a harmonious living arrangement while satisfying their friendship needs elsewhere. So try focusing on your ties to other people. Perhaps then you'll be less upset when she's unfriendly, she won't need to push you away, and the tension in the room may abate.

Q: I've tried everything to get along with my roommate, but it's still not working out. Now what?

A: Perhaps a third party can help. Have you asked your RA or a friend to act as a mediator? With someone else present, you and your roommate may be able to speak honestly, hear each other out and reach appropriate and acceptable agreements.

If even mediation doesn't help, the next step is a "divorce." Arrange through the housing office for a change of rooms. If you feel this needs to be done right away, explain your reasons to the housing office. If the change must be postponed until next semester, in the meantime spend time apart from your roommate. When you are together, try to make the best of a bad situation. A strained but peaceful coexistence is much better than open warfare.

FITTING IN

Q: My friend and I used to spend all our free time together, but lately she's been hanging out with a new crowd and saying she needs more time to herself. How can I get her back?

A: Are you sure you've lost her? All friendships have ups and downs, periods of more or less involvement. Your friend's recent pulling away doesn't prove your friendship is disintegrating.

Actually, one of you was due to back off sooner or later. Any inseparable, we-do-everything-together relationship is bound eventually to feel confining. When you limit yourself to one person, you do just that—limit yourself. You don't learn from other points of view, you don't express all sides of your personality and you don't feel like an autonomous person.

Q: What then should I do about my friend?

A: Give her space. Don't resent her for having other friendships. Enjoy the time she does spend with you without making a production out of the time she spends apart.

Meanwhile, try to develop other friendships. Not everyone can be your best friend or even a true friend, but many persons have something to offer: a shared interest, the same sense of humor, common experiences in your backgrounds. With more people in your life, you won't have to depend on one best friend to supply all your needs.

Q: In high school I was never one of the cool people, and it really bothered me. I thought all that would be over in college, but I see there's an "in" crowd on my hall pledging the same few fraternities. Doesn't this in-group, out-group stuff ever end?

A: No, not entirely. Whenever human beings socialize, some cluster into exclusive groups and others get left out. It's the same in employee cafeterias or health clubs or senior citizen communities. At every stage of life and in every setting, you'll find people vying to be accepted and jockeying for social position.

But, happily, the social hierarchy at college is looser than the one-party system you remember from high school. Football stars, cheerleaders and party-goers have status at college, but they're not alone at the top—or rather, there's more than one top. At most colleges there are also social sets for actors and musicians, radio jocks and computer whizzes, politicians and scholars, and an assortment of other like-minded individuals. No single group dominates the collegiate social scene. So if you don't make it with one clique, odds are you can find your place with another.

One question to ponder is your sensitivity to social rankings. Why did it bother you so in high school not to be "cool"? Perhaps as you mature and gain confidence you'll become less concerned about in crowds and social standing and won't need validation by high-ranking peers.

Q: I envy this one woman on my floor, who's got it all together. Why can't I be like her?

A: This question raises issues both about her and about you. About her, you need to understand that, impressive as she seems, there's more to her than meets your eye. She may be brilliant, poised, charismatic, beautiful—fill in your own adjectives—but for her, as for every student, there also exists an undercurrent of doubt and insecurity. Take the word of two seasoned college counselors: No college students feel, in their heart of hearts, that they've got it all together.

As for you, the issue concerns self-esteem. It's not unusual to admire a classmate, to wish you had some of her qualities. But when you elevate her above you, you correspondingly lower yourself. Envy erodes your self-respect. It would be healthier to see her and you—and everyone else—as different in particulars but fundamentally equal. Ideally, you would regard all your classmates as in some respects your superior and in other respects your inferior, but in basic human worth, no better or worse than yourself.

Q: Everyone at this college seems different from me.

A: In what way? Do you mean you're one of the few Latinos? International students? Gays? Nondrinkers? If so, then on one level maybe you're right. The very real challenges of being a member of a minority group on campus are covered at the end of this chapter and in subsequent chapters.

However, some students who say they feel "different" aren't referring to being Latino, international, gay, or whatever. These students feel *radically* different, alienated from everyone, as if there were two kinds of people on campus—themselves and everyone else. Students who harbor this core sense of differentness tend to feel like outsiders in each new situation, wherever they go. Unless given lots of reassurance, they assume people don't like them. The eminent psychoanalyst Karen Horney described this alienated mind-set as an "all-pervading feeling of being lonely and helpless in a hostile world."[2]

Feeling different can become a self-fulfilling prophecy. If you assume others are unlike you and won't accept you, your manner will be standoffish. Most people will then view you as conceited or unfriendly and won't bother with you. You make it happen that you end up alone, your sense of differentness confirmed.

Are we describing you here? If so, it's time to reevaluate. Whether or not your present college is right for you, an "everyone is different from me" attitude needs to be addressed—probably with the assistance of a professional counselor—for the sake of your future adjustment.

Q: But why should I waste my time with people here if I don't like them?

A: It may help to think of your classmates as an educational opportunity. Throughout your life, particularly in work settings, you'll be faced with all sorts of personalities, from all sorts of backgrounds. Like it or not, you're going to have to get along with them. College gives you a chance to learn how to do this. If you can figure out how to make connections here, even to deal with people you don't especially like, then you've got a head start on future success. The relationship skills you develop at college will prove as valuable as anything you learn in a textbook.

Besides, we predict that some people you initially don't take to will surprise you once you get to know them. They may even become your friends.

Q: I find it hard to resist doing what everyone else does on my hall. Is that a problem?

A: Like so much else, it depends on the degree. Conformity is a universal human phenomenon and ordinarily no cause for alarm. Doing what others do is an almost instinctive way to fit in. That's why certain expressions and hairstyles and fads sprout up on campus, and why in some circles everyone dresses so similarly that it's like a uniform. Nobody has to twist your arm to speak or act or dress that way. You follow the crowd almost automatically, because you want to belong.

Doing what your hallmates do is okay, as long as they're not up to anything self-destructive. Obviously, it's not a great idea to play copycat if that means excessive drinking or taking other drugs, or having sex when you don't really want to, or joining a cult (more about this later). When your well-being is in jeopardy, you need to have a mind of your own.

It's also not desirable to swallow ready-made values and opinions. Because you want to fit in, you may find yourself almost unthinkingly spouting your group's party line, being scrupulously politically correct, tailoring your ideas to fit the latest campus fashion. But that's not what an education is about. You are in college, after all, to learn to reason for yourself.

One suggestion to locate your own voice and keep peer influences in perspective is to write down your thoughts and experiences in a journal; this lets you make sense of the happenings in your life and draw your own conclusions. We also recommend venturing outside your social circle. You're less likely to tag along mindlessly if you expose yourself to diverse people and points of view.

Q: I find it very difficult to talk to anyone new. Why am I so shy?

A: You can blame your genes or your upbringing. Scientific studies have found that some people are genetically predisposed to be shy. Timid and passive even as toddlers, they have a biologically based tendency to retreat from unfamiliar situations. Other people become shy because of early life experiences. Bullied or teased by siblings or other children, ridiculed by parents or raised by parents who were shy themselves, they learned to be afraid of people and back away.

Does it seem that no one else is as shy as you? Don't you believe it. Most people know how to disguise social discomfort and put up a confident front, but that doesn't mean they feel inwardly relaxed. Surveys show that 40% of the population rate themselves as generally shy, while an additional 15% are shy in specific situations, such as going to parties or delivering a speech.

Q: Can I do anything about my shyness?

A: Absolutely. You may not metamorphose into the life of the party, but you can certainly come out of your shell. Here are some tips:

- **Take social risks.** Putting yourself in various social situations gives you practice that can increase your comfort level. So start a conversation with your neighbors; join a club; drag yourself to parties; take a speech class. Mingle!
- **Set small goals.** If you go to a party, plan to say hello to at least one person, to smile at somebody at least once and to stick around a full hour. Small accomplishments encourage you to continue developing social skills.
- **Focus on successes.** After an event, don't brood about the supposedly stupid things you said or the one person who snubbed you. Instead, think back to the conversation you initiated and the person who was friendly.
- **Forget yourself.** To reduce anxiety and self-consciousness during an event, pay attention to the conversation you're having, not to your performance. Socializing is like ice-skating: You can't do it fluidly if you're concentrating too much on how well you're doing.
- **Consider counseling.** Individual or especially group counseling can be helpful for shyness.

Q: When I approach people I often get shot down. What am I doing wrong?

A: It could be a number of things. Here are some basics on the fine art of making a good impression:

- **Show liking:** If you want others to like you, show you like them. Many friendships strike up primarily because one person conveys an interest in the other. To express interest, pay a compliment, ask questions about the person, suggest a get-together, be playful—anything to deliver the winning message, "I like you."
- **Listen well.** Make sure you really listen to what the other person is saying. A good listener is always welcome company.
- **Refrain from self-promotion.** Don't brag about your grades or your parents' connections, or monopolize the conversation with jokes and cleverness. The goal isn't to knock people's socks off. Let others discover for themselves what makes you worthwhile.
- **Refrain from self-belittlement.** Don't confess that nobody else likes you and that you're boring. If you refer to yourself— and too many "I" statements are tiresome anyway—do so with self-respect.
- **Don't come on too strong too fast.** Display an interest if you like someone, but don't be pushy about getting close. Let your friendships evolve naturally.
- **Try not to censor yourself.** Better to make some social gaffes— we all do—than to weigh everything you might say and rule out most of it. Conversations aren't graded like term papers. To connect with someone, simply look for common areas of interest: baseball, jazz, classes, even how you both hate small talk. Once you've found a common topic, let yourself talk freely about it.
- **Evaluate your nonverbal behavior.** Do you establish good eye contact, generally meeting someone's gaze but without staring? Do you stand appropriately close, neither crowding the person nor backing away in retreat? Do you speak clearly? Do you smile readily?
- **Pay attention to grooming and cleanliness.** There's no dress code for success in college, but that doesn't excuse you from washing your clothes, cleaning your fingernails or taking a shower. The way to make friends and influence people is not with body odor.
- **Get feedback.** Ask someone you trust to give you honest feedback on how you come across.

Q: Sooner or later, I always blow people off. Why do I do this?

A: Blowing people off affords a surge of satisfaction. For a short while, you enjoy the power of getting back at people who've hurt you and showing you don't need them. They can't fire you, you quit! Blowing people off also lets you jettison those unworthy souls who fall short of your standards. You can do better than them, you tell yourself.

But after the satisfaction fades, an empty feeling typically follows. You made your point and got rid of them—and now you're alone. For this reason, we urge you to hesitate before writing someone off. If the person is really wrong for you, by all means cut the tie. But if you're just feeling a bit disillusioned or temporarily hurt or angry or uncomfortable—and with everyone, sooner or later, these feelings come up—give the matter some thought before you toss the relationship away. The friendship may well be worth saving.

Q: How can I make friends when I'm a commuting student?

A: Some commuters do it simply by approaching people after class, at the student center or in the library. If you're not that bold, then we recommend participating in extracurricular activities. These let you meet other students naturally and can lead to binding friendships. Every college offers a full menu of possibilities: the campus newspaper and radio station; academic and career interest clubs; religious, ethnic and cultural clubs; informal theater groups; varsity and intramural athletics; fraternities and sororities; volunteer organizations; campus government; and on and on. Ask at the office of student affairs for a rundown of your campus's offerings.

GROUPS, ORGANIZATIONS AND CLUBS

Q: I don't consider myself shy one-to-one, but I'm uncomfortable in groups. Why is that?

A: Group dynamics are quite different from one-to-one interactions. When you're alone with one person, your role is assured. Whether speaking or listening, you are a participant. But in a group, the spotlight can be off you. You may not speak often or be noticed much, leaving you feeling ignored and out of it. When you do speak, it can feel strange to have everyone's eyes on you. In a group, you can never tell for sure how each individual is privately reacting to you.

Yes, groups can feel uncomfortable, but don't write them off. You'll be in many group situations in college and later in life—you simply can't escape them. It pays to learn group skills now.

One group skill is knowing how to inject yourself into the conversation. The trick is to react quickly when there's an appropriate opening, but not to interrupt anyone or hog the attention. Pay close attention to what's being said and then follow up on others' comments: "The same thing happened to me once. I was visiting this guy . . ." If someone cuts you off, don't brood and take it personally. Group discussions naturally have a disorderly, rough-and-tumble quality. Simply wait for a good moment and pipe up again.

Another group skill is reacting appropriately when you're not speaking or being spoken to. When this happens you need to remind yourself, and convey to others, that you're still very much part of the group. This you do by the quality of your listening. Show by your eye contact and body language, and by your comments when you get around to them, that you're following the exchanges. The spotlight is elsewhere, but you're still involved.

Q: I'm considering joining a fraternity. What do you think?

A: Fraternities and sororities have their good points. They provide a pool of potential friends, run parties and events you may like and give members a feeling of belonging. After you graduate, they may furnish business contacts and ongoing social connections. Additionally, in recent years many "Greeks" have raised money for charities and done volunteer work for social causes.

Yet fraternities and sororities also have a potential dark side. Many have a history of excluding blacks and Jews—not to mention the opposite sex—and in a subtler way they still exclude those who don't fit their particular image of jock, party animal or whatever. These practices raise ethical questions—are exclusionary clubs inherently discriminatory and wrong?—and they limit members' social opportunities. Diverse people attend your college, but in some social houses you may never get to know them.

Another concern is that some houses promote or at least tolerate irresponsible drinking and sexual behavior. Some subject "pledges" to hazing—physical abuse, humiliation and dangerous drinking practices—as rites of passage toward becoming members.

You are not alone in questioning the value of fraternities and sororities. Some colleges have abolished them entirely, others have pressured them to go coed and virtually all have made hazing illegal. In response to criticism, many fraternities and sororities have adopted more enlightened practices.

In making your decision, first weigh your feelings about fraternities in general, carefully considering the pros and cons we've outlined. Then if you remain interested, we suggest taking your time to investigate the particular fraternities on your campus. Each house is different, and it's critical to find one that fits your values and interests.

Q: These students who invited me to a prayer meeting now insist I stay with them all the time, even if I have class, and they're questioning my beliefs. I'm starting to feel uncomfortable.

A: Probably you should. Legitimate prayer meetings—there are many on college campuses—respect your right to think for yourself and make your own decisions. By contrast, a group that tells you how to think and behave and discourages other points of view is a cult. Cults use mind-control techniques of persuasion, pressuring you into spouting their party line, invalidating your objections, deceiving you about their true purposes and isolating you from your usual contacts. Once they've got their hooks into you, they may alienate you from family, friends and studies. All this can happen without your fully recognizing it.

Q: How can I resist being sucked in?

A: Retain a critical capacity when these people talk to you. Listen to them if you're interested, but remind yourself that no one has a monopoly on the truth. You're in college to learn from many sources, not to parrot some group's philosophy. Above all, don't let yourself be pressured. Make sure you're free to leave meetings, to decline invitations and to leave the group if it makes you feel too uncomfortable.

If in doubt about this group, discuss your concerns with an independent person you trust. Parents, a friend, a professor, a minister, priest or rabbi, or a counselor can help you sort out whether the group is a cult and, if so, help you break free.

DIVERSITY ISSUES

Q: Sometimes I find it hard on this campus to be from a racial minority.

A: We can appreciate that. As a member of a minority, you may sometimes find that your differentness influences your relationships, even if not addressed directly. People may be friendly and well intentioned but in subtle ways misunderstand you and even treat you differently. In turn, you may befriend them but still not feel wholly relaxed in their company or fully part of their world. Being a minority on campus can be like living in a foreign country. You may adjust well and fit in, but still not feel totally at home.

One interesting point, however, is that minority status is increasingly common in our pluralistic society. African Americans, Asian Americans, Latinos and Native Americans are all minorities. So, from different standpoints, are Orthodox Jews, devout Catholics, Muslims and Hindus, gay men and lesbians, international students and disabled students, and so on. If you tally all the individuals on your campus who are or feel themselves to be in the minority, you've probably formed a majority.

Are the experiences of all these groups the same? Of course not. Racial issues are quite different from issues of religion, sexuality and so forth. Still, it's worth noting that many students at college, even some who are part of the racial majority, inwardly share concerns about being different and in the minority.

Q: People look at me and think I'm like everybody else of my race. But people of my race came to the United States from different countries and cultural backgrounds. We're not all the same.

A: Each group originating from a particular country has its own identity, its own history, its own values and customs. Major differences exist, for example, between African-American students and Caribbean-American students, Japanese-American students and Chinese-American students, and Puerto Rican students and Mexican-American students. And within each group, it also makes an enormous difference when your family came to this country. If your grandparents were born in this country, you will see things much more like the mainstream student body than if you're a new arrival.

It is a truism that each of us is unique. To understand anybody, you need to factor in national/racial background, family background, gender, social class, religion, sexual orientation and perhaps a half dozen other variables. Once you've done all that, you're still only at the beginning of understanding the complexity of a particular human being.

Q: How can I know when people are treating me unfairly because of my race?

A: Sometimes there's no question about it. With luck this won't happen, but at some point in college you may encounter clearly patronizing or biased treatment, or even open expressions of hostility. A derogatory comment may be made about "you people" or slurs may be directed at your race. Such instances are blatant prejudice.

Other behaviors are unfortunate but are harder to categorize. Someone may betray ignorance about your group or assume all its members are alike. ("I thought all blacks listened to rap." "Don't Chinese people study all the time?") Such ignorance, though frustrating, may not be motivated by prejudice, which is rooted in hostility. Likewise, it's not necessarily prejudice if a professor gives you a surprisingly low grade, a classmate does not smile at you or your roommate acts selfishly. These disappointments and misunderstandings are a fact of life, regardless of one's race. Indeed, some people aren't racists but equal-opportunity pains in the neck, making life difficult for everybody regardless of race, creed or national origin.

All this confronts you with a challenge. How do you judge the intentions of someone who makes an uninformed comment about you or your race? How do you react to such comments? Learning how to interpret accurately and respond appropriately to the behavior of classmates and teachers is an ongoing struggle at college for any student from a minority racial group. On the one hand, you should be sensitive to prejudice and react accordingly, asserting your rights when necessary. Nobody has the right to mistreat you because of your race. On the other hand, it's unfortunate to be hypersensitive, confusing everyday social misunderstandings or even ignorance with racism. For your own peace of mind and to avoid misinterpreting others, it's important to be open minded about classmates and professors.

This challenge, as we say, is an ongoing process. Another challenge is to stay true to your goals even when you feel the burden of being in the minority—and even when you encounter prejudice. To bolster you during difficult times, consider joining "minority" student clubs and organizations, find out if your campus has an office specializing in minority student concerns and look into off-campus social and volunteer opportunities that involve others of your race. Faculty, graduate assistants and administrators who are the same race may also serve as mentors. These various connections can be a lifeline as you strive to pursue your goals of getting a good education, earning a college degree and having a full undergraduate experience.

Q: I like to have friends from all groups, but sometimes friends from my own race make me feel guilty for associating with outsiders.

A: While establishing connections with your own race is probably integral to your happiness at college, we believe it's also enriching to make friends with people from other backgrounds. That's one of the advantages of college. You can learn from other points of view and prepare to live in a multicultural society simply by reaching out to classmates.

Yes, it's hard to socialize with other groups if members of your own group frown on it. Perhaps you can explain that having diverse friendships is not intended as a rejection of them or of your racial identity. You want to broaden yourself, not deny who you are. If some people in your circle remain upset with you despite your explanation, maybe that's the price you have to pay to maintain a balanced social life.

Q: My parents are from two different racial backgrounds, and I don't know which one to identify with.

A: It's a special challenge establishing a sense of identity when you don't fall neatly into one of the traditional demographic categories—when, for example, your parents are Nigerian and Swedish, or Thai and Jewish, or any of the other once unlikely combinations that are now springing up in our society. Making the task even harder can be the reaction of others. In many cultures, biracial children are teased and shunned by people from both groups. Even at college, other students may seem uncertain about how to relate to you, heightening your own uncertainty about who you are.

Establishing a sense of identity is a gradual process for everyone, regardless of one's parents' backgrounds, so don't expect to work this out all at once. Your ultimate goal is to consolidate a sense of self, making room for both parents' backgrounds within a positive self-concept. In the meantime, we suggest socializing with students from both parents' backgrounds and with relatives from both sides. Doing so connects you to both your mother's and your father's heritage and helps you explore both these parts of your identity.

Q: I thought I wanted to come to the United States to study, but now that I'm here I'm very unhappy.

A: That's not surprising. Enrolling in an American college is quite a challenge if you're an international student. You are separated from family and friends and perhaps unable to visit home for many months or even years, unaccustomed to the American educational system and the American way of life in general, and perhaps burdened by English language difficulties, loneliness and financial pressures. Nevertheless you are expected to handle the same academic workload as American students. Under these circumstances, it's no wonder if you're having adjustment problems.

Too often unhappy international students suffer in silence, not knowing about or feeling uncomfortable using campus support services. Our advice to you is to take advantage of the support your campus has to offer. Visit the staff member or the office responsible for assisting international students, and attend social gatherings and support groups this person or office sponsors. Don't be afraid to ask your teachers for academic help or to approach deans and residence hall personnel for advice. Make contact, if possible, with others from your home country who live in your college community. Finally, don't hesitate to make use of your college's counseling service. Counseling may or may not be common in your own country, but in the United States it's a widely accepted resource for people who are under stress. You owe it to yourself to visit a counselor if you're unhappy.

FOR FURTHER READING

Robert E. Alberti and Michael L. Emmons, *Your Perfect Right: A Guide to Assertive Living.* San Luis Obispo, Calif.: Impact Publishers, 1995.

Philip G. Zimbardo, *Shyness: What It Is, What to Do About It.* Reading, Mass.: Addison-Wesley, 1990.

YOUR STUDIES

Studies aren't the only thing that matters for students, despite what parents may preach, but you can't ignore them either. You may be the class president, swim team captain or newspaper editor, but you still won't feel good about college if you're a bust in the classroom. Academic success means more than maintaining an acceptable grade point average. A truly successful student also enjoys learning, studies efficiently, keeps grades in perspective and makes sensible academic decisions.

This chapter proposes many straightforward remedies for academic problems. There are dozens of how-tos on organizing time, avoiding procrastination, memorizing, taking tests and much more. But study tips alone won't insure academic success. Many study problems aren't the fault of poor study skills but are due to internal conflicts, to hidden wishes, fears and resentments. Your studies suffer because you're holding yourself back, like a driver with one foot on the gas pedal and the other on the brake. So in addition to tips, this chapter delineates underlying reasons that may stand in the way of your working to full potential.

GETTING ORGANIZED

Q: Is the work at college much harder than at high school?

A: Although a few students swear college studies are a breeze (we're not sure we believe them), you will probably find college material is more challenging and abundant than you're used to. The concepts demand close concentration, and the reading load can be staggering.

Because the work is challenging, you'll need to approach it in a disciplined, organized fashion. Last-minute, haphazard study efforts that perhaps sufficed in high school won't cut it at college. Consider too that many college courses don't test your performance until the middle and the end of the term. Nobody is monitoring you; you're expected to work on your own. So to keep up on all your reading and assignments, you'd better learn how to be organized.

Q: How can I learn organizational skills?

A: Good organization depends on developing good habits. The idea is to use constructive study methods regularly until they become virtually automatic. For example, let's say you plan to study at the library every evening after dinner. Follow this plan for a few weeks, and pretty soon you won't have to think about it; after dessert your legs will practically carry you to the library. Thanks to the habit you've acquired, your evenings are now organized.

Organization also calls for use of calendars or appointment books. Many choices exist: computer calendar programs, handheld organizers or old-fashioned appointment books. Whatever product you choose, the procedure is the same. Enter into the calendar standing commitments for classes, meetings and appointments and the due dates for tests, papers and projects. This way you always know exactly where you have to be, what you have to do, and when.

Another essential organizational tool is the "to do" list. Again, it really doesn't matter whether you opt for a fancy computer program or a simple piece of scrap paper. Whichever you prefer, use the list to write down all your responsibilities—papers, homework assignments, materials to study before a test and so on. Whenever possible, break down each task into component parts. For example, rather than writing down "do history paper," divide the project into "choose topic," "research topic," "write outline," "write first draft" and "revise." Then as you finish each part of the task, cross it off the list.

Keeping a list lets you keep track of everything you have to do. Lists also help you set priorities; eyeballing the items should make clear which ones must be tackled promptly and which ones can be put off. Lists let you chart your progress too. Crossing off items shows you're making headway on your projects and motivates you to keep going.

One word of warning about calendars and lists. Make sure you really use them regularly. Make them a *habit*. The best organizational schemes are useless if they sit gathering dust on your desktop.

Q: Do you have any specific advice for getting organized during the final exam period?

A: Make out a time budget for the projects you must tackle. For example, you might set aside the first three days to prepare for one test, the next two days to prepare for another test, the following three days to write a term paper and so forth. Planning a time budget stops you from spending too much or too little time on any one project.

In planning the time budget, consider the actual time available to work. Usually you have less productive time than you realize. For example, three days to prepare for a test may seem like overkill, but it really isn't too much time once you subtract periods for sleeping, eating, bathing, traveling to and from class and so forth. So make sure you assign ample time for each project.

Q: I tried keeping a daily schedule but soon gave it up. I just can't stick to schedules.

A: Perhaps your system was too rigid and unforgiving. Time organizers should be assistants, not enslavers. If your system makes demands on your every waking minute, naturally you'll soon want to ditch it, and at the very least you'll feel like a failure if even temporarily you get off schedule.

Whatever organizational system you choose, build in flexibility. Your system should allow you to modify your plans or goof off for an hour or two. The goal is to organize your time, not control it so completely that you get fed up with the system.

PROCRASTINATION AND MOTIVATION

Q: I often fall far behind in my work, and then I feel panicky when I finally get around to it. Do you have any suggestions?

A: Students procrastinate for various reasons, ranging from poor organizational skills to low self-esteem. Whatever the root cause, once you fall behind, it's tough to get moving again because the undone work has piled up in your absence. It's intimidating to open the books when they're stacked up on the desk and you're running out of time.

The key to pulling out of procrastination, however, is precisely to get moving again—to take a small step forward. Success breeds success. Once you knock off one task, you are inspired to tackle the next and after that the next. So write down some ideas for a paper, read one chapter or do a short homework assignment. That one modest accomplishment may be the catalyst that gets you mobilized.

At the same time, be sure to speak constructively to yourself. Procrastinators discourage themselves through negative self-statements: "What's the point?" "There's too much and it's too hard." "I'll never get this done on time." "I'm too tired." In place of these downers, substitute encouraging words: "Good, I finished that." "I'm making progress." "That's something to cross off the list." One sure way to stay constructive is to focus on what you *are* doing, not what you *haven't* done.

Here's a grab bag of other tips to break the procrastination stranglehold:

- **Escapes:** Make yourself aware of your usual escapes from working—watching television, calling friends, surfing the Web, going out for a snack. Instead of automatically taking these escape routes, stop and ask yourself, "Is this what I really want to do?"
- **Time chunks:** Make use of small blocks of time. If you can read a few pages during a 20-minute period before dinner, you'll feel good about yourself and inspired to get back to work later.
- **Working conditions:** Pay attention to where and when you work best. Arrange the room and your desk just the way you like them, or find the library carrel that best suits you. Work at times when you have peak energy.
- **Pace yourself when you study.** Instead of long periods without studying followed by desperate all-nighters, try to jog along at a comfortable clip.
- **Reward yourself when you deserve it.** Before a three-hour stint of studying, promise yourself a visit to a friend when you're done.

Q: Since I've fallen behind in my assignments, I'm afraid to go to class.

A: This is a common self-defeating pattern. Since you haven't done the work, you're afraid to face your professor and classmates. And since that makes you feel further discouraged about the course, you miss more assignments, and soon you're academically paralyzed. The best way out of this vicious cycle is to face the music. At all costs, with or without completed assignments, make yourself go back to class. If you can't manage that, then make an appointment to talk to your professor, or at least send a note or an e-mail to the professor or the dean explaining your dilemma and asking for assistance.

Q: I don't feel motivated to do the work. Am I just lazy?

A: We doubt that it's pure laziness. In our opinion, inside every lazy student there's an enthusiastic learner struggling to get out. Think back to when you were a child. Weren't you eager to learn to read, to ride a bicycle, to find out about people and nature and how things work? How come you weren't too lazy to learn back then? Your innate love of learning has been stifled for some reason, but it's still there, lying dormant, waiting to be released.

There are many reasons besides laziness why you might feel unmotivated. One is lack of confidence in your abilities. If you're in doubt that you'll do well, naturally you'll lose interest in trying. And telling yourself that you're unmotivated also furnishes an excuse for poor performance. "Of course I get lousy grades," you tell yourself. "I'm sure I could be on the dean's list if I made a real effort."

Another reason for lack of motivation could be unhappiness with the field you're studying. You may not work hard at your current courses because your heart isn't in the subject matter. A battle with parents may be a factor here. Suppose they've talked you into studying engineering, but you really prefer liberal arts. Neglecting engineering classes—being "unmotivated"—is a way of protesting against their pressure.

Lack of motivation also could be due to worry about something else: a failed relationship, a family divorce, someone's illness. It could even be a signal of depression. The bottom line? There's more to motivation problems than meets the eye. If you've lost interest in your studies, you should consider consulting a counselor to ferret out what is interfering with your motivation.

READING

Q: I'm a slow reader and I don't retain what I read anyway. What do you recommend?

A: It may be that you're concentrating too much on each individual word. Maybe you even go back over words to make sure you haven't missed any. Not only does this painstaking, perfectionist approach slow you down, but you can lose the main argument this way; you miss the forest for the trees. Instead, try speeding up your pace and reading for overall comprehension, even if you miss a detail or two. You'll not only read faster but probably retain more in the bargain.

Some experts recommend breaking down the task of reading into separate steps. Here's a sample three-step system:

- **Pre-read:** Quickly skim the material, paying special attention to headings, first paragraphs within a heading and first and last sentences within a paragraph. Look over the chapter summary too. Pre-reading is like reading newspaper headlines before you read the article. You don't have the full story yet, but at least you've got the basic idea.
- **Read:** Now actually read the material, making sure as you proceed that you understand it. Key in on main points by selectively underlining critical sentences or jotting down notes in a notebook or the book margins. Don't underline or write down everything. Selective underlining or note taking helps you discriminate between the main points and peripheral material.
- **Post-reading:** Now go back and ask yourself questions about the material. If you don't understand or can't recall what you've read, briefly review the unclear sections.

The key to successful reading is actively engaging the material rather than passively plodding along from first word to last. Reading should be an interaction; you are both taking in and questioning what you read. Experiment with methods of pre-reading, reading and post-reading to see what works best for you.

TAKING NOTES

Q: What's the best way to take notes in class?

A: The trick is to decide what's important enough to write down. Recording the professor's every last syllable is not recommended, because then you're not really concentrating on what's being said or distinguishing what's important. But you have to write down the essential points or else you'll forget them. Most professors make it easy to identify essential points by putting them on the blackboard or calling attention to their significance.

Write quickly but legibly. You may find it helpful to employ symbols and abbreviations. Some examples are w/ for "with," w/o for "without," = for "equals," > for "greater than," WWI for World War One.

Also valuable are symbols or comments in the margins, whether you're writing class notes or taking notes from reading. For example, you might enter the number "3" in the margin when three points are being made, write "Q" for important quotations, write "Def" for a definition, write "?" when a point is unclear and write "!" for critical points. You can also underline or draw boxes around key points, or draw arrows to link related concepts.

Be inventive. Any abbreviation or sign that helps you make sense of the material is a plus.

Experts recommend reviewing notes regularly throughout the week and the term. That way you'll absorb the material as you go along rather than depending on heroic exertions right before the exam. Also, reviewing your notes right away alerts you if there's a topic you don't understand.

MEMORIZING

Q: What do you suggest to improve a lousy memory?

A: Is your memory really lousy or is it untrained? Many memory researchers believe that a good memory isn't an inborn capacity but a skill that can be developed. Here are some methods to strengthen your memory:

- **Put material from different sources—books, papers and classnotes—onto summary sheets.** It's much easier to memorize material condensed onto a few pages than material scattered over many sources.
- **Make sure you understand the material.** Clear understanding makes material easier to remember.
- **Organize the material into meaningful clusters or subunits.** For example, you might not be able to memorize all 50 states in random order, but you'll improve your chances if you divide them into the six New England states, five Middle Atlantic states and so forth.
- **Make an effort to remember.** An active process, memory doesn't just happen through reading or listening. You have to concentrate on remembering to commit material to memory.

- **Use mnemonic devices.** These are word or association tricks to aid memory. One trick is to arrange the first letters of a set of items into easily remembered names, nonsense words or acronyms. Experiment with mnemonic devices that work for you.
- **Question yourself on what you've learned.** Ask, "What are the six New England states?" "What are the five Middle Atlantic states?" The more you recite answers, the stronger your recall.
- **If during a test you're stuck trying to recall something, don't panic or give up.** Try to remember any part of the missing material or any related material. Once any piece comes back to you, you may be able to retrieve the rest. ("It was Connecticut, Rhode Island, . . . Oh yes, Massachusetts . . .") Also, try to visualize how the material looked on the study sheet. Being able to "see" a missing item may help you to recall it.

WRITING

Q: Do you have any advice for someone who hates writing?

A: First, practice as much as you can. Through practice you build up skills and confidence and make writing a natural activity. You may even find yourself starting to enjoy it. So sign up for courses that emphasize writing, and look for additional opportunities to write, like keeping a journal.

Efficient writing, like efficient time management or reading benefits from a plan. Here's ours:

- **First give careful thought to your topic.** Exactly what do you want to write about? Topics that are too broad or hazy are setups for failure. Equally bad are topics that don't interest you. To succeed at writing, you need to find something specific you want to write about.
- **Next, research the topic.** Take notes on what you read. While you're doing the research, jot down your ideas stimulated by the reading.
- **After the research is finished, write down or enter into the computer all the ideas you can think of to go in the paper.** Be inventive; put down everything that comes to mind. What might you possibly say—what's interesting—about this topic?
- **Next, play with these ideas.** Which ones belong together? (Draw arrows.) Which ones are primary and should go first? (Note them.)

Which ones are irrelevant and should be excluded? (Cross them out.) From this exercise you should start forming an image of your paper, like an architect's preliminary sketches of a building.

- **Continue manipulating your ideas,** starting on new sheets, until you've put together an outline. This is a step-by-step plan, from introduction to conclusion, of what you intend to convey.
- **Now, follow your outline and put down your thoughts,** section by section. This should be done quickly and fluently, without worrying about perfect expression or consistency.
- **Finally, set aside ample time for revising.** Check your draft for clarity, consistency, logic, spelling and grammar. When a section needs rewriting, try it again. It may take considerable reworking before you've got the paper pretty much as you want it, every idea snugly in place. You'll probably be quite relieved and even proud of your product and motivated to write again.

Q: Nothing I write comes out the way I want, so I usually give up in frustration.

A: Severe self-criticism is one of the major causes of writing problems. Some students can't write down two successive sentences without telling themselves "This is crap" and deleting everything. Needless to say, you can't get very far this way. It's hard enough collecting your thoughts on paper without hearing a chorus of boos in the background.

If at all possible, try to silence the critical inner voice, especially during the draft-writing phase. Strive to get something down on paper—anything! It may help as you're writing to pretend you're speaking to someone, letting words and sentences flow as they would in a conversation. If the writing isn't great, so be it. There'll be plenty of time to rework the material later, during the final, revision phase.

PARTICIPATING IN CLASS

Q: A quarter of my grade is based on class participation, but I'm terrified to raise my hand.

A: Talking in class is like standing on the proverbial high diving board. The longer you hesitate, the harder it is to jump in. Our advice is to forget about being brilliant and simply blurt something out, preferably at the beginning of the very next class. Ask a question (you

probably have some), ask the instructor to repeat a comment or state your opinion. Once you've made your speaking debut, silently congratulate yourself—you did it! Then do it again. Say something else—anything—later in that same class. Now that you've broken the ice and established yourself as a participant, it should be easier to participate from here on in.

If this doesn't do the trick, you may want to talk to a sympathetic professor about the problem. Perhaps he or she can help you make a contribution in the classroom. Also, see the information on performance anxiety (pages 71–72), which has several suggestions that also apply to class participation.

Q: In my culture we were taught to sit quietly in class and take notes. But if I say nothing in American classes I'm penalized for not participating.

A: It's true, in the United States students are expected to participate in class. Speaking up is not considered rude or a challenge to the professor's authority, as in many other countries. Rather, the assumption is that class discussions stimulate learning and demonstrate students' understanding of the material.

It's difficult to put aside a lifelong custom of polite, passive listening, but it can be done. Take the plunge and start talking in class. Eventually you may find yourself chattering away like a native of New Jersey or California.

TEST ANXIETY AND TEST TAKING

Q: Whenever I take a test I go into a panic and freeze. Are there any remedies?

A: Yes. Most likely you're psyching yourself out with negative thoughts like "I'll never be able to do this," "Oh no, I'm getting anxious again," "I can't think" and "I'm going to fail." To reduce test anxiety, instead talk to yourself in a confidence-building manner. Say to yourself, "Good. I know I got that one right," "I'm doing fine" and "This test isn't as bad as I thought." These constructive thoughts can calm you.

Test anxiety can begin long before you enter the classroom. Hours or days in advance, you may make yourself frantic by imagining all sorts of catastrophic scenarios: "Suppose I botch up this exam. Then

I'll fail this course, my academic record will be ruined, and I'll never make medical school." Challenge such thoughts, as follows: "This one test won't decide my chances for medical school." Corrective reasoning will ease pretest jitters and put you in a calmer frame of mind when you actually take the exam.

It also helps to be prepared for some rough moments during the exam. Of course you'll be anxious—who isn't?—so there's no point getting upset when it happens. You will run into questions you can't answer, so here again there's no reason for alarm.

Relaxation exercises may alleviate test anxiety before the exam (see page 84). For anxiety during the test itself, you can spend a moment taking slow, deep breaths and silently reciting the word "relax."

Q: What good are constructive thinking and relaxation techniques if I haven't studied for the test?

A: Good point. Trying to cram material the night before gives you good reason to be anxious. The best anxiety-reduction method of all is thorough studying beforehand and really knowing the material.

In studying for exams, it may help to consolidate lecture and textbook material onto summary sheets. Include on these summary sheets the course's essential points rather than every last detail. Don't just read the sheets; question yourself about them: "What were the main causes of World War I?" "What do these French verbs mean?"

Q: My grades on tests never reflect what I know.

A: Sounds like you're not test smart. There's no substitute for hard studying, but you can definitely improve your grades by knowing test-taking strategies:

- **Scan the whole test at the beginning to work out a time budget for each question.** For example, an hour's exam containing four equally weighted questions allows you roughly 15 minutes per question; an hour's exam with 60 questions allows you one minute per question. On any given item try not to spend much more time—or much less—than you've planned.
- **Read the overall directions and the exact wording of each question.** If the question asks for "two causes" or "three examples"

or wants you to "compare and contrast," make sure you provide just what's requested.

- **When you draw a blank on an item, skip it and come back to it later.** Answering the easy questions first puts you in a confident, effective frame of mind. You may also see clues or get reminders from subsequent questions that enable you to answer the ones you've skipped.
- **If there's no penalty for wrong answers, put down something for every question,** even if you're unsure of the answer. You may guess right on a multiple-choice question or get partial credit on an essay.
- **With multiple-choice questions, eliminate the obviously incorrect answers first.** Watch out for overstatements containing words like "all," "none," "always" and "never." These choices are usually—but not always—wrong.
- **Essay questions are like miniature term papers, and like papers they benefit from a plan.** First, briefly outline your answers on scrap paper. Second, write the essay. Third, check and revise it as necessary and as time allows.
- **In writing essays, make sure you're clear about what you're trying to say.** Sometimes it's helpful to explain what you will say, then say it, then summarize what you have said. After writing the essay, check and revise as time allows.
- **Don't rush to be the first person out the door.** If you go through the test quickly, put extra time to good use by going back over the exam and checking your answers.

MATH ANXIETY

Q: What do you suggest for math anxiety?

A: With math anxiety—or science, computer or language anxiety—part of the problem is a vicious cycle of fear, avoidance and more fear. You're afraid of the material and so give up; by giving up, you remain afraid of the material. Coupled with avoidance is a defeatist mind-set in which you tell yourself you can't do math and so set up failure when you do try. Another factor behind math anxiety is the cumulative nature of the material. Since each topic in math builds on preceding topics, any last-ditch attempt to catch up is bound to seem too little, too late.

Overcoming math anxiety requires a combination of steady work and self-encouragement. From the earliest days of the course, you need to read material closely, ask questions in class, attend tutoring sessions and do anything else it takes to ensure your grasp of the coursework. You need to stay on top of the material. At the same time, it's critical not to give in to self-defeating thoughts. Tell yourself you *can* do math. Keeping up throughout the course and maintaining a positive attitude can turn around math anxiety.

LEARNING DISABILITIES AND ATTENTION DEFICIT DISORDER

Q: I do fine in math and science courses, but no matter how hard I try I can't seem to succeed in writing classes or keep up with my reading.

A: Then it's possible you have a learning disability. A learning disabled person has a specific deficit in learning despite an overall normal or high IQ. Dyslexia, the most common learning disability, involves deficits in one or more of the following areas: reading, spelling, writing, speaking or listening. Other learning disabilities involve deficits in math (dyscalculia), handwriting (dysgraphia), memory for names and words (dysnomia) and fine motor skills (dyspraxia).

Dyslexia and the other learning disabilities are chronic, presumably neurological conditions—the structure and function of the brain is somehow impaired. Learning disabilities can frustrate your efforts in a class no matter how determined, motivated and intelligent you are or how well you do in other classes.

Q: I have a different problem. I daydream during lectures and I can't pay attention when I study at night.

A: Although you'd need testing to be sure, it's possible you have attention deficit disorder (ADD). The main characteristics of ADD are distractibility, inattentiveness, disorganization, forgetfulness, and confused or jumbled thinking. Often, but not always, ADD is also associated with hyperactivity (being fidgety and always needing to be on the move) and impulsivity (blurting out answers, having trouble waiting on lines, interrupting others). These symptoms, which vary from person to person, can wreak havoc on academic performance.

ADD has a lot in common with learning disabilities. Both are presumed to be caused by a neurological defect. Both can persist into adulthood. And many people have both conditions. The world isn't always fair. Imagine how hard it is to take a heavy reading course confronted with the double whammy of both dyslexia and ADD!

Q: How can I know if I have a learning disability or ADD?

A: The only way is to be assessed by a specialist. Your college may have an office that provides assessments or gives referrals for an assessment. If not, you can get a referral for off-campus testing of dyslexia by contacting the International Dyslexia Association in your state or the national office. For other learning disability referrals try the Learning Disability Association of America, and to obtain referrals for ADD testing try Children and Adults with Attention Deficit Disorder (see Appendix 2).

Testing for these conditions can be time consuming and expensive. But the advantage of testing is gaining a clearer understanding of your strengths and weaknesses, even if it turns out you have neither a learning disability nor ADD. If you are diagnosed with one of these conditions, you'll probably feel a sense of relief—there's a *reason* for your academic frustration. Then you can pursue a strategy to find help.

Q: What can my college do if I have a learning disability or ADD?

A: Once it's been documented that you have one of these disabilities, your college is obligated according to the Americans with Disabilities Act to provide an equal educational opportunity. The same holds true for students with other types of disabilities, for example, those who are in wheelchairs, have visual and hearing disabilities, or have disabling psychiatric conditions. Every college has an office or a staff person in charge of helping disabled students obtain reasonable accommodations. It's important to find out who has this responsibility on your own campus.

How can a college assist you? Tutors may be available for note taking, explaining assignments and checking papers. Courses and workshops may be offered on developing study skills. The learning disability specialist may intervene with professors to help them understand and respond to your needs, for example, making arrangements to take tests in a quiet environment or have more time to finish tests or writing assignments. Deans or department chairpersons may let you substitute alternative educational experiences for requirements you are unable to handle. In these and other ways, colleges can provide accommodations giving you a fair chance to succeed.

Q: Is there anything I can do on my own if I have a disability?

A: Yes, various compensatory strategies are appropriate depending on your particular disability. For example, you can tape-record your professor's lectures (check with the professor first). You can use a word processor with a spell check, have material read aloud to you or listen to tape-recorded textbooks. Also, experiment with the tips given earlier in this chapter for time management, motivation, note taking, memory and writing. Keeping lists, for example, can be a lifesaver for those who struggle with attention and organization difficulties.

Since having a disability can have emotional consequences such as shame, embarrassment, low self-esteem, anger or discouragement, another avenue to consider is professional counseling or a support group. Medications, for example Ritalin, may also be helpful specifically for those who have ADD.

One caution: Make sure the professional counselor or the physician who evaluates you for medication is an expert on your kind of disability. As psychologist James Lawrence Thomas points out, some professionals are uninformed or skeptical about ADD and therefore can't help someone who has that disability.[1]

ACADEMIC PROBLEMS OF DIFFERENT GROUPS

Q: Am I at a competitive disadvantage as a female student in college?

A: Unfortunately, you may be. Research studies have found that professors are more likely to remember the names of male students than of female students and to take the answers of male students more seriously. And males are quicker to participate in class discussions than females.[2]

But you don't have to play along with this unequal arrangement. You can be firm and persistent in asserting your right to be heard in class. If a professor seems to ignore or devalue you, privately point this out to him—or her!—and if that doesn't bring results, discuss the problem with the department chair.

Q: As a member of a racial minority, I feel as if everyone prejudges how I'm going to perform.

A: Unfortunately, society's racial stereotypes can seep into the classroom. If you're African American or Latino, some professors and classmates may underestimate your academic preparedness and studiousness, leaving you feeling that you must work harder than other students to prove your academic worth. If you're an Asian American, you may confront the opposite stereotype, that you're a single-minded scholar who cares only about studies and career.

Such stereotypes can be enormously hurtful. All of us deserve to be judged as individuals. Fortunately, most professors and fellow students will open their eyes once they come to know you, forming an opinion based on your actual performance and individual personality.

However others may prejudge you, it's important to remain clear about your own goals. It's not your responsibility to prove others wrong if they underestimate you. It's not your responsibility to live up to their preconceptions if they assume you'll get all A's. And it's not your responsibility to take on the burden of representing your entire race. Your responsibility is to yourself, to get a good education and have a full college experience. Others will simply have to figure out for themselves who you are.

Q: My classmates and professors don't take me seriously because I'm still learning English.

A: Here's another common stereotype. If you're struggling with the language, it's not unusual that others fail to recognize how much you know, how serious you are about studies and how much you have to contribute.

Once again, try not to let the stereotypes be a distraction from your goals. As for others' opinions, your best strategy is to apply yourself academically, reach out to those persons who are receptive and of course continue improving your language skills. Eventually, perceptive people will look beyond the language barrier and appreciate what you have to offer.

GRADES

Q: I'm a good student but I can't stop worrying about grades.

A: Some concern about grades is inevitable. After all, grades are important in your life. You need to maintain a certain grade point average (GPA) to be accepted at graduate or professional schools, to keep a financial scholarship and simply to satisfy yourself that you've mastered course material. So you should take grades seriously—up to a point.

What you shouldn't do is overvalue grades, attaching meaning to them that they don't deserve. Grades are simply estimates, nothing more, of your course performance. They are not the equivalent of an intelligence test. Still less are they a yardstick of your worth as a person. If you think about it, grades leave out most of what makes you human. There are no grades to reflect your creativity, sensitivity and judgment, no grades for your special interests, physical grace, integrity, warmth or humor. So don't fall into the trap of measuring your self-worth by the fluctuations in your grade point average.

Also, bear in mind that your entire future does not turn on whether you get a B or a B+ in French. Yes, graduate and professional schools do consider performance in college, but grades are only one among several factors that enter into their admissions decisions. In the long run, your college GPA will fade in importance. When you're a dentist, teacher, editor or sales manager some day, nobody will ask at a cocktail party what grades you made in college.

Q: But I've always had this need to be perfect, to get straight A's.

A: Aspirations are fine. By all means set goals to do well in your studies. Insisting on perfect A's, though, is a treacherous aim. Perfectionism limits you as a person and actually can sabotage your academic performance.

One trouble with perfectionism is that you may become single minded and driven in the pursuit of your goal. Like a miser who only cares about hoarding money, your attention is focused so much on your grade point average that you lose sight of whatever and whomever falls outside your narrow line of vision. Besides, you probably won't even enjoy a perfect 4.0 GPA if you get it, because the pressure will be on for a repeat performance next term. You can never relax, never pat yourself on the back when you feel driven to be the best.

When you strive to be perfect, it's difficult knowing where to draw the line. You may read course material over and over, endlessly rewrite sentences, try to memorize every fact, all because you're afraid of getting some tiny detail wrong. And since you'll never get everything just right, you're apt to be anxious and dissatisfied no matter how hard you try or how well you do.

Ironically, perfectionism can pave the way to underachievement. Since your goal is set so high, you may feel intimidated and give up studying altogether. Better not to try hard, you erroneously think, than to do your best and almost certainly fall short of perfection.

Q: But if I give up trying to be perfect, aren't I settling for mediocrity?

A: Nobody is saying you have to settle. You can still set goals and push to do your best, but the trick is to do *your* best, to compete with yourself, rather than worrying about being perfect. As long as you continue to make progress, you have reason to be pleased with yourself whether or not you're perfect. It also may help to base your goals on knowledge and skills rather than grades. You can't guarantee a particular GPA, but you certainly can set your sights on mastering new material.

You might also want to consider the loaded word *mediocrity*. Do you regard good results, or even very good results, as mediocre? We don't. In our view, there's a huge gap between conscientious work and sloppy work, between good performance and so-so performance. Something you do conscientiously and well, though not perfectly, hardly deserves to be dismissed as mediocre.

Q: No one besides me seems to work so hard to get good grades.

A: Don't be too sure. It's no fun being called a grind or a geek, and for that reason many of your classmates keep their studying a secret. They'd like you to think their good grades just materialize somehow, no effort necessary. But no one, no matter how bright, can succeed at college without hard work. You can't bluff your way through term papers and final exams merely by flashing superior intelligence. And what goes for college holds doubly for your future. Though not glamorous, effort and persistence are indispensable qualities that often separate the successes from the also-rans in life. So it's fine to work hard. Usually it's necessary.

Q: Yes, but I'm at the library 10 hours a day 7 days a week. Am I overdoing it?

A: Probably. Everything has its limits, hard work included. When you overwork, your performance eventually deteriorates. You get so weary and tired or so tense and distraught that you're unable to concentrate, and eventually you may feel burnt out and want to drop studying altogether. Completing an academic semester is like running the marathon. You have to pace yourself or else you'll never make it to the finish line.

Overstudying is a driven behavior—something you feel *compelled* to do—not unlike overeating, overspending, starving yourself or feeling compelled to drink or have casual sex. Like these other problem behaviors, it may be rooted in other issues such as low self-esteem. If you have trouble moderating your study habits, consider consulting a counselor.

CHEATING

Q: I'll never meet the deadline in my history class unless I copy my friend's paper. Everyone else cuts corners to get good grades. Why shouldn't I do it?

A: While it's not true that everyone does it, admittedly cheating—let's call it by its right name—is widespread. The usual reason students give for cheating is the pressure to get good grades, and the usual excuse is "Everyone else does it too." Cheating isn't very hard to do, whether you're copying a friend's paper or copying answers on a test. You can even cheat without realizing it. Using information in a paper without noting or citing the source is cheating; so is citing references you haven't read to pad a bibliography.

But even though cheating is fairly common and easy, it's still not in your best interest. For one thing, you might get caught. Every year on every college campus some students suffer the humiliation of being discovered, and often they wind up flunking classes or getting expelled. Second. cheating shortchanges you. When you use someone else's work rather than your own, you deprive yourself of an opportunity to learn, and if you don't learn, then what's the point of paying thousands—or tens of thousands—of dollars for college? Third, you probably won't like yourself if you cheat. Inevitably, cheating causes you to think of yourself as a cheater. No matter how strenuously you defend your actions or varnish the truth, on some level cheating chips away at your self-respect. Bottom line: It's not worth it.

FAILING

Q: I'm already on probation, and now I think I'm about to flunk out. What now?

A: Before you do anything, first see if there's a way to salvage the term. Can you drop a course? Get extra help? Take an incomplete? Get an extension? Talk to your professors and your dean before any more time goes by. Possibly you don't have to flunk out after all.

But if failing is inevitable, don't let yourself panic. There's nothing disgraceful or catastrophic in what has happened. You're not the first college student to flunk out, and you won't be the last. At least now after a long struggle you know where you stand and can get on with your life.

Your immediate task is to decide how to use your time productively after the term is over. Will you enroll at another school? Take time off to go to work? Travel? Join the military? The sooner you make sensible plans, the better you'll feel.

In planning for the future, it helps to analyze what went wrong this time. Possibly you were enrolled in a program of study or at a college too difficult for you. If so, you're wise to face up to this now rather than planning to come back later—and failing all over again. It's also possible that college itself isn't right for you; it's not for everyone. Being honest with yourself about this will enable you to make realistic career decisions that don't require a college education.

Maybe you failed because of some underlying problem. Perfectionist standards, lack of self-confidence, rebellious feelings toward your parents, an alcohol or drug problem—issues like these may be sabotaging your performance. If so, we urge going into counseling before resuming a full-time course of study. You need to understand and work through your other problems before you'll be ready to resume college.

ACADEMIC DECISIONS

Q: I'm going crazy trying to choose an academic major.

A: Then you're probably attaching too much significance to the decision. True, choosing a major is an important decision and may point toward a particular career, but it's not a lifelong commitment.

You can major in French and end up as a doctor, or major in biology and become a French teacher.

To choose a major, sample widely different kinds of courses. Ideally, you'll eventually find an area where you feel an interest and have an aptitude. Feelings are the best guide here. Do you really enjoy these courses? Would you look forward to studying these subjects in depth? If you can answer in the affirmative, then you've probably found a good major.

Q: I'm a second-term sophomore, and I want to switch my major. Should I?

A: Of course. As a sophomore you're certainly not locked into your original major. Many students change majors, sometimes more than once, in an ongoing process of discovering their academic interests. It's much better to start on a desirable new path than to trudge along in an unwanted direction.

There may be a few obstacles to overcome. When you switch to a new major, you need to work out distribution requirements—minimum course totals in the humanities, social sciences and natural sciences—to make sure you're on track for graduation. Sometimes it's necessary to take an extra term to meet the requirements for a new major. Deans or advisors can help in setting up a new program.

Our advice would be different if you were a first-term senior, because working out distribution requirements might be impossible. As a senior, your best bet is to complete your present major and then after graduation take an additional year or two of courses to pursue your new interest.

Our advice would also be different if you were contemplating, say, a *third* change of majors. This would suggest a fear of committing to one area, or a fear of finishing college. We'd suggest then that you talk this over with your advisor and perhaps a counselor.

Q: My college doesn't have the program I'm interested in. Should I consider transferring?

A: Yes. No college can meet everyone's academic needs. If your current school doesn't offer the program of your choice, then switch to another college that does.

However, transferring to another college is a big decision that shouldn't be made lightly. Suppose you were going through a personally unhappy or difficult spell or you had vague doubts about your college's suitability for you. Our suggestion then would be to take your misgivings seriously but not to transfer right away. Instead, allow time for the problem to resolve itself, and in the meantime try to gain perspective by speaking to parents, a friend, a dean, an advisor or a counselor. You also might go on leave for a term and take classes at another college that interests you.

Transferring *is* sometimes the right thing to do. But be confident about the move before you burn your bridges behind you.

Q: I only came to this college because I didn't make my top choices. I like it here now, but I'm still considering transferring to one of my original choices. What do you think?

A: We think it would help to shed light on your motives. Do you want to transfer to improve your education? Are you hoping to take advantage of intellectual and cultural features lacking at your current college? In our opinion, these are valid reasons to transfer.

But suppose after all is said and done, your reason boils down to prestige. Your current college meets your intellectual and personal needs, but another college has a more elite reputation. Here we caution you to think twice before transferring. It may not be worth it to walk out on a good situation simply because of another college's name value.

Q: I made plans to study abroad next year, but now I'm having doubts about going because of all my personal problems.

A: Studying abroad is a wonderful opportunity—if you're up to it. You learn about another culture (and gain perspective on your own), discover memorable people and places and perhaps learn a foreign language. But living in another country can be stressful too. Far from both family and college ties, you may feel lonely and out of place and come down with a fierce case of homesickness. Daily affairs can be complicated too, whether you're trying to explain yourself to an impatient bus driver or persuade your stomach to accept the local cuisine.

And if you are in need of support, the resources are usually less complete than back in your college community.

Common sense suggests delaying plans to study abroad if you're actively struggling with an eating disorder, substance abuse, depression or suicidal urges. These problems will probably cross the ocean with you, and you may have trouble in your new location finding therapists and medical professionals to treat them. If your problems are less acute, then by all means study abroad. Even if the initial adjustment is rocky, your new surroundings eventually will become familiar, and chances are you'll start to feel at home.

TAKING TIME OFF

Q: I'm burnt out with school and would love to take time off. But if I do this, I'm afraid I'll never make my way back to college.

A: There's no assurance, of course. Once out of academia, it's possible you'll settle into your new life and never want to be a student again. However, most students who spend a semester or a year away from college do make a successful return. The time off lets them recharge their batteries, clarify their priorities and come to appreciate, if they didn't before, the value of education and a diploma. Not only that, the job or travel experience gained while on leave often proves a valuable educational experience in its own right.

Your parents may be uncomfortable with your taking time off, fearing, as you do, that the detour will become permanent. You'll need to reassure them about your long-term educational objectives and inform them that most students who leave college eventually go back. Point out that it's foolish to put time and money into college when you're not really taking advantage of it. You'll return when you're ready to make full use of the opportunity. Point out too that the average student nowadays takes longer than four years to get a degree. So if you finish "on time," you are actually—statistically speaking—abnormal!

Before taking time off, discuss the financial implications with a financial aid administrator or other informed advisor. Will any loans start coming due while you're away? Are you jeopardizing a scholarship by leaving? What health insurance plan will cover you? Such questions should be asked well before you make the decision to leave.

Q: I'm under a lot of stress for personal reasons, and I can't study for my finals. What should I do?

A: You have several options. One is to talk directly to your professors, who may let you postpone assignments or tests until later in the term, grant you an incomplete to finish the work after the term, or even let you drop the class. Alternatively, you can speak to a dean or faculty advisor, who may help you to work out an arrangement with your professors. Either way, act quickly rather than waiting until after assignments are due.

Another possibility is to go to the counseling center to work on the emotional problems interfering with your studies. Counseling can't accomplish sudden miracles, but it's possible some insight or a boost of support can get you back on the academic track.

At many schools, another option is to talk to a dean or counselor about going on a medical leave of absence. This option lets you drop the term's classes and so preserves your grade point average. After taking time off and fulfilling certain conditions—often a course of therapy is required—you then are eligible to be readmitted to school and resume your studies. Because the term *medical leave* is nonspecific and can refer to anything from pneumonia to a broken leg, your permanent record is not blemished. No one can tell later from inspecting your transcript that you went on leave because of emotional difficulties.

FOR FURTHER READING

William H. Armstrong and M. Willard Lampe II, *Study Tactics.* Hauppage, N.Y.: Barron's, 1983.

Albert Ellis and William Knaus, *Overcoming Procrastination.* New York: Signet, 1979.

Sara D. Gilbert, *How to Do Your Best on Tests.* New York: Beach Tree Paperbacks, 1998.

Kenneth A. Green, *Making the Grade in College.* Hauppage, N.Y.: Barron's, 1990.

Charles T. Mangrum and Stephen S. Strichart, *Colleges with Programs for Students with Learning Disabilities and Attention Deficit Disorders,* 5th ed. Princeton, N.J.: Peterson's, 1997.

James Lawrence Thomas, *Do You Have Attention Deficit Disorder?* New York: Dell, 1996.

FEELING DOWN AND GETTING BACK UP

Depression is a condition that overlaps with nearly every other problem area discussed in this book. If you feel homesick at college, if you feel academically overstressed, if you have concerns about romance or sex or diet or career, then you can end up depressed. Conversely, if you are depressed, you'll surely struggle with socializing, studying, forming relationships, performing sexually and so forth. Depression is both a cause and a consequence of personal difficulties. It is a common denominator, sometimes unrecognized, of widely differing problems.

In this chapter we explain the nature of depression, list its warning signals and give coping strategies. Also covered are the related subjects of mood swings, low self-esteem, identity confusion and suicidal feelings. These are not cheerful topics, but knowing about them furnishes a toehold in case you or a friend falls into a major slump.

DEPRESSION VS. SADNESS

Q: I get sad a lot. Is that normal?

A: It depends on what you mean by "sad" and "a lot." If all you have are passing downshifts in mood, episodes of feeling blue, then you're probably no different from anyone else. If, however, you have long bouts of feeling downcast or your down periods are intense and incapacitating—you can't study, eat, sleep, socialize—that's different. You probably are depressed.

Q: But what's the difference between sadness and depression?

A: It's not entirely clear if sadness and depression come from the same root and basically differ in degree, or if they're essentially unrelated phenomena. Either way, it's important not to confuse the two. Sadness—a temporary state of feeling down—is a limited experience, and for that reason it's not a problem. In fact, it can feel satisfying sometimes to feel sad and have a good cry, to listen to melancholy music or watch a tragic drama. Sadness adds a fitting solemnity to human existence; life would seem shallow without it. Sadness also has lessons to teach. Through recognizing sadness you may discover that a relationship is empty, a need is unfulfilled, a potential has been wasted. You can discover when you're sad who and what matters to you.

Depression—especially the more severe varieties—is on a different scale. Depression isn't satisfying; it doesn't uplift or teach. A debilitating condition, depression casts a pall over every aspect of life. In its stronger forms, depression can make you unable to continue in college and can cause you to think about suicide.

You can't eliminate sadness from your life. You can, and should, take steps to fight off depression.

Q: I've known lots of people who say they're depressed, but they don't all seem the same to me. Are there different kinds of depression?

A: Yes, there are. To begin with, depressions differ in severity. One severe kind is called *major depression.* Usually coming on relatively suddenly and lasting several weeks to many months, major depressions are paralyzing conditions that often make it impossible for students to remain in school. The effects of this disorder are devastating and dramatic; something is obviously very wrong—at least to observers. *Dysthymia,* by contrast, is a milder, subtler, longer lasting condition. Dysthymics manage to get by from day to day; they can bring themselves to study and socialize, and they're not always recognized by others as depressed. The dysthymic's inner world, however, is somber and gray. One psychologist compares dysthymia to "a low-grade infection. Dysthymics never really feel good."[1]

Major depressions and dysthymia are both *unipolar* mood disorders, meaning the abnormal moods travel in only one direction: south. *Bipolar disorder*—also called manic-depressive disorder—is different in that there are both depressed periods and abnormally high periods (mania). Each emotional extreme is dangerous. Depressive episodes bring despair and the danger of suicide. Manic episodes are characterized by inflated self-esteem, racing thoughts, impaired judgment and lowered inhibitions that can lead to reckless acts like gambling away money or shirking responsibilities. Although seriously impaired, manic persons often strenuously resist treatment, as depicted in Kay Jamison's moving memoir *An Unquiet Mind*. (For an equally gripping memoir about major depression, read William Styron's *Darkness Visible*).

A variety of other depressive conditions has also been identified. *Seasonal affective disorder (SAD)* strikes perhaps 5% of the population during the winter, especially in the colder, cloudier climates. Apparently caused by lack of sunlight, SAD consists of chronically depressed mood, social withdrawal, excessive sleep and a voracious appetite that leads to weight gain. Depression can also be associated with *physical illness, psychological disorders,* and *alcohol* and *drug dependence*. (Depressed people often turn to alcohol and drugs to self-medicate; alcohol and drugs, in turn, can cause depression.) Finally, an *adjustment disorder with depressed mood* is a fancy label for an emotional tailspin triggered by a major stressor, such as academic failure or a romantic breakup. Although adjustment disorders are by definition less severe than full-scale depressions, they are still depressing. Probably more students who feel depressed fall into this category—adjustment disorder—than any of the other depressions.

WARNING SIGNS

Q: Sometimes I wonder if I'm depressed and don't know it. Is that possible?

A: Very much so. You may not recognize depression if it creeps up on you or if you're chronically depressed (dysthymic) and therefore have no normal emotional baseline as a comparison. If you're severely depressed, your thinking may be so clouded that you don't recognize your condition.

Here are some classic signs and symptoms to identify depression:

- Prolonged sad or depressed mood, crying spells, irritability or an inability to feel anything at all. (Note: You can be depressed without feeling sad.)

- Loss of interest and pleasure in activities and other people.
- Significant weight loss or weight gain, or marked increase or decrease in appetite.
- Low self-esteem; feelings of worthlessness, guilt and self-blame.
- Poor concentration; you can't read, write or study for a test.
- Difficulty making decisions.
- Feelings of hopelessness; a belief that the future won't be any better than the present.
- Fatigue and loss of energy, or agitation and restlessness.
- Problems with sleep; inability to fall or stay asleep, waking up early and being unable to get back to sleep, or sleeping too much.
- Worries about health, and physical symptoms such as digestive disorders and nonspecific aches and pains.
- Recurrent thoughts of death or suicide.

FAMILY INFLUENCE

Q: Both my parents sometimes get depressed. Will the same thing happen to me?

A: It could. Research shows that a vulnerability to depression can be inherited, particularly for bipolar disorder.[2] Parents can also raise depressed children by serving as role models demonstrating depressive behaviors or by failing to provide the love, attention and structure a child needs.

However, there is nothing certain about any of this. Children take after each parent in some respects, and not in others. It's good to be aware of the risk of depression so you'll seek treatment if the need ever arises. But don't assume because of your parents' history that your own fate has been sealed.

Some students are so afraid of following in their depressed parents' footsteps that they won't let themselves feel sad or upset. One student we know wore a constant smile, as if a cheerful face could ward off evil moods. She was determined not to be like her mother, who'd once been hospitalized for depression. Then her boyfriend broke up with her, and she could no longer muster the smile. This raised terrifying questions. Did her sorrow indicate severe depression? Was she turning into her mother after all? Thanks to several counseling sessions, she saw that suffering after a breakup is normal, not a sign of emotional illness.

HELPING YOURSELF

Q: What should I do if I'm feeling down?

A: If it's just a question of sadness—a low mood—then no major remedies are necessary. Time is your ally. No matter how bad you feel, chances are all will be better in a day or two. In the meantime, you might let out what's troubling you to someone you trust. A bit of support and blowing off steam can work wonders for a mild case of the blues. You may also take a break from the usual routine by going to a movie or leaving campus for the weekend.

Choose wisely, however, in selecting a break. Don't soothe bad feelings by getting drunk, taking other drugs, bingeing on food, missing classes, having careless sexual experiences or making credit card purchases you can't afford. Such excesses may distract you for the moment, but you're only substituting a new, nastier problem for the one that got you down in the first place.

Alcohol is particularly treacherous when you're down. Because chemically it acts as a depressant, it can make you feel even worse than before. And since it lowers inhibitions, alcohol increases the likelihood of risky, self-destructive acts, such as unprotected sex or suicide attempts.

Q: How about more lasting down periods? Is there anything I can do on my own to feel better?

A: Yes. One method, popular among counselors and therapists, is to identify and challenge self-defeating thoughts and beliefs. According to this "cognitive" approach, depression is caused by talking yourself into disturbed feelings and self-defeating behaviors. You have distorted, negative views about yourself, the world and the future, you repeat these views to yourself, and that's why you're depressed. What's more, these internal communications are so familiar, so automatic, that you may not be aware of them; you're giving yourself subliminal messages to be unhappy. To battle depression, then, you need to replace these messages.

The first step in breaking out of this rut is to identify your depression-inducing thoughts. Pay close attention next time you feel down or discouraged. What thoughts are crossing through your mind? What were your thoughts when the mood began? Keep a written record of these thoughts. The goal is to expose this hidden self-sabotage to the bright light of conscious awareness.

Next, evaluate the thoughts. How realistic do they look on paper? Chances are you'll notice lots of unreasonable, exaggerated statements, such as the following:[3]

- **Dwelling on the negative.** You zero in on the negative aspects of a situation while downplaying or explaining away positive details.

    "Sure I got three B's, but that D is going to ruin my average."

    "He's only being nice because he feels sorry for me."

- **Thinking in all-or-nothing terms.** You interpret events as all good or all bad. Either you perform perfectly (which is unlikely) or you perform horribly; events are either completely wonderful (also unlikely) or they're terrible.

    "I said something stupid in that seminar. The whole class must think I'm an idiot."

    "I've gained five pounds. Now, I'm so fat!"

- **Overgeneralizing.** You draw general conclusions based on minimal information. Clues to this pattern are absolute-sounding words like *always, never, only, just, everyone, everything* and *completely.*

    "I knew I wouldn't make the tennis team. I always screw up at tryouts."

    "Of course she wouldn't go out with me. Everyone thinks I'm a loser."

- **Catastrophizing.** You expect the worst outcomes imaginable and dwell on disastrous future possibilities.

    "I'll never make any good friends at this college."

    "What if I fail this test and never make it to medical school?"

- **Overassuming.** You assume you know what people are thinking and feeling. In particular, you assume their actions have personal, negative meanings for you. (Taken to an extreme, overassuming becomes paranoia.)

    "He didn't call me tonight. He must think I'm boring."

    "She didn't return my sweater yet. She probably plans to keep it."

- **Having unrealistic expectations.** You refuse to accept others, yourself or conditions as they really are and hold the view that things should be better. To express your indignation, you pepper your talk with "shoulds" and "shouldn'ts" and "it's awful" and "it's not fair."

"He should treat me better than he does."

"It's not fair that Harvard Law School rejected me."

The next step after recognizing negative thinking patterns is to challenge and replace flawed thoughts whenever they crop up. Counter each depressive thought by asking yourself, "Is this an accurate view of the situation?" "Am I being fair and reasonable?" Then replace the original thought with a realistic, constructive alternative. Use your reasoning abilities to restore perspective—and ward off depression.

As an example, imagine a friend doesn't smile as she passes you on campus. This really bothers you and sticks in your mind (that's dwelling on the negative). You have the thought she doesn't like you anymore (that's overassuming). Analyzing the event further, you catch yourself thinking most people don't like you very much (now you're overgeneralizing) and wondering what's wrong with you (more overgeneralizing). The end result? After all this gloomy cogitation, you won't feel too rosy.

How do you work your way out of this morass? The remedy is to recognize the negative thoughts, identify the errors they contain and inwardly substitute constructive alternatives. Here's a sample corrective inner dialogue: "Wait! Am I being realistic here? Do I really know what she was thinking when she passed me? Usually when I run into her she's friendly, so there's no reason to assume she doesn't like me anymore. Maybe she was preoccupied and didn't see me. And there's certainly no point dwelling on this little thing or concluding I'm unpopular. That's just me making myself miserable. Actually, I have a pretty good relationship with her, and besides I've made good friends here at school."

Can a dose of constructive self-talk cure a funk all at once? Maybe not. Once you're ensnarled in a depressed state, it may take awhile to work yourself free. Still, the cognitive way of identifying and refuting negative thoughts can get you started feeling better. If you really learn to watch your thinking and make it a habit to correct negative thoughts, you won't stay depressed as long and you'll be less likely to get down in the dumps in the first place.

Q: What else can I do to fight a slump?

A: Check out the stress management suggestions on pages 82–83. These ideas also may help with down periods. Reducing an over-crowded schedule may work; so may adding meaningful activities to an unchallenging schedule. Regular exercise, healthy eating and plenty of sleep are also recommended.

Depression is also often associated with social isolation. Although some solitude is good for you, too much time spent alone is demor-alizing and can spawn irrational thinking. (Solitary confinement is used as the ultimate in prison punishment.) If, then, you can make one friend, or schedule even a single social activity, you may give yourself a vital boost. For tips on social skills, review the material in Chapter 1.

Valuable as all these measures are, they may not work for you. This would suggest that you're not just going through a "normal" down period but are depressed. Depression calls for professional assis-tance. We recommend in this case contacting your campus counsel-ing service.

Q: What can I do to prevent mood swings?

A: Again, it depends on the severity. Some emotional variability comes with being human. You think diverse thoughts, you have ever-changing experiences and so naturally you have shifting moods. So for minor ups and downs, nothing special needs to be done.

For more frequent or pronounced emotional swings (perhaps a friend can help you judge this), try the cognitive approach explained above. All-or-nothing thinking, overgeneralizations, unrealistic expec-tations and other flawed thoughts can propel you on an emotional roller coaster. Substituting realistic thoughts can restore emotional equilibrium.

Keeping on an even keel also requires readying yourself for chang-ing fortunes. Life, after all, is a deliverer of mixed messages. In any given week, count on it that some people will be friendly and others cool, on some matters you'll shine and on others you'll screw up. Good, bad and indifferent will all come your way. If you learn to expect these fluctuations, you won't do emotional flip-flops when your fortunes turn.

Another suggestion is to build routines or habits into your schedule. Practice consistency in your sleeping schedule, eating habits, exercise program and times of study and leisure. Don't hit the books for 10 hours and then blow off the next three days (while perhaps drinking too much). Don't binge today and starve yourself tomorrow. Consistent practices will cause you to view yourself evenly, and that in turn may stabilize your moods. If these tactics don't help and your emotional swings feel out of control, then consult a professional at your campus counseling service.

SELF-ESTEEM

Q: I don't like myself very much. Why is that?

A: How you feel about yourself reflects a lifetime of experiences. Partly your parents and siblings have molded your self-image. If they were harshly critical, no doubt you internalized their messages, converting their disapproval into self-disapproval. Teachers, peers and others have also left their mark. How each of them related to you has become part of how you now see yourself. In addition, you've been your own judge through the years. All those countless times when you've thought "I'm doing great" or "I'm screwing up" are material you've used to construct an image of the sort of person you are. If you struggled first learning how to read or hit a tennis ball, somewhere inside those experiences of failure may still be with you.

Self-esteem is not a uniform judgment, however. All of us feel better about ourselves in some ways than in others. You may not think of yourself as a competent or capable person but still feel well liked and lovable, or maybe it's the other way around. You may not like your body but think your face is attractive. You may question your intelligence but take pride in your way with animals and small children. Everyone can find some qualities to like and to dislike.

Q: What can I do to improve self-esteem?

A: We have some suggestions, but you'll need to be patient waiting for results. After all, your feelings about yourself have had two decades to take root. Here are the suggestions:

- **Identify and replace self-belittling thoughts.** Self-esteem problems, like depression, are fueled by negative thoughts. For example, you may dwell on your faults and discount strengths. You may overgeneralize from a single setback and conclude you're worthless. You may disparage yourself for failing to be perfect. Watch for these thinking traps, challenge them each time they appear and substitute fairer and more realistic self-appraisals.
- **Take an inventory of your positive points.** What do you like about yourself? What would others say they value about you? Write down on a piece of paper all your assets, large and small: "Responsible. Friendly. Sympathetic. Honest . . ." Study this list. Seeing these qualities in black and white may give you an appreciation for your strong points.
- **Catalog your negative points.** In what ways are you deficient? How would others say you might grow and improve? Be as honest as you can, neither exaggerating nor glossing over the truth, and write down what you find. Carrying out this exercise helps build self-esteem because it shows you can look at yourself honestly and unflinchingly. There's nothing so horrible about you that you can't admit it, nothing so dreadful that you can't look yourself in the eye.
- **Accept those negatives you cannot change.** Are you unhappy with your height? Your basic body type? Your family's circumstances? A learning disability? These are the givens in your life, the cards you've been dealt. As much as possible, work on accepting these conditions. Reconcile yourself to your limitations. If you can live with them, neither blaming yourself, cursing the fates nor wishing you were somehow different, you'll take a big step toward self-acceptance.
- **Work on negatives you can change.** Ultimately, self-esteem has to be earned. To respect yourself you need to behave in ways that yield self-respect. This may sound obvious, yet surprisingly many students fail to grasp the principle. They act contrary to their goals and values, and then they find that they don't like themselves. So examine where you've been slacking off. Are you badly out of shape? Start working out again. Have you been cutting classes? Start attending regularly. Have you neglected to write your high school friends? Drop them a note. Have you been unfair or cruel to your roommate? Resolve to stop. Each such constructive act, no matter how small, pays a dividend in self-esteem.

Q: But if I start building up self-esteem, won't I become conceited?

A: We doubt it. In fact, often it's the people who don't like themselves who come off as conceited. They have an exaggerated sense of their own importance or abilities, or at least they try to convince you they're something special, because they're compensating for inner feelings of inadequacy. In contrast, people who have self-esteem are comfortable with their real selves, warts and all. Because they basically like who they are, they don't have to inflate their importance. So it's safe to work on building your self-esteem; you won't turn into an egotistical monster.

Q: I keep hearing this voice saying, "You're stupid, you can't do this, you're a jerk." Why do I do this to myself?

A: Our bet is that you learned it from someone in your past. If you listen carefully to the voice, you may recognize the words or intonation of a critical parent or sibling, or hear again the teasing that made your life miserable in elementary school. You're now saying to yourself what used to be said to you.

Oddly enough, you also may *want* to criticize yourself. Your harsh words may be intended to goad you to action. ("Try harder, stupid!"). They may be a backhanded way of declaring that you're really wonderful. (Thinking "I'm so dumb" when you get a B+ implies that you really consider yourself an A student.) They can also be meant to inoculate you from outside criticism. Since you've already said the worst to yourself, you feel no one else's negative words can hurt you.

Despite such subtle motives, you still probably don't enjoy this critic residing inside your head. To get rid of him (or her), employ the cognitive strategy for eliminating negative thinking patterns: Make yourself aware of the self-criticisms. Challenge unfair statements— talk back! Substitute fair self-assessments in their place.

It also may help to imagine being a parent someday. Do you want to criticize, find fault, always harp on the negative with your child? Or do you hope to be a supportive parent, patient and encouraging when your son or daughter takes on a challenge? You want the second way, of course. Why then be any less humane toward yourself? Why mistreat the child inside you—we all have one—when this method is obviously counterproductive?

If you can, try to be a good parent to yourself. Like your future child, you too will perform better and feel happier hearing "Come on, you can do it" rather than "You can't do anything, stupid."

IDENTITY

Q: I feel as if I don't really know who I am.

A: That feeling is not uncommon in people your age. According to Erik Erikson, the renowned psychoanalyst, identity concerns are characteristic of adolescence through the college years. Erikson described a sense of identity as complex, combining many dimensions—career direction, political and philosophical views, comfort with one's body, a sense of oneself sexually and in relationships.[4] Discovering yourself in all these areas and putting the "pieces" together is a slow and complicated process. So it's natural at your age still to question who you are and sometimes to feel rather uncomfortably confused and divided.

Besides your youth, the college experience itself also can cause self-uncertainty. At college you are exposed to other students, professors and writers who call into question your ideas and beliefs. Your classmates come from differing backgrounds and have differing values and practices. You have more decisions to make than before, more responsibilities, more freedom. All this can shake your earlier convictions—and your sense of self.

As with other topics in this chapter, the seriousness of identity questions depends on the degree. A few students have a severe deficiency in their self-image or sense of self. They may be aware of strong feelings, wishes and needs, but what's lacking is any overall sense of self, any feeling of coherence and stability. It's as if they are one person on one occasion, and someone entirely different the next. If this picture of instability applies to you and causes you distress, here again we recommend consulting your campus counseling service.

Q: If I act inconsistently, does that mean I've got serious identity problems?

A: Not necessarily. All of us have various facets to our personalities. We might act silly with a friend, feel serious with an elder, express our emotional side with a loved one. Each situation and each individual may draw out subtly distinct aspects of our many-sided selves. As long as there's an overarching sense of "I" embracing these components, there's nothing abnormal about this. There's still a basic organizing principle—a self—that contains the many parts. As the poet Walt Whitman wrote: "Do I contradict myself?/Very well then I contradict myself,/(I am large, I contain multitudes.)"

Q: How can I form my identity?

A: There's no one foolproof method. In fact, the process of identity formation isn't fully conscious anyway; mostly it happens as a by-product of life experience. However, most of the tips already suggested concerning depression, mood swings and self-esteem are also applicable to identity formation. We've separated these topics for purposes of discussion, but in actuality they are closely related. So if you're working on avoiding emotional slumps or steadying your moods or improving your opinion of yourself, simultaneously you're doing the work of identity formation.

In addition to these efforts, we recommend pursuing creative interests. Writing, drawing or painting, taking up dance or doing any other creative activity can aid self-discovery. Relationships can also help you form your identity. Becoming close to a friend or a romantic partner helps you discover and develop aspects of yourself. Another idea is to keep a diary or journal. The process of writing down thoughts and capturing reactions to experiences helps you learn who you really are.

COUNSELING AND MEDICATIONS

Q: How do I know if I should see a counselor for one of these problems— down moods, mood swings, low self-esteem or identity confusion?

A: One test is duration. If you've felt depressed for several weeks or more, or if you've had many episodes of depression during the past few years, consult a counselor. The same holds true if your mood swings, self-esteem or identity problem has troubled you for a long time.

A second test is lack of success resolving the problem through your own efforts. If you're getting nowhere on your own, then by all means turn to a professional.

And a third test is other people's concern about you. Depressed people are often unable to recognize their condition. Therefore if a friend, RA, parent or professor voices concern, we suggest taking the warning seriously and getting a professional opinion.

Q: I feel so depressed I can't believe I will ever get better, even with counseling.

A: You probably will, though. Most cases of pronounced depression eventually run their course—especially when they're professionally treated. The trouble is, time passes slowly and the future seems hopeless when you're depressed, so of course it's difficult to imagine feeling better. But try to remind yourself that depression is skewing your current thinking. You can eventually improve, even if that seems hard to believe right now.

Q: If I see a counselor about depression, will I be given medication?

A: In the majority of cases, the answer is no. The combination of support and insight that counseling provides is sufficient.

Sometimes, though, the "talking cure" is not enough. Major depression—the most severe "unipolar" mood disorder—often requires medication, and bipolar disorder—manic-depressive disorder—almost always does. Often these conditions respond best to a combination of psychotherapy and a prescribed drug.

There are dozens of antidepressant medicines, with new ones introduced regularly. Adding to the confusion, each drug has both a chemical name and a brand name. The most popular antidepressants in recent years have been the selective serotonin reuptake inhibitors (SSRIs), such as fluoxetine (brand name: Prozac), sertraline (Zoloft) and paroxetine (Paxil). Another class of antidepressants is the tricyclics, such as desipramine (Norpramin), imipramine (Tofranil) and amitryptiline (Elavil). A third class, the MAO inhibitors, such as phenezine (Nardil) and tranylcypromine (Parnate), are usually prescribed for so-called atypical depressions (patients eat and sleep too much) but are less commonly used these days due to side effects and the need for dietary restrictions. Some newer antidepressants with unique mechanisms of action, such as venlafaxine (Effexor), buproprion (Wellbutrin) and mirtazapine (Remeron), may be tried when other antidepressants cause unwanted side effects or are not effective.

Usually, however, the first antidepressant that is prescribed is tolerated and proves effective.

To stabilize the extreme mood swings of bipolar disorder, the drug of choice has long been lithium carbonate, similar chemically to table salt. A more recent alternative, particularly useful for rapid mood cycles, is the anticonvulsant drug (originally developed to treat epilepsy) sodium valproate (Depakote). Unlike the antidepressants listed above, lithium carbonate and Depakote are mood stabilizers, preventing extreme highs. Usually patients stay on these drugs for at least a year but in some cases longer. Both drugs have to be closely monitored through periodic blood samples to insure safety and effectiveness.

Antidepressants work by altering the levels of brain chemicals, called neurotransmitters. Prozac and the other SSRIs, for example, increase the availability of the neurotransmitter called serotonin. Though each antidepressant operates differently, the exact mechanism of action is not always clearly understood. When effective, antidepressants improve a person's mood within roughly 10 to 14 days, but may take up to four to six weeks.

Q: Won't I grow dependent on them if I take one of these drugs?

A: No, these drugs are not the type that lead to physical dependency. To assure your recovery from depression you may stay on an antidepressant for six months or even longer, followed by a gradual tapering off. But you will not become physically addicted.

Q: Does taking a drug mean I'm crazy?

A: Absolutely not. Medications are simply aids intended to help you feel better, think more clearly and use counseling more productively.

Q: Will drugs change my personality?

A: No, again. If anything, the right medication may make you feel as if the clouds have lifted and your true personality is at last shining forth. For a thoughtful discussion of this issue, read Dr. Peter Kramer's *Listening to Prozac*.

Q: What about side effects?

A: This is an important issue. Although the SSRIs have fewer problems than the other antidepressants, all drugs have potential side effects. A particular medicine may cause such effects as fatigue, headaches, anxiety, sleeplessness or an upset stomach; it depends on the drug and your individual reaction. These side effects are typically short lived, lasting one to two weeks. Additionally, a small percentage of patients experience sexual side effects such as decreased libido or delay in orgasm during the course of their medication treatment.

Sometimes side effects can be reduced or eliminated by changing the dosage, switching medications, using a combination of medications, or, of course, stopping medications altogether. Therefore you, your counselor and your prescribing doctor need to think through the issues carefully before you undertake drug treatment, balancing possible benefits against potential problems.

When taking a prescribed drug, never try any other prescribed or nonprescribed drugs—including alcohol!—without your doctor's approval. Drugs tend to interact with each other in unpredictable and sometimes dangerous ways.

Q: If I can take pills to recover from depression, why should I bother talking to a counselor?

A: Although a quick fix may sound appealing, we believe taking drugs without counseling is doing yourself a disservice. For one thing, it's not a given that pills alone will lead to a full recovery. Medications affect brain chemistry, but unlike counseling they do not target distorted beliefs, childhood hurts, environmental stressors or ineffective patterns of behavior. Medications treat depression's symptoms, but counseling—for most people—addresses depression's causes.

Consider also the risk of relapse. Suppose erroneous beliefs, early losses or maladaptive habits make you vulnerable to depression. If you don't work on these issues now, what's to stop them from blindsiding you again? Only counseling can give you the tools to ward off future bouts of depression.

Medications are literally lifesavers for some depressed people, but in our opinion they should always be combined with counseling.

Q: My family doctor gave me a prescription in August for an antidepressant medication, and he told me to check in for another appointment when I return home for Christmas holiday.

A: With all due respect to your doctor, we don't think that's a hot idea. For one thing, his plan leaves out counseling, and we don't think students should be on medication without also speaking to a counselor. Second, four months sounds far too long to be on an antidepressant without visits to a doctor. You need to find somebody in your college community to monitor the medication. We'd recommend choosing a psychiatrist, not a general practitioner, to monitor you, since depression and medication call for the expertise of a specialist.

Q: What if the antidepressant my doctor gives me isn't working and I want to stop taking it?

A: Then talk to your doctor. There's no reason to take something that's ineffective or uncomfortable. You should take an active role in your drug therapy, asking questions, reporting your reactions and stating your preferences. However, don't go off the medicine or change the dosage without consulting with the doctor.

SUICIDE

Q: This girl down the hall swallowed a bottle of pills last year and had to be hospitalized. Why would anyone do that?

A: We assume there was an immediate crisis in her life or a buildup of problems. Perhaps she had a romantic breakup, an unwanted pregnancy or word of her parents getting a divorce. Along with the bad news, no doubt her reasoning abilities were impaired too. Suicidal thinking, it's been found, involves a narrowing of options, a tunnel vision, so that suicide is seen as the only solution to ending psychological pain. The person regards his or her situation in either-or terms: "Either my problem resolves itself, or there's no reason to live."

For example, a political science major in his junior year told his roommate about suicidal feelings after he failed a history midterm. His reasoning process had narrowed dangerously: "I have to get at least a B in this course to get into law school. And I have to become a lawyer, since that's what my parents and friends expect of me. If I botch up this course, all my plans are ruined—I might as well end my life."

Another contributing cause to a suicide attempt, besides current problems and impaired reasoning, is the desperate wish to get help. Suicidal persons often don't know appropriate ways to signal their distress. They've learned, usually because of unhappy childhood experiences, that nobody responds when they're in pain. Suicide, then, affords a dramatic method to get attention—nobody can ignore their suffering now. Sometimes the desperation for help is mixed with feelings of rage or vengefulness. The person thinks, "When I die, you'll be sorry."

Another point we should stress is that college students who attempt suicide are often acting impulsively rather than carrying out a long-planned event. Typically they are reacting to an immediate disappointment—perhaps a fight with parents or a romantic breakup—which before long will fade in significance. That's why it's critical to take action immediately when a classmate feels suicidal. If you can stop the person now, before long he or she probably will feel better and very much want to live.

Q: Lately I've been worried about a friend who seems very depressed. How can I tell if he's suicidal?

A: Look for the following warning signals and risk factors:

- **Hints about suicide or death:** "You won't see me for long." "Maybe I'll kill myself" [even if said jokingly]. "I wish I were dead." "I'm going away for a long time."
- **Withdrawal:** From friends, family, classes and favorite activities.
- **Signs of depression:** See pages 48–49.
- **Giving away of prized possessions.**
- **Alcohol and other drug use:** These lower inhibitions and so greatly increase the likelihood of acting on a suicidal impulse.
- **History of family suicide or suicide of a friend.**
- **Self-destructive behavior**—accidents, reckless driving, trouble on campus or with the police.
- **Giving up:** Grades, personal hygiene and responsibilities have been neglected, as if the person is saying, "I don't care anymore."
- **Previous suicide attempts.**

Q: But people who talk about killing themselves don't really do it, right?

A: On the contrary, most suicide attempters reveal their intentions beforehand, although usually in disguised fashion. The sad part is, their warnings often are ignored. Since just talking about suicide does get a serious response, they feel desperate and carry out the threat.

Another myth about suicide is that you don't have to worry about people who've made a previous attempt—obviously they didn't really want to die. In fact, 30% to 40% of people who take their own life have made one or more previous attempts.[5]

Q: How often does it happen?

A: About one in every 10,000 college students takes his or her own life each year. Perhaps 10 times that number make a suicide attempt. Fortunately, completed suicides are statistically rare, but each one is one too many. A life has been tragically lost and family, friends and others are afflicted with enormous pain.

Q: If my friend has some of the warning signs of suicide, what should I do to help him?

A: First, take your own fears and intuitions seriously. Don't dismiss the signs and tell yourself, "No, it's not possible." Every year countless suicidal students are brought to professional attention only because friends cared enough to follow through and get them help.

You have two choices about how to proceed. One is to go directly to residence hall staff, a dean, faculty member, administrator or your college's counseling center. They will then contact your friend to assess the suicidal risk. If a suicidal threat arises at night, most colleges have an on-duty residence hall manager or counselor. The campus police or security office can help you locate them.

The second choice is to speak to your friend first before enlisting outside help. To do this right you must sit down with him and ask what's wrong. Show by your patience and concern that you won't be brushed off with a curt, "Nothing, I'm fine." Lead up to the topic of suicide and then ask directly, "Have you been thinking of killing yourself?" Don't be afraid to use these very words. Suicidal persons appreciate the opportunity to speak openly about suicidal feelings and intentions. By the way, there's no danger that you'll give your friend the idea of suicide simply by asking about it. If he doesn't intend to commit suicide, your questioning won't drive him to it.

How you respond next depends on your friend's answers. If he convincingly demonstrates that your fears are groundless, then you needn't take further action. But make sure the person has said in so many words that he or she is definitely not planning to kill himself. Make sure you're 100% convinced!

If, however, he admits to having suicidal wishes, or if his answers are evasive and unconvincing—if you're left with any doubts at all—then get help. Either escort your friend to a residence hall manager, dean, administrator or counselor, or go directly to that person yourself.

Q: My roommate asked me to keep a secret, and then she told me that she wants to kill herself. What should I do?

A: The value of human life far outweighs the importance of keeping a secret. Even after making the promise, you still need to inform someone in authority. Otherwise you'll be burdened by a terrible responsibility that no college student ought to shoulder. Your studies and peace of mind will be ruined, and you'll be afraid to leave your roommate's side. And if she does kill herself, you'll end up feeling terribly guilty.

For both your sakes, immediately tell someone in authority about her suicidal plans.

Q: Suppose after I tell a college authority it's decided that she can continue to remain in our room with me?

A: Then you can relax. Her remaining in your room would mean that professionals have determined she's not at risk of killing herself. True, your roommate's situation could change. It's conceivable that she might say or you might observe something next week or in several months that suggests she is feeling suicidal again, in which case once more you should alert someone in authority. Generally speaking, however, once you've contacted school officials, you should not feel obliged to continue watching over her, and you should not feel obliged to be her counselor. Once the professionals are involved, it's their job, not yours, to guarantee her safety.

It's possible your roommate may resent you for a while for having reported your fears. Ultimately, though, most students in her situation are grateful. They recognize the caring and concern that motivated you to get professional help.

Q: A woman on my hall threatened to cut her wrists last night. I'm the only one who knows. She begged me not to tell anyone, saying she's really okay now, and her parents would take her out of school if they found out. Should I leave well enough alone?

A: Again, the answer is no. Her response is quite typical of suicidal people, who often resist any intervention and ask others to do the same. However, you're in no position to judge if this person really is in the clear. You should contact a school official immediately.

Q: I sometimes think about suicide. Does that mean I'm likely to go through with it someday?

A: Probably not. Practically every human being has wondered about suicide. College students wonder more than most, since late adolescence and early adulthood are times of asking large questions about the meaning of life and personal identity. But we need to draw a sharp distinction between thoughts and behaviors, between casual reflections and serious intentions. So long as you're not at all tempted to act on your thoughts, you are not in danger. So long as you have no intentions of carrying out a suicidal thought, it's most unlikely that you'll do it.

The time to start worrying—and get help—is when your suicidal thoughts cross over into serious, hard-to-control urges, or when you find yourself thinking of ways to carry it out. Likewise if thoughts about suicide are persistent and won't go away or if they're an expression of depression, it's time to seek professional help.

Q: Sometimes when I feel upset I take a razor and make little cuts in my arms and legs.

A: Self-cutting can have a different purpose than a suicide attempt. Students who cut themselves may be seeking distraction from emotional pain or trying to make themselves feel *something* in lieu of their numb inner state. In these cases, self-cutting is not a suicidal act but a search for psychological relief.

But even when not life threatening, self-cutting is obviously a serious matter, and only partly because of the physical wounds. That you're in such pain or feel so emotionally numb is a concern. That you'd resort to self-damage to feel better is also concerning, suggesting it's hard for you to tolerate distress. If not already in treatment, we urge you to make an appointment at your college's counseling center.

Q: I've been having strong suicidal urges. I know I should seek counseling, but I don't see how that will help me get over the wish to kill myself.

A: Fortunately, almost nobody has a 100% wish to end his or her life. The fact that you've resisted suicidal impulses says loud and clear that a strong part of you clings to hope and wants to live. It's that life-affirming side of you that counseling can support and reinforce.

How can counseling help? It can enable you to see your situation in perspective, widening your field of vision beyond your immediate problems. It can provide empathic support during a lonely time and encourage you to get support from others. Your counselor can teach coping methods to resist suicidal impulses. For example, you may learn when you feel suicidal to call a friend, arrange for an immediate visit to your family or get someone to take you to the hospital.

In the long term, counseling can also help you achieve a fundamental change inside. You may still endure episodes of depression, and you will still have setbacks and losses. But you can change your attitude toward life itself. You can eventually decide that life is too precious to give up, no matter what the situation. It will take hard work in counseling, but ultimately you can learn to give up the option of suicide once and for all.

FOR FURTHER READING

A. Alvarez, *The Savage God: A Study of Suicide.* New York: W.W. Norton, 1990.

Kay Redfield Jamison, *An Unquiet Mind.* New York: Knopf, 1995.

Peter D. Kramer, *Listening to Prozac.* New York: Penguin Books, 1997.

William Styron, *Darkness Visible.* New York: Vintage Books, 1990.

DEALING WITH ANXIETY, INDECISION, ANGER AND STRESS

This chapter deals with four common problem areas. Anxiety, the first, is similar to fear. Both are unpleasant reactions to the idea of danger, and both have a psychological side (apprehension, uneasiness, worry) and a physical side (trembling, pounding heart, sweating). They are normally distinguished in that anxiety, unlike fear, is triggered by something ill defined, irrational or unrecognized. You know what frightens you but not necessarily why you're anxious—and that can make you more anxious still.

Anxiety is an inescapable part of the human condition; just observe your own rapid heartbeat whenever you make a speech in class, talk to someone you're attracted to or walk into an exam. But although anxiety can't be eliminated, it shouldn't reach crippling dimensions or cause intolerable suffering. The following pages suggest ways to alleviate the anxiety felt in a variety of situations.

Indecisiveness, anger and stress are also inevitabilities. You can't make it through a single term, much less your college career, without feeling stuck sometimes on a decision, furious with someone or stressed out. It helps to think of these difficult occasions as opportunities to develop coping skills that will serve you throughout life. You can learn how to make decisions, handle anger and manage stress, as we explain in these pages.

ANXIETY

Q: Several times recently my heart started to race, and I began to tremble. I thought I was having some kind of attack and was going to die. What's wrong with me?

A: It sounds like panic attacks—sudden episodes of intense anxiety. Panic attacks consist of dramatic, uncomfortable symptoms like shortness of breath, dizziness, racing heart, sweating, stomach distress and hot flashes or chills. They arise so suddenly, powerfully and inexplicably—you never know when they're coming—that you may be convinced you're going crazy, are losing control or are about to die. But panic attacks aren't a sign of insanity or losing all control, and they're not medically dangerous. They're basically an intense form of anxiety.

The cause of panic attacks appears to be the misinterpreting of bodily sensations—like shortness of breath, racing heart, sweating—to mean something terrible and catastrophic. These bodily sensations may arise due to increases or decreases in carbon dioxide in the body, or they may be due to anxiety itself. In other words, the physical symptoms of anxiety can trigger more anxiety, even terror. When panic sufferers become anxious for some reason (we all do), they fearfully overreact to the physical consequences and unknowingly set off a panic attack.

Q: What can I do to avoid ever having one again?

A: For starters, don't make that your goal. When you tell yourself "Never again," you make yourself worry about a recurrence, and the worry itself can bring one about. And if you do have another panic attack, your dread of it adds to its intensity, so don't fight against panic attacks. Strive to *accept* them, to let them occur if they must and run their course. (Panic attacks usually last only a few minutes.) In addition, experts recommend these other responses:

- **Oppose irrational, catastrophic thinking during attacks.** Thoughts like "I'm going crazy!" and "I'm having a heart attack" increase your dread. To calm yourself, instead tell yourself: "These are only anxiety symptoms—nothing more," "I'm not going crazy," "I can handle this" and "This will be over soon."
- **Deliberately induce symptoms.** Crazy as it may sound, consider inducing panic-like symptoms by running up stairs or breathing rapidly. Once your heart pounds and you're out of breath, calm yourself with the soothing, constructive thoughts listed above. This trial run gives you practice coping with an actual panic attack and demonstrates that the panic-like symptoms are

merely bodily sensations. (Of course if the trial is too uncomfortable or medically risky, stop it.)

- **Take slow, deep, regular breaths from the belly.** Panic attacks are often associated with either excessive breathing (hyperventilation) or holding your breath. In contrast to these extremes, slow, deep, rhythmic breathing counteracts the physical symptoms of anxiety (midwives have known this for years). It also may help to say to yourself "Relax" each time you exhale.
- **Train your attention on something outside yourself**—a chair, children playing outside the window, the person you're with, a song on the radio. With your mind otherwise engaged, you won't feed your panic by worrying about the symptoms.
- **Get a medical checkup.** Though it's unlikely, occasionally panic-like symptoms are brought on by a medical condition, medication or withdrawal from medication, premenstrual syndrome, mitral valve prolapse (a heart disorder) or—rarely—hypoglycemia (low blood sugar).
- **Don't self-medicate with alcohol.** Heavy drinking can cause a hypoglycemic reaction that 12 hours later produces panic symptoms. One student we know drank 10 beers every night to stave off panic attacks. Once he stopped his drinking, the panic attacks eased up too.
- **Experiment with eliminating coffee, tea and cola drinks.** Caffeine is a stimulant that can cause anxiety and even panic.

Q: Suppose nothing I try relieves my panic attacks?

A: That may happen. Panic attacks can be rooted in underlying psychological conflicts, irrational thought patterns or an inherited susceptibility. In these cases, the above remedies may not suffice.

If underlying conflicts or irrational thought patterns are the problem, psychological counseling may be needed (although you can work on your own to correct negative thinking, as we discuss later). In counseling, you may discover that you have a panic attack whenever there's a hint of anger—yours or someone else's—or perhaps whenever you feel sexually aroused. Maybe you panic because you overreact to stressful situations—thinking "I'm going to fail," for example, when coursework piles up—or because of conflict in a relationship. Understanding such themes demystifies panic attacks. Instead of seeing them as a curse visited on you for no reason, you realize they're a predictable reaction given what you fear and how you think. Understanding the meaning of the attacks may point the way to their disappearance.

Another recourse is drug therapy, often effective in combination with counseling. Several of the common antidepressant medications can reduce or eliminate panic attacks at least so long as you take the medication. You need to work closely with your doctor to discuss possible side effects, interactions with other substances and other implications of drug treatment.

Q: Whenever I have to make a speech in class I get sweaty palms and a dry mouth, my heart goes a mile a minute, and I want to run out the door. Does this happen to other people?

A: It certainly does. Of all human fears, stage fright, or performance anxiety, is the most common. Almost everyone feels a little uncomfortable standing in front of an audience, and many others besides yourself have a hellish time of it. Some famous athletes and entertainers report being sick with anxiety before every performance of their careers.

Q: What can I do about speech anxiety?

A: To combat speech anxiety, or anything else you fear, make up your mind to hang in there and confront what frightens you. This approach, "exposure therapy," is based on the premise that avoiding a situation perpetuates fear, while facing the situation reduces fear. So look for opportunities to participate in groups or, better yet, to speak to them. Possibilities include participating in classroom discussions, enrolling in a public speaking class, becoming a teaching assistant who leads classroom discussions or taking a Dale Carnegie class. At first with these activities you'll notice your heart pounding (that's normal!), but soon anxiety may taper off as public speaking becomes routine.

A second general fear-fighting strategy, the cognitive approach, challenges negative, irrational thoughts and substitutes constructive, realistic alternatives. Do you say discouraging things to yourself before and during a talk? "Oh no, I'm getting scared again." "Everyone will be bored." "People will know I'm nervous." "I'm going to really screw up." In place of these anxiety-producing messages, substitute comforting, constructive statements: "Just relax, you're doing fine." "The anxiety is getting better already." "This isn't so bad." With the cognitive approach, you use your reasoning powers to restore perspective, and you coach yourself to a more relaxed performance.

Here are other suggestions:

- **Practice your talk beforehand until you know it well.** But don't memorize it, because then you'll panic if you forget the exact words.
- **Stage dress rehearsals in front of a few supportive friends.** If that's not possible, imagine an audience in front of you when you rehearse the speech.
- **View your speech as a communication rather than a performance.** Your purpose is not to wow your audience, it's to inform them. This mind-set takes the pressure off—you don't have to be a brilliant orator—and allows you to speak naturally.
- **Focus on your message, not yourself.** Whenever you start paying attention to your voice (is it quavering?) or your hands (are they shaking?), shift your focus back to the message you're trying to convey.
- **Take slow, deep, regular breaths.** Don't breathe too fast or stop breathing.
- **Remind yourself that observers probably can't tell if you're anxious.** Your symptoms of anxiety are much more obvious to you than to anyone else.
- **Remind yourself too that anxiety peaks at the beginning of a talk and soon subsides.** If you're fearful at the beginning, this is to be expected; it will soon get better. And actually, some initial anxiety is desirable. It means you're up for the task.
- **Bring notes in case you get lost.** But don't read your talk, if possible. Your audience will remain more interested if you talk rather than read to them.
- **Speak to one member of the audience at a time.** Pick out friendly faces in different parts of the audience and direct your remarks to them.
- **Go slow and easy.** The tendency when you're anxious is to hit the fast-forward button. Slowing yourself down to normal speed makes for a better talk and calms your nerves.
- **As a last resort you can try medication.** A beta blocker such as propanolol reduces racing heart, sweating and other physical effects of speech anxiety, and can be taken on an as-needed basis.

Q: I get anxious every time I take the train. What should I do?

A: Your problem is called a *phobia*, an excessive fear of something coupled with the powerful urge to get away from it. There are lots of phobias, each with imposing Greek- and Latin-derived names: claustrophobia (fear of closed spaces), acrophobia (fear of heights), mysophobia (fear of dirt), cynophobia (fear of dogs) and agoraphobia (a more general fear of crowded or open places or travel), to name only a few. By definition, phobias evoke fear out of proportion to the real danger. In your case, it's true trains can crash, but the probability is very small.

The general strategy to reduce any fear is to confront it. Sometimes it helps to proceed gradually. In the approach called "systematic desensitization," first you learn to employ a relaxation technique (see below). Then you create a hierarchy of scary situations and face them one by one, from least frightening to most frightening, all the while making sure to maintain a relaxed state. For example, you might start with the relatively nonthreatening task of imagining riding the train while you're sitting in your room. After completing this step, next time you might view the train station from a distance, then next time walk closer to the train itself, then several steps later take a ride for one stop. Finally you'd be ready to go for a full trip. This method depends on your advancing slowly through the hierarchy of situations, feeling comfortable and relaxed every step of the way. This way you learn to associate trains with relaxation, not fear.

The principle of systematic desensitization is worth a try with anything that irrationally scares you. Just remember to start with the easy tasks and build up gradually to the most scary, while staying relaxed all along the way. If your own efforts don't succeed, then of course consult a professional. Therapists have a high success rate alleviating phobias either through systematic desensitization or "flooding," another, more intense behavioral method which involves confronting the most frightening situations right from the start.

Q: How can I stop having this fear that my father is going to die?

A: Unwanted thoughts or images that won't go away are called obsessions. The most common obsessive thoughts concern dirt and germs, aggressive and sexual impulses, fears for someone's safety and doubts about whether you've done something, such as locking the door. The commonsense reaction to obsessions is to try to stop them, which is called suppression. Suppression can be effective at shutting out everyday thoughts in the short term. During a test, for example, it makes sense to block out thoughts about dinner.

As a permanent solution to unwanted thoughts, though, suppression tends to backfire. When you say to yourself, "Don't think about this," on some level you keep yourself aware of the thought, which paves the way for its return. As an experiment, concentrate for a few moments on *not* thinking about dogs. What happens? Chances are you can't help yourself from imagining something furry and barking.

Rather than forbidding the thought about your father dying, one recommended approach is simply to let the thought pop up when it will. Don't fight it, don't dread it. Just allow the thought to come. You might even try the paradoxical technique of *encouraging* such thoughts, planning 15-minute sessions for that purpose. By encouraging these thoughts you rob them of their power to torment you. You grow used to them, they prove harmless—and gradually they may fade away.

Also important is maintaining perspective on unwanted thoughts, seeing them for what they really are. A thought is not an action, not a prediction. Your father suffers no harm because of what goes on privately in your head. If human beings were held accountable for all the strange, criminal and wayward thoughts that flit through their minds, every last one of us would be in jail. So tell yourself whenever the troubling thought occurs, "It's just a thought. Everyone has strange thoughts. Nothing has really happened to my father."

Although everyone has unwelcome thoughts from time to time, in severe cases a person is tormented by obsessions much of the time and to a disabling degree, disrupting performance and personal life. More about this condition, obsessive-compulsive disorder, is in the next question.

Q: I know this is crazy, but I sometimes feel driven to do weird things. For example, whenever I enter a building I have to count to 100.

A: What you're describing is a compulsion, a repeated urge to perform a meaningless behavior. Obsessions and compulsions often occur together, the compulsion serving to reduce anxiety caused by the obsession. For example, the obsessive thought "I'm dirty" may be accompanied by the compulsive ritual of constantly washing your hands. Like obsessions, compulsions are difficult to stop. If you prevent yourself from performing the action, your anxiety level rises until you give in to the impulse.

While some obsessive thinking and compulsive behavior is adaptive and common, especially among bright people (like college students), 1.5% to 2% of the population suffers severely from these symptoms and warrants the diagnosis of obsessive-compulsive disorder, or OCD.[1] Having OCD does not mean you're going crazy. On the other hand, obsessive-compulsive disorder can be long lasting and disabling.

Two treatments can be effective with compulsions. One is drug therapy; several of the newer antidepressant medications relieve obsessive-compulsive symptoms. With the second, a behavior therapy treatment called "exposure and response prevention," you deliberately place yourself where you normally perform the ritual (that's the exposure) but then restrain yourself from going through with it (that's response prevention). After a period of anxiety, often not only the compulsive behavior but also the associated obsession fades away.

To try exposure and response prevention on your own, you need to prevent yourself from counting when you enter a building. Your anxiety level will rise and you'll be sorely tempted to start counting; if you can, ride out these feelings. Later, go in again and resist counting once more. If this proves too difficult at first, try the gradual approach by first counting only to 70, then next time to 50 and so forth. Eventually, after enough trials, your overpowering urge to count may weaken and fade away.

This self-help method can work—if your problem isn't severe. However, OCD, if that's what you have, is a serious condition requiring professional assistance. If you have no success on your own curbing compulsions or obsessions and if they're interfering with your life, those are clear signals that you should consult a counselor.

Q: Every week or so I have a nightmare. Does that mean I have deep emotional problems?

A: Probably not. Studies show that college students average one nightmare every one or two weeks—the frequency subsides as you get older—and nightmares usually don't betoken psychological disturbance. One exception is if nightmares are the result of a traumatic event, like a severe accident, rape, or childhood sexual or physical abuse. Nightmares then are a sign of "post-traumatic stress disorder," and counseling is indicated. Counseling is also recommended if nightmares make you afraid or unable to sleep. Otherwise, bad dreams in and of themselves are probably nothing to worry about.

This is not to say you should dismiss your dreams. Dreams are remarkably revealing; Freud called them the royal road to the unconscious. To understand dreams, write them down immediately and in detail when you wake up, rather than waiting to recall them in the morning (warning: you can lose sleep this way). Then next day play with possible meanings, paying special attention to feelings (were you angry? scared?) and plot lines (were you trying to go somewhere? get away?). One dream in isolation may not make much sense, but a series of dreams may yield powerful truths about your wishes, fears and conflicts.

Q: I'm a worrier. I worry about my grades, my girlfriend breaking up with me, you name it.

A: Worry is an easy habit of mind to acquire. If you're at all imaginative, talented at fantasizing and inventing stories, then it's a simple mental exercise to concoct "what if" disaster scenarios: "What if I fail this exam?" "What if my girlfriend breaks up with me?" "What if this cough turns out to be bronchitis?" A good worrier doesn't even need to rely on future calamities; the present moment is rich in disappointments if he or she wants to see things that way: "I wish I had got into Princeton." "I wish I had more money." "I wish I were ten pounds lighter." To a talented worrier, the world is full of glasses, and they're all half empty.

Once you learn to worry it's hard to stop, particularly because the habit has psychological payoffs. For one thing, the act of worrying gives you the illusion of preparing for the worst. By worrying about a potential disaster, you feel as if you won't be hurt if it happens. (You still will, though.) Also, worry gives you the illusory sense of doing something positive to avert bad outcomes. You feel when you're worrying as if you're *working* somehow, putting in effort, similar to the effort of praying. Unless you make yourself anxious before a test, for example, you may feel as if you haven't prepared properly. In truth, of course, worry doesn't really accomplish anything; worrying about a test is no substitute for studying. Worry also takes the sparkle out of life. Too much of it and you make yourself dull and miserable and test the patience of those around you.

To curb the worry habit, the first step is to be aware of it, to catch yourself in the act. So notice how often your mind almost automatically slips into worry mode. Then give yourself a reality test each time it happens. "Are my fears rational?" "Is there anything else I can do to improve the situation?" If the answers are no, encourage yourself to relax about the issue at hand. Remind yourself that further worry is useless.

That's the reality-testing approach. A second approach is the paradoxical technique of deliberately worrying *more*. Make yourself worry, set aside time for it, exaggerate the disasters that await you. Ultimately, the absurdity of so much self-imposed distress may get to you, and you'll weary of the mental exertion.

INDECISIVENESS

Q: How can I learn to make a decision? I'm going crazy deciding between two majors that both appeal to me.

A: Making decisions is a skill that can be learned. Like any other skill, it improves with practice. Here are recommended steps:

1. **Gather information.** Find out about each choice. This may mean asking others' opinions, doing background reading and if possible testing out each option—for example, sitting in on classes for each major. Keep doing this until you have a good—not absolute—understanding of both sides. When you have a good fund of information, go on to the next step.
2. **Evaluate the information.** To bring order to the process, it may help to put down on paper "pro" and "con" columns containing the positives and negatives of each choice. It's essential to form your own conclusions here—how do the choices seem to *you*? Ideally a decision should be your own, based on your own judgment, and it may or may not coincide with what others would have you do.
3. **Be prepared for mixed feelings, conflicting thoughts and competing motives.** You may feel torn between what you "should" do and want to do, or between a safer route and a riskier, more exciting one. You also may feel torn because either choice means giving up the other. That's the nature of difficult decisions; they tug at you both ways. Don't wait for a feeling of 100% certainty or an overwhelming mass of evidence all on one side—that rarely happens.

4. **Don't insist on knowing the future.** As you evaluate, also remember that you can't know for sure how each choice may turn out—you don't have a crystal ball. The best you can do is go with the information available to you at the present time.
5. **Let yourself decide.** Once you've gathered and evaluated evidence, you're ready to make a choice. Remember, your task is to make a *good* decision, not the "right" decision.
6. **Don't second-guess yourself.** Having made a tough, sensible, reasoned choice, now support yourself and give it a fair chance. If future events add new information that calls for a change of plans, you can always reconsider; few decisions in life are irrevocable. For now, respect your judgment and support the choice you've made.

Q: These steps aren't going to work for *me*. I can't even choose what clothes to wear in the morning. What's my problem?

A: It could be a number of things. Depressed and risk-averse students have difficulty making decisions. So do chronically anxious students, who think in catastrophic, "what-if" terms ("What if I change my major and then hate it?") and so resist taking any course of action. If you can't make even little decisions or if there's a big decision that you feel incapable of making, then you may have one of these difficulties and should consider counseling.

ANGER

Q: I get angry a lot, sometimes outwardly but mostly inside. In my mind I'm always furious and telling somebody off. Why am I like this?

A: Anger is a basic emotion, like sadness and fear and joy, so it's no mystery that you feel it sometimes. Anger can be thought of as a source of energy with both constructive and destructive potential. When used constructively, it mobilizes you to correct wrongs and overcome frustrations, to fight for yourself when necessary. But when uncontrolled, misdirected or unrelieved, anger destroys relationships and injures mental and physical health. In recent years, studies have linked chronic anger to heart disease and early death.

Why do you get angry? Certainly, sometimes angry feelings are justified. There's no shortage of selfishness and cruelty in the world, no lack of frustrations. But anger also can be a by-product of flawed thinking or misinterpretation of events. For example, you may guess what's in people's minds and assume they mean you harm or don't respect you. You may consistently assign people to the same depriving or victimizing roles, even if they don't deserve it. Viewing others in these biased ways assures you'll end up angry.

Anger can also grow out of feelings of hurt, disappointment, powerlessness or frustration. If someone rejects you romantically or a professor gives you a bad grade, your mind may automatically shift gears to anger and fantasies of retaliation. It isn't exactly fun to be angry, but on balance indignation feels better than hurt and disappointment.

Q: What can I do if I'm often angry?

A: For starters, we recommend being cautious about expressing it. Instead of making you less angry, openly releasing anger tends to make you angrier still—not to mention antagonizing the other party. A better approach if you have a legitimate grievance is to bring it up assertively (see pages 5–6). Focus on the issue and what you want to happen in the future: "John, you forgot to give me the message when my friend called. Next time, please try to remember, okay?" Don't attack, accuse, bring up extraneous issues, threaten or raise your voice. You don't even have to stress that you're angry. Stick to the issue at hand, communicating as one reasonable, well-intentioned adult talking to another.

We also recommend a delay before expressing your concern. Folk wisdom says to count to 10 when you're angry; we say take several hours, a day or even longer to get perspective on the issue. Go off by yourself to think, or better yet talk the matter over with an objective friend. This is your chance to apply the cognitive approach of identifying irrational thoughts and replacing them with realistic alternatives: "John probably didn't deliberately forget to give me the message. That's an assumption on my part. He's forgetful, not mean, so I shouldn't get too worked up about this. And it's not that big a deal that he forgot." During this cooling-off period you can think through how to deliver an assertive message, if that's what you decide to do.

Since disproportionate anger is often a sign of flawed thinking, poor self-esteem or painful early life experiences—notably a disproportionately angry parent—you may not be able to lick this problem on your own. In that case you should consider consulting a counselor.

Q: Being angry makes me so uncomfortable. What can I do to prevent this feeling?

A: You can get a handle on excessive or inappropriate anger, as we explain on the previous page. But for appropriate anger, whether it's mild annoyance or full-blooded wrath, we have no solutions. You can't simply make feelings go away because you don't approve of them. You can't mold yourself into having only the "right" feelings. As long as you are human, you will have emotional reactions to experience—a succession of feelings will well up—and sometimes this means you'll feel annoyed or even angry.

Let us expand on this point. Many people are intolerant of one kind of emotion or another. Those who pride themselves on niceness are uncomfortable experiencing any anger. Those who think of themselves as tough tend to reject feelings of sadness, tenderness and fear. Independent personalities disown their dependent side; dependent personalities are out of touch with their longings for autonomy. All these strategies are limiting, making people strangers to themselves and cardboard figures to others. When you deny the full range of your emotional responsiveness, you negate parts of yourself.

So, do work on curbing unrealistic angry thoughts and uncontrolled angry outbursts, if that's a problem. But experience and "own" anger when you feel it. That way you know the real you and are genuine in relating to others.

STRESS

Q: What is stress?

A: Stress is the arousal of your mind and body in response to the demands of life. Taking tests, keeping up with reading lists and writing term papers cause stress. So do family problems, dating pressures, roommate conflicts and misunderstandings with friends. Stress is unavoidable, and, up to a point, healthy and desirable. Without sufficient stress life lacks zest. Over vacation, for example, you may find yourself feeling restless and unhappy for no apparent reason. The problem may be a lack of challenges to engage you—a shortage of stress.

Too much stress, however, and you suffer the consequences. That's because stress turns on your body's emergency response system. Your nervous and hormonal systems prepare for fight or flight—your heart, blood pressure and breathing rates speed up, muscles tense, digestion slows—as if you were a cave dweller threatened by a wild animal. But in today's world, where the challenges come from reading loads and roommates rather than saber-toothed tigers, your emergency response system may not turn off promptly. The stressors keep coming, you can't get rid of them by fighting or fleeing, and so you may remain mentally and physically aroused far longer than is healthy for you.

When stress becomes excessive, the goal is to reduce it to manageable levels. You can do this by cutting down on outside pressures, by inwardly responding to pressures in healthful ways and by learning to relax and develop healthy habits.

Q: How do I know if I'm under too much stress?

A: Look for the following signs:

- You always feel rushed, under time pressure.
- You can't slow down or relax.
- You feel a need to be perfect.
- You're irritable, moody, tense or anxious.
- You can't stop worrying.
- Your mind races; you're caught up in too many details to concentrate well.
- You turn minor matters into major concerns.
- You have difficulty sleeping.
- You have headaches, backaches, an upset stomach, hives or other physical problems.

Q: If I'm under too much stress, what can I do about it?

A: The most straightforward approach is to lighten your load. Pare down external demands until you feel challenged but not overwhelmed. For example, you might drop a course, pass up an extracurricular activity or cut down on the hours of a part-time job. Even minor adjustments can make a difference. Say your roommate is adding to your stress by playing music late at night. Request that he or she stop the music after a certain hour—be friendly but direct—and you may start to feel less burdened. Or a friend may ask for a drive to the airport. If you don't have the time to do the favor, say so: You'll feel less stressed and you also won't resent your friend afterward.

For some students, cutting back is easier said than done. "I can't drop a thing," they say, explaining why it's absolutely unthinkable not to take 18 credits, visit a dozen friends, run for campus political office, compete on the varsity swim team and do 15 hours per week of volunteer work. If this is you, we suggest stepping back for a moment and examining your motives. Are all your activities truly indispensable? Or do you feel *driven* to do them, compelled by some psychological need?

What might psychologically drive you to take on too much? The reason could be to compensate for inferiority feelings. If you juggle a dozen responsibilities, then you quiet that nagging inner voice of self-doubt. Or overinvolvement may make you feel less empty: Rushing around is better than the uneasy feeling that overtakes you the moment you slow down. Or perhaps you're frightened to let anything go for fear of never having another chance. You must do everything at once, lest opportunities disappear forever.

As you can see, various motives drive students to take on too many responsibilities. If you feel impelled to overextend yourself, consider talking it over with a counselor. Once you understand yourself better, perhaps you can slow down to a good cruising speed.

Q: I work 40 hours per week to pay for college while taking a full course load. How can I avoid feeling stressed out?

A: Cut back on either work or studies, if possible. If you can arrange to have either a part-time job with full-time studies or part-time studies with a full-time job, the schedule may be quite manageable. In fact, some students thrive on work-and-study combinations; having a job helps them to organize their time and study efficiently. If you're considering switching to part-time student status, however, first talk to a financial aid administrator and an academic advisor. Don't inadvertently lose financial aid or fail to fulfill academic requirements because you were uninformed of the consequences of changing your status.

If financial pressures dictate that you absolutely must both work and study full-time, then at least do everything possible to lighten your stress level otherwise. Eat and sleep well, use alcohol moderately or not at all, and try to get regular exercise and squeeze in time for relaxation and socializing. Also, have realistic expectations of yourself and keep a sense of perspective. A backbreaking schedule won't allow you much time to study; you probably won't earn the highest grades. Recognizing what's academically feasible will make you feel good about your achievements, and that in itself reduces stress.

Q: Is it stressful to study too hard?

A:
It can be. All work and no play is not a sound regimen; neither is all play and no work. A balanced schedule, like a balanced diet, is healthiest. Years ago, one of us counseled an extraordinarily tense freshman who spent virtually all his waking hours in the library. He didn't see friends, he didn't date, he didn't play sports. The only reason he made time for counseling was because he hoped it would help him study. After a discussion in counseling, he agreed to try an experiment. He would cut down on library time and instead visit friends, ask someone out and exercise at the gym. The results were dramatic. When he returned the following week, not only did he report enjoying these other activities, but he also felt less tense and better able to concentrate at the library.

Q: I don't think I've taken on too many responsibilities, but I still feel rushed and tense. What now?

A:
The problem may be in your thoughts and beliefs. If you send yourself irrational, negative messages, your stress level surges. For example, suppose you say to yourself before a test, "I have to perform brilliantly or the professor won't respect me," or tell yourself before a job interview, "I know I won't get it, and if I don't get this one I'll never get a good job." Think in these ways often enough, and naturally you'll soon feel stressed out.

To reduce stress, employ the cognitive approach. First, identify flawed thinking (see pages 51–52 for common negative thinking patterns). Whenever you notice such thoughts—they may come fast and furious—try to banish them from your mind. Then replace the thoughts with reasonable, constructive alternatives. For example: "I don't know for sure what my professor thinks, but probably she'll respect me even if my work isn't brilliant." And, "I don't know what will happen at the interview, but I'll give it my best shot. Besides, if this job doesn't work out, another one surely will."

Employing the cognitive approach is like being your own counselor. You talk yourself into keeping perspective and thereby lower your level of stress. When this isn't enough, another option is to talk to someone else—a roommate, friend, parent or counselor. Another person can show you how you've lost perspective on your responsibilities, and it's amazing sometimes what a relief it is just to let out what's troubling you. Finding a sympathetic ear is perhaps the oldest stress reduction method of all, and it's still among the best.

Q: I'm always tense and I get headaches. Will relaxation exercises help?

A: Very possibly. Relaxation techniques are another major strategy of stress management. Here are suggested methods:

- **Take deep, slow, regular breaths from the abdomen.** Do this for 10 or 20 minutes alone in your room, or even for a moment or two in a classroom or at a party. You'll notice an immediate lowering of tension.
- **Practice deep muscle relaxation.** This involves systematically squeezing and then releasing large muscle groups in the body, one at a time: forehead muscles, jaw, neck, shoulders, each bicep, each forearm, each fist, chest, stomach and so forth. After you tense and then relax each muscle group, pay attention to the sensation. Not only will you feel thoroughly relaxed at the end of this exercise, but you'll learn to recognize tension in any part of your body.
- **Learn meditation.** Take a course to do this, or try these steps on your own. Alone in a quiet place, seat yourself in a comfortable position. Then, focus on a repeated word or phrase like "peace," "calm" or "let it be," silently reciting it each time you exhale. At the same time, gently let other thoughts, images and feelings drift out of awareness. This form of controlled meditation, practiced for 10- or 20-minute sessions, is described in detail in *The Relaxation Response*.[2]
- **Practice visualization.** Imagine a pleasing scene: a beach, your parents' living room, a friend's face. You can do this in conjunction with other relaxation techniques.
- **Try a warm bath, good book or music.** Activities and hobbies are also excellent ways to relax and counter stress. Finally, sometimes you can attain peace of mind simply by "vegging out," doing nothing.

Q: Can an unbalanced diet add to my level of stress?

A: Anything unhealthy increases your stress level. Eating too much, too little, erratically or poorly (junk foods) is stressful. So is not getting enough sleep or keeping wildly irregular sleep habits.

Another contributor to stress is lack of physical exercise. Since stress arouses your nervous and endocrine systems for the exertion of fight or flight, regular exercise provides the physical release that restores your body to a relaxed state. The standard recommendation is at least four or five 20-minute sessions per week of aerobic exercise, such as jogging, swimming, basketball, rowing or biking. Build up to strenuous exercise gradually, and check with a physician if you have a medical condition that makes exercising hazardous.

Q: Sometimes I take a drink or two to relax. Is there any problem with that?

A: Drinking may help in the short run, but it won't change your situation or teach new coping skills. The same goes for tranquilizers prescribed by a doctor. Except in severe cases where a psychiatrist may recommend medication, we suggest you refrain from medicating away stress.

FOR FURTHER READING

Herbert Benson with Miriam Z. Klipper, *The Relaxation Response.* New York: Avon, 1996.

Edward A. Charlesworth and Ronald G. Nathan, *Stress Management: A Comprehensive Guide to Wellness.* New York: Ballantine, 1985.

Daniel Goleman, *Emotional Intelligence.* New York: Bantam Books, 1995.

John H. Greist, James W. Jefferson and Isaac M. Marks, *Anxiety and Its Treatment.* New York: Warner, 1987.

Christopher J. McCullough and Robert Woods Mann, *Managing Your Anxiety.* New York: Berkley Publishing, 1994.

Martin E.P. Seligman, *What You Can Change and What You Can't.* New York: Fawcett Columbine, 1993.

R. Reid Wilson, *Don't Panic: Taking Control of Anxiety Attacks.* New York: Harper Perennial, 1996.

COPING WITH
YOUR FAMILY

Students who go into counseling sometimes grow impatient when questioned about their families. "I came here to talk about my room-mate and study problems," they say. "What's my family got to do with it?" The answer is that family issues have a long reach. After all, your parents and siblings were your first teachers. They influenced your basic opinions about yourself and the world; they helped create, for good or ill, your capacities for trust, love and independence. Even now, when events back home may seem remote, current family prob-lems still work their influence. You don't slough off two decades of emotional involvement just because you've gone off to college.

Family concerns, then, are important not only in their own right. To understand current problems at college, often you must under-stand what used to happen, and still happens, back home.

The material in this chapter is divided into three sections. First we address "normal" family concerns voiced by students from healthy families. Even good family relationships are strained sometimes, especially when students leave home for college. Next we consider the disruptive consequences of parental divorce and the death of a parent. Lastly, we focus on troubled family interactions and the effects of growing up with critical or unloving parents, emotionally disturbed parents and other dysfunctional households.

PROBLEMS OF A "NORMAL" FAMILY

Q: Over Christmas vacation I started fighting with my sister, snapping at my mother and running to my room in tears. I felt 14 years old all over again.

A: Your reaction is not atypical. Maturation is not a straight-ahead march to adulthood, where you advance step by step and leave behind old ways forever. Psychologically speaking, a 14-year-old still exists within you, and for that matter so does a 7-year-old and a 2-year-old. And there's no one like family to push the buttons that bring out these earlier selves. Your sister's whining, your mother's nagging, the noisy way your father chomps his food—these, for you, are old stimuli that trigger deeply ingrained responses.

Don't be surprised or too concerned if you misplace a few years of maturity when you go back home. Actually, you can even enjoy being a 14-year-old again and take a break from the sometimes confining role of college student. There's something comforting about being with people who still accept you even when your most obnoxious qualities surface.

But if you're really unhappy with yourself at home, make an effort to practice assertive communications (see pages 5–6). Expressing feelings and needs in plain language is one mark of the mature individual. Also, consider if there's any way your family can help you behave maturely. For example, request that they *ask* you to do chores rather than order you. If you point out ways they can treat you like an adult, maybe you'll find it easier to act like one.

Q: Why don't my parents see how much I've changed at college?

A: They're at a disadvantage if you live away from home. Not having a chance to observe you regularly, they remember you as you were back in high school. Also, it seems to be a law of human nature to expect consistency and predictability from others. Since you've acted certain ways before, naturally your parents assume you'll continue acting those ways. Otherwise they'd feel as if they didn't really know you.

Assuming your parents have generally viewed you accurately in the past, their perceptions of you should eventually catch up with reality. After you've spent a long vacation living again at home, they should come to recognize how much you've grown.

Q: My parents say they want me to phone every Sunday night, but sometimes I can't get around to it, or I just don't feel like it.

A: Once a week doesn't seem unreasonable, especially if you're a first-year student who's just moved away from home. Your parents understandably want to know you're alive and hear about your doings.

If the every-Sunday arrangement seems too inflexible, maybe you can work out a compromise where sometimes you'll write or e-mail rather than call, or your calls may have to wait for a Monday or a Tuesday.

Q: My mom calls me every day, sometimes twice. We've always been close, but I wonder sometimes if we're overdoing it.

A: There are two ways to look at this. The traditional thinking is that college is a time to separate from your family and turn your attention to peers. According to this view, either you or your mother, or both of you, are finding it hard to let go, and that spells trouble for your personal development. But your closeness can also be interpreted as a blessing. Some students constantly fight with their parents or hardly speak at all. If you and your mother are best friends, possibly you're just lucky.

So which is it? One test is what your mother asks of you. Does she turn to you because she's lonely and unhappy, as if you're her spouse? Does she burden you with her problems, as if you're the parent? If in these ways she imposes her emotional needs, then the relationship as it stands is not healthy. You can't live your own life if you feel responsible for hers.

A second test concerns your involvement in college. Do you call your mother instead of reaching out to make friends? Are you on the phone with her rather than pursuing romantic opportunities? Relying on family for emotional fulfillment and missing out on a full social life on campus is not in your best interests.

So, the issue is more complicated than how often you speak on the telephone. You may want to explore any guilt or insecurity aroused by the thought of becoming less involved with your mother. It also may help to raise the issue with her. She may have insights into your relationship and be sympathetic to your concerns.

Q: Every time my parents ask, I always say everything's "fine." Actually, I'm not doing very well in some classes, but I don't want them getting all bent out of shape. Is it wrong to lie to them?

A: In our opinion, you're entitled to keep some things to yourself, but it's a mistake to lie. Most lies come out anyway; you can't hide your grades forever. And when your parents catch on to the truth, they'll become less trusting of you and question you even more in the future.

Do your parents pry into your affairs? Then point this out and say you'd prefer bringing up matters on your own. Tell them you'll keep them posted on what they need to know. Do your parents overreact to your problems? Then explain that their worry and anger are counterproductive, making you reluctant to confide in them. Tell them you'll volunteer more if they respond calmly.

Such an honest face-to-face discussion will serve you far better in the long run than attempting a cover-up.

Q: I hate to admit this, but I wish my parents wouldn't come for Parents' Weekend. They speak with a thick accent and they always say and do the wrong thing in public. How can I control them around my friends?

A: Probably you can't. Parents say the darnedest things, and there's little you can do to stop them. If it's any consolation, you're not the only one who's embarrassed by your folks. Even young children, according to Freud, have an adoption fantasy that their real parents were royalty and were replaced by much inferior caretakers.

Will your friends really judge your parents harshly? Probably not. What to you seems incredibly gauche behavior may just strike your friends as appealing and unpretentious. Besides, your friends will be too preoccupied with their own concerns on Parents' Weekend to give much thought to your parents.

Here are a couple of tips about making the best of parents' visits:

- **Expect strong and possibly conflicting feelings.** In addition to possible annoyance or embarrassment, you may experience an upsurge in homesickness, pride and excitement as you show off your college life or keen disappointment because your parents don't seem equally excited. Expecting such reactions will prevent you from being overwhelmed by the feelings.
- **Plan ahead.** Work out the best time for them to come, and discuss what they will do during the visit, where you will take them, when you will be together and when apart. This will help make your visit more comfortable.

Q: My parents are good people, but they're really old-fashioned. I know it hurts them that I'm changing my religious views and attitudes about dating and sex. How should I deal with them?

A: This is a difficult question. Obviously, you don't want to alienate your parents. You also shouldn't take their opinions lightly. Many
of their ideas that you now call old-fashioned may eventually, as you
gain maturity, start to make sense. To paraphrase Mark Twain, parents can seem ignorant when you're young, but when you get older
it's astonishing how much they've learned.

On the other hand, trying out new views is inevitable at college—
that's why you go there. You have to learn to think independently in
order to grow up. And in a sense, you show gratitude to your parents
when you rethink your views. They sacrificed to get you an education,
and now you are thanking them by figuring things out for yourself.

If you haven't already done so, try explaining what you believe in a
frank discussion with your parents. Perhaps the differences between
you are less wide than they think. For example, your parents may fear
you've become an atheist when actually you're only questioning a few
church teachings. They may have exaggerated notions about your sexual exploits and will feel reassured when they learn the truth. Talking
openly with them may clear the air.

But some differences can't be explained away. When you and your
parents have basic disagreements, our advice, in most cases, is to stick
to your guns. Ultimately, you must decide about religion, dating and
sex. You have to conduct your life as you see fit. Your parents may disapprove for now, but eventually they'll probably come around. In the
long run, most parents accept the fact that their sons and daughters
must follow their own natures.

Q: But I come from another country, and in my culture children are supposed to
obey parents' wishes.

A: That complicates matters. If your culture considers obedience
to parents a paramount virtue, it will be enormously difficult for you,
even as a young adult, to oppose their wishes. Not only won't they
understand why you're disobeying them, but you won't feel at peace
about it. By opposing them you are in a sense untrue to yourself, since
parental obedience is one of your own deepest values.

Sometimes if you're patient, though, these seemingly impossible
situations sort themselves out. With the passage of time parents may
surprisingly shift their position; students have been known to change
their position too. But if the impasse persists, consider consulting a

clergyperson, professor, or counselor. With such a deep-seated, emotionally loaded conflict, a disinterested listener can at least help you calmly examine the issues.

Q: My oldest sister is the brains in the family, my next sister is the athlete and the next one is creative. There's nothing left for me.

A: Talents and interests aren't real estate. Your siblings can't claim exclusive ownership of them. No matter how impressive your sisters' accomplishments, you still should explore all your own potentials. You can be a scholar, jock or creative artist—or choose not to be—even though your older sisters got there first. You can either follow in their footsteps or take a new path, whether or not you're as successful as they are.

If comparisons to your sisters deter you, it may help to examine and question family messages you have received. Have your parents implied that you shouldn't compete with your sisters, or only compete if you're their equal? Have your sisters delivered one of these messages? Such family communications can be particularly powerful if you've never stopped to question them. Question them now, though, and you'll see that they are unreasonable. You have to follow your own bent regardless of family expectations.

Some students who feel limited by comparisons to older siblings—or to a twin or parent—elect to attend a different college than their relative. There they feel free to fulfill themselves without being haunted by their siblings' past achievements.

Q: Everyone says I'm exactly like my father and nothing like my mother. Is that unusual?

A: No, it isn't. Quite often children superficially take after one parent much more than the other. These resemblances don't always respect gender lines. A son may be quiet and subdued like his reserved mother, his sister a scene-stealer à la her theatrical father.

Resemblances and differences become a problem only when they become rules of behavior, limiting who you can be. If you feel compelled to be everything your father is—say you must always be strong and in control like him—then you may deny other parts of yourself. The same holds true if you feel compelled to be totally *unlike* your mother; because, say, she gets violent, you never let yourself feel angry.

Similar to your father you may be, but look closely and you'll recognize yourself as your mother's child as well as your father's child. With genes and parenting from both of them, you can't escape either heritage. But look again and you'll see you're more than the sum of their influences. Ultimately, you are an individual, complex and unique, not quite like them or anyone else.

Q: Nobody in my family has ever even finished high school. How will that affect me at college?

A: It's a challenge being a first-generation college student. Your family can't prepare you for the college experience—you're a pioneer—and they won't fully understand it once you're there. They may unrealistically expect you to make A's easily or imagine the worst about the college social scene. They may even resent you for draining family resources or supposedly putting on college airs.

Since your parents aren't familiar with college life, we advise you to invite them to your school. Introduce them to friends and professors, and show them your classes and samples of your work. This way college becomes less alien, and they can view your experience more realistically. At the same time, look for on-campus mentors such as more advanced students, advisors or counselors who can serve as role models and offer guidance about college that your family can't provide.

Q: I'm adopted and I've always gotten along really well with my parents. Lately, though, we seem to argue all the time.

A: All children, adopted or otherwise, go through rough patches with their parents. All have bitter moments of hating their parents and questioning their parents' love. The tensions in your case may have nothing to do with the adoption, which is but one factor among dozens that have shaped your relationship. On the other hand, the issue of adoption can cause stress between children and parents, even in basically healthy families.[1]

As an adoptee, naturally you'll have questions about your origins. What were your biological parents like? In what ways do you take after them? Why did they give you up? Should you try to contact them? You'll also wonder why your parents wanted to adopt you, how they arranged to do it and whether they'd treat you differently if you weren't adopted. These are normal questions for adopted persons, especially during the identity-questioning period from adolescence to early adulthood. Normal, too, are various emotional reactions to adoption, possibly including sadness, shame and anger.

If the arguments continue, address the problem with your parents. This may be the time to have another frank discussion about the adoption.

YOUR PARENTS' DIVORCE

Q: I always thought my parents had the greatest marriage. Now they're thinking about a divorce, and I feel devastated. What do I do?

A: Not only young children are shaken by news of parents' divorce. College students can feel the shock just as acutely. In fact, in some ways younger children have it easier, since at least they have the continuity of still living at home with a parent. But you have already left home, which was one loss, and now comes a second loss. All of a sudden the family you regarded as a haven doesn't exist anymore.

With your parents divorcing, you need to prepare for a difficult time and a welter of powerful, disturbing feelings. Expect to be angry: "Why didn't they tell me about their problems?" "Why didn't he treat her better"—or "Why didn't she treat him better?" Expect confusion and uncertainty: "Will Dad move away?" "Will the house be sold?" "Is Mom having an affair?" Above all, expect a pervasive hurt, a wrenching sense of loss. One of the worst scenarios imaginable has happened, and of course it has left you reeling.

To cope during this difficult time, we recommend the following:

- **Get support from friends and other relatives.** Parents, for obvious reasons, may not be much support to you now.
- **Be patient with yourself.** Don't blame yourself for having strong emotional reactions or for being below par in your studies.
- **Search for constructive activities and outlets:** exercise, extra-curricular activities, hobbies, volunteer work.
- **Watch out for destructive activities and outlets:** drugs and alcohol, compulsive eating, indiscriminate sexual activities.
- **Consider going to your college's counseling center** or to a private counselor for support and perspective.

- **Be realistic about your capabilities.** If you can continue with your current course load, great. But if you need to drop a course or even take a medical leave of absence, be open minded about these options.

Q: My parents got divorced six months ago, and now my mother doesn't want me to have anything to do with my father. What should I do?

A: Your parents divorced each other, not you. You're still as much your father's child as your mother's child, and you shouldn't have to choose between the two. And you shouldn't stay away from your father based solely on your mother's say-so. Assuming you're no longer a minor, the decision to see him is one which you, at your stage of maturity, can and should make for yourself.

If you do choose to visit him or even write or speak to him on the phone, you'll need to calm your mother and make your position clear. Tell her you are *not* taking his side. You are *not* betraying her. What you are doing is fulfilling your own need to maintain relations with both your parents.

Q: My father insists that I spend Christmas with him and my stepmother in London. My mother wants me to come home to San Francisco. Help!

A: A familiar problem, unfortunately. Divorced parents often play tug-of-war over their sons' and daughters' college vacations, just as they may play hot potato over who pays for college expenses. Sometimes it seems each side wants you home as much as possible while spending as little money on you as they can get away with. The conflict partly concerns you—they genuinely want to see you—and partly it involves the two of them. Though legally parted, your parents still may feel angry and use you to get back at each other.

Like Solomon confronted with two women claiming one baby, you obviously can't satisfy both your parents at once. Some sort of compromise needs to be worked out where you first visit one of them and later the other. In the meantime, explain to both sides the dilemma they are causing. Tell them that their pressure frustrates you and casts the vacation as a duty rather than a pleasure. Explain that you want to visit both of them; where you go first shouldn't be interpreted as choosing a favorite. With luck, they'll hear this message and allow you to work out vacation plans.

Q: My parents recently separated, and now they're not speaking. Instead, they ask me to relay messages and pump me for information about each other. How much should I tell them?

A: Ideally, nothing. Whatever your parents need to say to each other, they should do so directly. Your interactions with each parent should be confined to matters that just concern you and that parent.

Q: But why can't I help them communicate and perhaps bring them together?

A: For one thing, you'll probably do a poor job of it, positioned as you are in the midst of family dynamics. That's why there are marital counselors, trained professionals who are not emotionally involved with the family and can view issues objectively. So if you really want to assist your parents, encourage them to consult a counselor.

There are also dangers for you in the go-between role. Remember, in ancient days messengers were executed for being the deliverer of bad news. How will your mother or father treat you—and how will you feel about yourself—if you report something that hurts that parent? And how will they feel later if you decide instead to slant the news and withhold painful information? Being the intermediary is a no-win proposition whichever way you play it.

Your best bet is to declare up-front that you won't pass along messages or give out information from one parent to the other. Explain that you want to be helpful, but not in that way.

Q: But if I don't help solve my parents' problems, I feel guilty.

A: There are a couple of explanations for this feeling. Perhaps one or both parents has always placed undue responsibility on your shoulders. Now they are asking you to save the marriage or to care for them, in effect to be a surrogate parent or spouse. If that's what's happening, you need to determine for yourself and clarify for them your appropriate role within the family.

The other explanation for guilt is that you feel responsible somehow for breaking them apart. You fear you've been too close to one parent, or have been a financial burden, or have disappointed them in grades or behavior or in not being lovable enough. Since you believe you've caused the separation, now you feel it's your job to patch things up.

If this is your thinking, you need to understand that children don't dissolve marriages; husbands and wives do. It wasn't you who stopped them from loving each other—you couldn't if you tried. And now you don't have the power, or the duty, to rekindle their love. The problems they are having are not your responsibility.

Q: My mother recently remarried and moved in with her new husband and his two daughters. Now I feel out of place when I visit her.

A: An understandable reaction. You have a new stepfather and stepsisters, and your mother has a new dwelling and new claims on her affection. With so much that's unfamiliar, no wonder you feel strange when you visit her.

Here are some thoughts about dealing with the situation:

- **Be patient.** It will take a good while and many visits before you come to know your stepfamily and get used to your mother's changed circumstances. Only gradually will you start to feel at home in this household.
- **Be open-minded.** Although inner misgivings are inevitable, try to be accepting of these new people and the changes in your mother's life.
- **Open lines of communication.** If possible, discuss with your stepfamily everyone's reactions to the recent events. Doing so may bring you together and help instill a sense of family.
- **Avoid warfare.** If after getting to know your stepfamily you still don't feel comfortable or even like them, accept your feelings but try to keep matters civil.
- **Seek time alone with your mother.** While you shouldn't begrudge her time with her new family, she's still your mother. Spending time alone with her will lessen your sense of loss and help you accept the changes.

Q: My parents divorced 10 years ago. Could that be connected to my current adjustment problems at college?

A: It's certainly possible. Judith Wallerstein has done research showing that many children have difficulties—underachievement, worry, self-doubt and anger—years after the divorce. Sometimes the damage isn't apparent until the college years, when romantic and sexual relationships begin—and students become frightened of following in their parents' footsteps.

Divorce, Wallerstein found, delivers children a series of blows. First there are parental battles or coldness before the divorce, then comes the disruption caused by the divorce itself, and finally the parents have a reduced capacity to parent after the divorce. In addition, children often feel rejected by one of the divorcing parents, especially the father if the children remain in the mother's custody.

Not every divorce causes children lasting damage. However, if you are having problems in a relationship, are depressed, are an academic underachiever or have other inexplicable difficulties, there may be a connection to this decade-old divorce of your parents.

DEATH IN THE FAMILY

Q: My father's dying of cancer, and I don't feel a thing. Is it that I just don't care?

A: Your seemingly callous reaction is probably just numbness. We suspect it hasn't fully hit you yet that your father is dying.

Although there is no uniform, correct way to mourn or grieve, reactions to a loved one's death tend to follow a certain sequence. In the beginning you can expect to feel shock, numbness and a sense of disbelief. Later comes a period of intense suffering, of despair, as the reality of the loss sinks in. In the next stage, depending on your style, you may cling to others or withdraw, and may obsessively dwell on your father's memory or avoid ever thinking about him. You also may experience strong, seemingly inexplicable anger and feel a profound sense of aloneness.

These reactions are all part of active mourning. Mourning can last as long as several years, although some of the pain endures for a lifetime. Mourning is a healing process, painful but necessary. When you've successfully mourned, you can remember the dead person without being overwhelmed by your feelings, and you feel emotionally ready to get on with your life.

Q: I've never really been close to my father. Maybe that's why I'm reacting so calmly.

A: Maybe. Eventually, though, your distant relationship may actually intensify your suffering, not reduce it. Now he will never fulfill the promise of a father. Now you and he will never become close. As these realizations gradually hit home, you may find yourself feeling bitter and profoundly sad, and perhaps blame yourself for your own role in shutting him out. It can be especially painful to let someone go when so much between you is left unsaid.

Maybe, however, you do still have some time. Are there things you want to say to him before he dies? Are there things you want to hear? If so, we encourage you to open up the dialogue. Confronting the death of your father requires confronting your relationship with him in life as well. We also recommend seeing a counselor to sort out these issues and begin the necessary task of mourning.

Q: My mother is critically ill. Should I take time off from college?

A: It all depends. Certainly you should take time off if you feel unable to concentrate or engage in college activities. You also should go home if being at college prevents you from attending to your parent and helping your family. On the other hand, some students find the best place to be during this crisis is at college. They can still visit home as needed, but for their own sake and the family's sake they're better off remaining enrolled as a student.

If you do need to take time off, speak to a faculty advisor, dean or counselor about the options, making sure to consider any financial repercussions. Postponements, incompletes, waived assignments or a medical leave of absence may prove best in your particular case.

TROUBLED FAMILIES

Q: My younger brother has always been in and out of psychiatric hospitals, and now he's getting out of control again. What can I do to help my parents? They're going crazy with worry.

A: You're asking the "$64,000 question": What *can* you do? This same issue comes up when parents go through a divorce, a parent has a substance abuse problem, a single parent is lonely and needy, or the family has a financial crisis. In each case, you have to decide whether to get involved, and if you do, what you can accomplish.

In making the decision, review what you've tried and achieved in the past. Have you been effective speaking to your brother during his crises? Did you succeed in consoling and encouraging your parents? If in such ways you've been helpful before, then maybe it makes sense to pitch in again.

But most likely your influence is limited here, as it usually is when college students get caught up in family tangles. Though almost grown up, you're still a child in this family, not a parent—only a lay person, not a professional. Realistically, there may be nothing you can do to help. You may even make matters worse. As a family member yourself, you can't be objective about disturbed family interactions and may unintentionally exacerbate the very problems you're trying to solve.

And then there's yourself to think of. Let's say to help your family you make sacrifices—frequent phone calls, personal anguish, weekends spent at home, withdrawal from college. In the end, you may forfeit your educational opportunity without improving the family situation, and that won't please any of you.

Q: My father says that either I become a premed major or he'll pull me out of school. In the past he's told me where I should go to college, who my friends should be and what jobs I should take. How do I deal with such a rigid parent?

A: Let's first place this in context. In the normal course of events, your parents would relax control as you got older. By the time you entered college, you'd mostly make your own decisions *and* your own mistakes. But some parents don't let this happen and continue managing their children's lives. Not only can this feel suffocating, but it makes it hard to know your own mind and enjoy your own triumphs. It deprives you of the opportunity to learn to care for yourself.

So where does this leave you with your father? One issue to explore is the signals you send to him. For example, have you always ducked decisions in the past, inviting him to make them for you? In that case, explain that you are growing up and feel capable now of deciding on matters such as your own choice of a major. Have you typically reacted to his authority by shouting, crying, being sarcastic or sullenly withdrawing? Such immature tactics naturally provoke him to act like an authority. Much more effective is to speak reasonably about the choice of majors, listening to his position while calmly presenting your own.

If better communicating doesn't do the trick, another possibility is to bring a knowledgeable third party to the discussion. Perhaps with your mother, aunt, uncle or grandparent as a negotiator, you and your father will hear each other and work out a compromise.

If none of these tactics budges your father from his hard-line stance, you have a tough choice ahead. One option is to respect his authority and switch your major. This will maintain the peace at home, although at the considerable cost of abandoning your own wishes. The other option is to defy your father, try to finance college yourself and prepare for an angry, guilt-inducing rift within the family. This is a difficult judgment call, and you should consult with trusted friends or professionals before making it.

Q: No matter what I do or accomplish, my mother has always criticized me. I've never been good enough in her eyes—I'm stupid or lazy or selfish. How can I deal with such negative feedback?

A: Criticism from parents is not exactly headline news, of course. All parents criticize their sons and daughters sometimes, and almost always the children get through it. But when the criticism passes a certain threshold—when the negative words are too harsh and persistent, too unloving and disapproving—then it's no longer the usual parental badgering, but verbal abuse. Parental verbal abuse can maim you emotionally.

Some children who grow up hearing excessive criticism react by trying everything to please their parents, always searching for the key to approval. Others give up the effort to please and sometimes deliberately invite criticism—it's the only parental attention they know. That's what one student did in high school, when he infuriated his critical, old-fashioned father by dyeing his hair purple, cutting classes and dropping hints about taking drugs. "Go ahead," the student's actions said. "Now you've really got a reason to yell at me."

As for your mother, you probably can't change her much. You can try, if you wish, to confront her when she laces into you, pointing out what she's doing and asking her to stop. You can ask her to praise you and acknowledge your successes as well as your faults. This straightforward, assertive approach is certainly worth a try.

Most likely, though, she will at best tone down her words, not adopt a new attitude. You can spend your whole life hoping she'll change—and feeling deflated each time she doesn't. A better plan is to come to terms with who she is. Try to face the reality of her limitations, the fact that whatever you do she'll never be loving and accepting. This truth may hurt, but false hopes hurt more. Once you give up the vain attempt to win your mother over, you'll be free to look elsewhere—to friends, lovers and teachers—for the acceptance you rightfully desire.

Having a critical, disapproving parent undoubtedly has influenced how you relate to other people. You may have grown up submissive and overpleasing, or unduly sensitive to criticism, or defiant and aloof. You also may be self-critical and self-disapproving, having taken your mother's harsh judgments to heart. If in such ways your mother's verbal abuse has proved damaging, we advise you to consult a counselor. Counseling can help you accept yourself as well as look into your parental and other relationships.

Q: My father has never been interested in me. Once or twice he's said he loves me, but in truth he just doesn't seem to care.

A: Sadly, what you describe is an oft-told story. Some parents, especially fathers, appear cold and remote within the family. They may show passion for their job or the dog or television football, but with spouses and children they tune out. Other parents are emotionally involved with certain family members but not with others, or up to certain stages of children's development but not afterward. Any way it happens, indifference and rejection from a parent wounds deeply.

What's to be done about your father? As with the hypercritical parent described above, you can experiment with how you relate to him. Possibly you're now as distant with him as he is with you, and so a friendlier approach is in order. If you try reaching out by telling him about college or asking about his job, maybe you'll spark some interest.

But again as with the critical parent, you need to have realistic expectations. Getting him to chitchat is a possibility, but more than that may be unlikely. He may never be warm, never show a real interest in you or allow himself to get very close. Learning to acknowledge this bitter fact can spare you further disappointments. The essential goal is to face his limitations squarely and give up hoping he'll miraculously start to take an interest in you.

Lastly, take a close, honest look at yourself. Are you lacking in self-worth? Are you wary of getting close to others—or are you overdependent, hanging on for dear life? Do you gravitate toward emotionally unavailable people and then try, as with your father, to win them over? Consequences like these call for exploration in counseling.

You can't transform your father, but you can do something about yourself and your other relationships.

Q: I never know what to expect from my mother. One minute she loves me, the next I'm the cause of her divorce. One minute she's bubbly and joking, and the next she's in tears.

A: Irrational, unpredictable parents can do as much damage, in their own way, as verbally abusive or cold parents. The tendency in such a home is to grow up insecure and apprehensive, always fearful about what's coming next. In reaction to your mother's erratic moods, you may have become a people pleaser, who does almost anything to head off an ugly scene. Another possibility is you learned to shy away from people. You also may have developed a moodiness problem of your own.

Your mother's instability strongly suggests emotional disturbance. Even if you already suspected as much, this still can be hard to accept. Your mother brought you into the world, she and your father were your caretakers and first teachers, and naturally part of you still wants to believe in her. We recommend speaking to a counselor to understand and come to terms with her difficulties. In counseling you can look at her objectively and see how she distorted reality. You can also repair your self-image and relationships—both of which, unfortunately, have surely been casualties of your mother's disturbance.

In the meantime, we have a few thoughts about surviving visits home. When you see your mother, train yourself if you can to expect the unexpected. Her mood may shift at any moment, like a child's, and bearing that in mind will ease your distress when it happens. Remind yourself, too, that her emotional storms are not your doing, they're her nature, and therefore it's not your responsibility to pacify her nor your fault when she has an outburst. Finally, try to be as consistent, predictable and calm with her as you can. Since she is emotionally like a child, it may steady her a bit if you conduct yourself almost like a patient parent or teacher.

Q: My father has an alcohol problem. How has that affected me?

A: Alcoholic families differ. However, it seems safe to say that neither your father, focused as he was on the bottle, nor your mother, burdened by his problem, provided consistent caring and structure.

Being raised in an alcoholic family, especially if his problem was severe, has almost surely deprived you of a normal childhood.

Children's reactions to parental alcoholism also differ. Some adult children of alcoholics (ACOAs) thrive despite their upbringing, and in fact ACOA college students in general have been found to be remarkably resilient. On the other hand, some ACOAs are thought to have low self-esteem, judge themselves harshly and have difficulty trusting others and forming relationships. ACOAs are also at risk of becoming alcoholics themselves and of marrying an alcoholic.

Certain therapists believe that children of alcoholics learn a role in order to survive in their family. For example, the "hero" is a high achiever but inwardly is prey to insecurity, in terror of being wrong and in constant need for approval. The "scapegoat" is hostile, defiant and prone to alcoholism, and so manages to shift the family's focus of attention away from the alcoholic. The "lost child," detached and shy, avoids attracting attention—or getting his or her needs met. The "mascot," the humorous and cute family clown, laughs on the outside and cries within.

These roles may help some children of alcoholics get by in their families, but they are limited, rigid ways of relating, maladaptive for making genuine connections outside the family.

Q: If I'm an ACOA, how can I change?

A: We're not sure you have to. Again, many college student ACOAs appear to be doing fine. If, however, you recognize in yourself some of the problems mentioned above, we recommend attending ACOA meetings either in your community or on campus. There you'll find others who have had similar experiences, and you'll have a chance to see your past realistically and explore current concerns. In the group you can experiment with giving up limited roles and discover what genuine relating is like. Reading about growing up in an alcoholic home may help put your own experience in perspective. Finally, consider counseling in order to understand family experiences and work on honest communications, healthy relationships and self-esteem.

Q: There's something I've never told anyone. For a couple of years when I was in elementary school, my teenage brother used to touch me and make me touch him sexually.

A: You're not alone, unfortunately. Studies tell us that in the United States 25% of girls and 10% of boys have been sexually abused, typically by someone known to them.[2] While sex play between same-age children is common and usually harmless, sexual acts imposed on a child by an older person can cause lasting harm, especially if the abuse continues over time. Many sexually abused children grow up with severe problems in self-esteem, relationships and sexuality. Some wind up abusing their own children or marrying an abuser.

You've never told anyone? Then we recommend confiding in a counselor or joining a support group for survivors of sexual abuse. In these safe settings you can allay feelings of guilt or shame. Tragically, many victims blame themselves for permitting the abuse or wanting the abuser's attention—even though the older person bears full responsibility for sex with a child. You also can examine your complex feelings toward your brother and toward your parents, who failed to notice and protect you. You love these people but in different ways they all failed you, and that can be emotionally confusing, to say the least. These are difficult topics, but better to face them in counseling than let them fester inside you.

Even in counseling, don't expect to resolve these issues right away. It can take months and even years to undo the pervasive harm that was caused long ago.

Q: I'm furious at my parents for all the psychological harm they did to me. Is that unhealthy?

A: Any counselor worthy of the name will tell you that it's good to know your feelings. So if you're furious with your parents, by all means admit it. Anger may be necessary and appropriate as you first face up to hurts from the past. Anger declares that you deserved better from your parents. Anger asserts that you are a worthwhile human being and shouldn't have been mistreated.

But anger is an emotion that should reach toward resolution. If you remain angry, you keep yourself in emotional turmoil. You can't fully get on with your life while looking back in anger; you have less energy for other enterprises. And if you wallow in anger, you also may see yourself as a victim, which holds you back too. At some point, you'll need to resolve your anger and put the past behind in order to get the most from life.

Your ultimate goal with damaging parents should be to let past injuries heal, like a mourner who lets a deceased person go. You need to accept who your parents are—even if you can never approve of what they did. Associated with acceptance comes a sense of perspective. You may come to realize that your parents struggled with their own misfortunes, including perhaps inadequate parents of their own. Your parents hurt you, but perhaps they loved you too. They failed you, but perhaps they tried, in their own way, to do well by you.

Ultimately, acceptance and perspective will serve you far better than lifelong resentment.

FOR FURTHER READING

Ellen Bass and Laura Davis, *The Courage to Heal: A Guide for Women Survivors of Child Sexual Abuse.* New York: Harper Perennial, 1994.

Susan Forward and Craig Buck, *Toxic Parents: Overcoming Their Hurtful Legacy and Reclaiming Your Life.* New York: Bantam, 1990.

Howard M. Halpern, *Cutting Loose: An Adult's Guide to Coming to Terms with Your Parents.* New York: Fireside, 1990.

Judith S. Wallerstein and Sandra Blakeslee, *Second Chances: Men, Women, and Children a Decade After Divorce.* New York: Houghton Mifflin, 1996.

Sharon Wegscheider-Cruse, *Another Chance: Hope and Help for the Alcoholic Family.* Palo Alto, Calif.: Science and Behavior Books, 1988.

Janet G. Woititz, *Adult Children of Alcoholics.* Deerfield Beach, Fla.: Health Communications, 1990.

HOW TO SURVIVE
FALLING IN LOVE

If you're like most undergraduates, your mind is very much on romance while you're in college. Your studies are important, yes, but you also want to date others. You want a relationship.

None of this boy-meets-girl business is easy, however—and neither is boy-meets-boy or girl-meets-girl. Though you're surrounded by potential partners and most of them want an involvement too, college relationships can be tricky every step of the way. Here we discuss the insecurity-ridden beginning of the process—Why doesn't anyone ask me out?—right up to the nervous excitement of possible marriage. In between we take up such charged matters as fear of rejection, choice of partners, lovers' quarrels, jealousy and breaking up.

FIRST STEPS

Q: Guys always want to date my roommate but with me it's "Let's be friends." Why won't anyone ask *me* out?

A: The world of romance isn't strictly fair. Some favored beings, like your roommate, generate interest without even trying. Blessed with striking looks or whatever else it takes, they're always being pursued by an admirer or two (which presents its own difficulties). But that's not the case for the average college student. The typical experience is more like yours, where you go through lean periods when it seems no one wants you, at least no one you really like.

Q: But what can I do to interest somebody?

A: We wish we could give you a surefire formula, but in our experience romance begins unpredictably. There's no "right" way to go about attracting someone; all sorts of personalities, carrying on in all sorts of ways, manage to meet and pair off. So partly you just need to be patient. Your turn may come next week or next semester, or you may have to wait quite a while longer.

But while there isn't a recipe for finding romance, we can offer a few modest suggestions. First, review the tips on relating presented on page 14. These don't tell you exactly what to do, but they do suggest some social pitfalls to avoid. It's possible you're doing something basic to defeat yourself, and by correcting that you'll stop driving potential dates away.

Second, give some thought to the partners you've considered. Have you been open minded about all the eligible candidates? This is not to say you can't be discriminating. You have a right, the same as anyone else, to like and be attracted to a romantic partner. But liking somebody doesn't require that he or she be gorgeous, or popular, or a certain height, or meet any such rigid standard. Liking somebody simply means that you *like* him or her. So check whether you've been focusing your search too narrowly, and, if so, open your eyes. Very possibly in your classes, dorm or club activities there are some promising sleepers you haven't given a fair chance.

Third, make sure you're sending off the right signals to people you like. Have you successfully shown interest, either by letting them know or at the very least by managing to *be* with them? If not, you risk losing out because they assume you're not available. Have you presented yourself as more than friendship material? If instead you just pal around, people will think of you that way, as a sidekick rather than a potential romantic lead.

Again, please don't misunderstand: We're not suggesting that you have to behave in a particular way. To interest someone, you don't have to flirt or play it cool or be different than you are. The best romantic strategy of all is that timeworn cliché—Be yourself. But while being true to your personality, do try to convey that you like the person and are receptive to something happening between you. That way you give yourself a fighting chance.

Q: But when I'm with someone I like, I get all tongue-tied.

A: That can happen. Anxiety about pleasing can make anyone awkward and uptight. It's easy to be charming and natural with people you're not attracted to, but in the presence of someone special it's not unusual to fumble and falter like an actor with stage fright.

The best advice we can offer is to hang in there. If you spend time with this person, you'll soon start feeling comfortable and your true personality will emerge.

Q: My life seems empty without a relationship. Suppose I'm alone forever?

A: We sincerely doubt you'll be alone forever if you really want a relationship. In the meantime, let's examine your reasoning. By imposing a condition on life—"I must have a relationship or else"— you guarantee yourself misery for as long as your condition isn't met. By dwelling on what you don't have, you lose sight of what's already yours: friends, family, studies, activities. In short, you *think* your way into suffering.

And please note, thinking this way doesn't get you to your goal one day sooner. On the contrary, others may sense your great need and run the other way. Both men and women are attracted to self-sufficient individuals who also happen to like them, not to desperate souls who feel miserable and incomplete on their own. Friends too will grow tired of your I-want-a-relationship spiel. So your desperation for a partner may keep you without one.

Relationships are important, but not all-important. We encourage you to put this part of your life in perspective.

Q: But what can I do if nobody at this college appeals to me? All the people here are geeks and losers.

A: All of them? You certainly are painting with a wide brush. Surely in an entire institution of higher education there must be one or two desirable persons lurking around somewhere.

Earlier we alluded to the problem of being too picky in choosing a partner. Let's look now at a few possible reasons. One reason may be lack of self-esteem. If inwardly you don't have a favorable opinion of yourself, then it may seem that anyone who likes you must also be a loser, as in the famous Groucho Marx line: "I don't want to belong to any club that will accept me as a member."

Another reason is fear of rejection. If you spurn all possible partners first, no one can spurn you. Your unreasonably high standards shield you from being hurt. Similarly, you may fear getting involved. If you had a relationship, you and this person would depend on each other, and you'd lose a measure of freedom. If that's not what you want, a good solution is to be dissatisfied with all available partners. That way you can tell yourself you'd like a relationship without running the risk of actually forming one.

These motives tend to be deep seated and aren't easily laid aside. If you recognize one of them in yourself, consider consulting a counselor. Deficient self-esteem, excessive fear of rejection and fear of involvement are all worthy subjects for self-exploration. In the meantime, try to go beyond your first impressions and get to know some of your classmates better. Make a concerted effort to see individuals for the complex human beings they are. If you can put aside your prejudices and fears, some of these "geeks and losers" may grow on you.

Q: How do I know if I should go out with someone?

A: If you're not sure, you don't have to rush into anything. You can get to know someone casually first, without making it an official dinner-and-a-movie date. So if someone has sparked your interest, arrange to chat in a study lounge or meet for ice cream at the snack bar. After a few informal get-togethers you should start having an idea whether you want to pursue this further.

Q: How do I approach someone I like? What's a good opening line?

A: How about "Hi," or anything else you can think of to break the ice. The truth is that opening lines are vastly overrated. A person will either respond to you or not based on who you are, not the cleverness of your first half-dozen words.

Q: But I can't just say hello. What should I talk about?

A: Once again, there is no formula. You can't prepare a dialogue or follow a script. Simply talk about things that interest you, listen to things that interest him or her and see how the conversation flows. The talk may be a bit strained at first if you like the person and want to impress. Even so, you should get an idea early on whether the two of you click.

If you do, the conversation will proceed and pursuing matters further will seem natural. If not, the problem isn't that you're saying the wrong things but that you and this person probably aren't right for each other.

In their anxiety to impress, some students ask someone out by turning in a kind of performance. They do a comedy routine or show off their sensitive natures or advertise their superior intelligence. Now if you're naturally funny or sensitive or brainy, that's great, but you don't have to stage a show. You can express yourself without working so hard at it. Besides, a performance places so much attention on you—you're working so hard on your act—that you don't get to know the person you're so busy impressing. You can't learn about someone while consigning him or her to the audience.

Q: There's this friend I'm attracted to, but we've always dated other people. Do you think I should ask her out?

A: Tough question. Certainly you can make a case for taking a chance. Many couples originally get to know each other as friends, without the pressure of romance, and gradually develop an intimacy that leads to a relationship. On the other hand, you have a lot to lose if your gamble fails. She may not want to go out with you in that way, which will be awkward for both of you. And if she does agree to go out, you may not make it as lovers and you risk losing her as a friend.

In case you do ask her out, our advice is to move slowly. (This isn't bad advice for any couple, of course.) Start seeing her if she's willing, but don't hurry into sexual relations. Going slowly doesn't ensure that no one gets hurt; feelings are on the line from the moment you ask her out. But a slow pace does enable you to take stock of the relationship, and perhaps, if it isn't working, salvage your friendship in time.

REJECTION

Q: I really like this person, but I can't seem to ask her out. How can I get rid of my fear of rejection?

A: You can't, not entirely anyway, any more than you can rid yourself of fear of heights or of dangerous animals. Being afraid of rejection is a natural response, an outgrowth of the fundamentally social nature of human beings. All of us want to be accepted. Yet all of us have tasted rejection. So it's only natural when asking someone out to feel some trepidation.

The real issue here is not what you feel—of course you fear rejection—but what you do. You don't have to shy away when you're frightened any more than you must slug somebody when you feel angry. You can still ask her out, even though you're afraid. Good judgment, not feelings alone, should decide your course of action.

Although you can't eliminate fear, sometimes you can cut it down to size by performing the very act that frightens you. If you ask this person out, it will probably be easier to ask out somebody else next time. Similarly, you might go to a party and set a goal of asking three people to dance. The purpose is to show yourself that rejections aren't unbearable, that you can endure a "no." (With luck you'll also get a "yes.") Armed with this knowledge, you're now free to ask out anyone you wish.

Q: There's this guy I like. When I finally got up the nerve to speak to him, he blew me off. I felt mortified.

A: We didn't say rejection was fun. No matter how often it happens, getting turned down always stings. But here are a few ways to salve your wounds:

- **Visit a good friend or call your parents.** When someone does not want you, it helps to be appreciated by people who do.
- **Remind yourself that what you did was fine.** You have the right to approach anyone you want. When you do, inevitably you'll get rebuffed sometimes. But you still have the right to try.
- **Applaud your effort.** It takes courage to approach someone. You deserve credit for trying. The only mistake would have been chickening out and never giving yourself a chance.
- **Repudiate negative thoughts.** If you're having negative thoughts after the rejection ("Nobody will go out with me." "I'm a loser."), ward them off and substitute constructive alternatives ("Others will want me." "I'm still attractive and desirable, whatever this guy thinks.").
- **Keep rejections in perspective.** A refusal communicates very little about you. You can't know if this guy said no because he only likes short blonds, he's already interested in someone else, you remind him of his dreaded ex-girlfriend—or you're too attractive!

You can be turned down for any of a hundred reasons. As psychologist Judith Sills points out, rejections are "nothing personal."

- **Gauge the intensity of your reaction.** Yes, rejections do sting, but they shouldn't batter your self-esteem or threaten your sense of identity. If your reactions threaten to overwhelm you, too much is at stake here and you may want to explore the issue in counseling.

Q: How do you let someone down easy if you don't want to go out with him?

A: The kindest course is to be gentle but straightforward. Tell him you're flattered he asked, but you're not interested in a dating relationship. Perhaps then you can move on to a friendly conversation about other matters. He'll appreciate that you're willing to talk to him even if you don't want to go out.

When you turn someone down, you're not obligated to explain your reasons. All you have to say is "Thanks, but I don't want to," even if he presses you for an explanation. You also don't have to apologize or put yourself down with comments like "I'm just too mixed up to see someone right now." To explain your refusal, it's not a good idea to invent an off-campus boyfriend. This familiar white lie can come back to haunt you if later you want to date someone else on campus. It's also not recommended that you simply avoid your admirer until he gets the message. Staying out of sight spares you from having to say no, but it's crueler to him than confronting him directly and simply telling the truth.

Turning someone down is one of the more unpleasant chores in life, almost as bad, but not quite, as being the one turned down. But remember, everyone plays both roles sooner or later, and everyone survives. Meanwhile, you can keep an awkward situation from getting any worse by stating your refusal tactfully but honestly.

Q: But suppose someone doesn't take no for an answer? This guy keeps showing up at my door, stopping me on campus and calling me. Does he have the right to do that?

A: Of course not. He has the right to ask initially, but you have the right to accept or decline. You don't have to go out with him or even have a casual friendship, if you don't want to. And he should respect your wishes.

Have you clearly expressed how you feel? Some people interpret any kindness, hesitation or ambiguity as a sign that your defenses are weakening. At this stage, you need to be blunt. Tell him to leave you alone, and then have nothing further to do with him.

If he persists even after you've made your wishes clear, then he's harassing you. Speak to an RA, a dean or another college official about your problem.

PROBLEMS COUPLES FACE

Q: I'm not really sure how I feel about my boyfriend. How do you know when you're in love?

A: We can't give a definitive answer, because the concept of love is impossible to pin down. Certainly your own experience must tell you that being in love feels differently at different moments, at different stages of a relationship and with different partners. There are quiet loves and stormy loves, tender loves and loves tinged with hate. There is falling in love, a frenzied, short-lived phenomenon; ongoing romantic love, less intense and partaking of affection, passion and commitment; and platonic love, which has caring without passion. When you say you love someone, you may mean any of these experiences, or perhaps none of them quite captures what you feel.

Love is an elusive concept, but let us try to answer your question with some questions of our own. Do you continue feeling as close to your boyfriend, or closer, as time goes by? Do you consider him a true friend, someone you can be intimate with? Do you feel physically attracted to him? Do you generally enjoy his company? Do you often think in terms of "we" rather than "I"? Do you sense your commitment is deepening?

If the answers are yes, then you are, by any reasonable standards, in love.

If the answers aren't clear cut and you have reason to doubt your love, one step to consider is slowing down for a while or even taking time off from the relationship. From a distance you may see things more clearly that appear muddled in the thick of day-to-day interaction. Of course, you'll need your boyfriend's understanding and agreement to do this. He may feel rejected by your request to slow things down, and you'll need to address his concerns.

Q: How can I know how my new boyfriend feels about me?

A: You can't know for a certainty, and what's more, he may not exactly know either. Lovers' feelings can be complex and changeable. Your boyfriend may cherish your vivacious personality but wish you were a different physical type, or love to be with you alone but feel uncomfortable when you drag him along to a party. He may pine for you on Thursday but hardly give you a thought on Friday. Asking him to pin down his feelings, especially at this early stage, may be asking for more clarity than is possible.

Another reason you can't be sure where you stand is because people are cautious, especially early in relationships, about expressing their true feelings. They don't want to frighten away or hurt their partners or get prematurely involved in a relationship, so instead of speaking directly they use what Judith Sills calls "coded communications." Any behavior can be a coded communication: a gift or a compliment, an unreturned phone call, a sexual come-on or refusal, lateness, teasing. The trouble is that codes are tough to crack; you can easily misinterpret your partner's signals. If your boyfriend doesn't call, that may mean he doesn't care, but equally it may mean he's afraid to appear too eager, or he feels hurt and thinks it's your turn to call, or possibly he was tied up and couldn't get to the phone. You can't be sure what his not calling means, and so it's hard to infer from this behavior how he feels about you.

Eventually, your boyfriend's position will become clear. As you come to know him better, he'll have sent a great many coded communications, and you'll know how to decipher them, and meanwhile he'll probably start expressing himself directly. But for now, you have to live with ambiguity. You can have an idea about how he feels, but you can't know for certain.

Q: But shouldn't I be more direct and *ask* him how he feels?

A: You can, and with luck you'll get an honest answer and spare yourself either needless worries or false illusions. Open, assertive communications are often best. But bear in mind, again, that he may not yet know his answer or feel ready to deliver it. Pushing for a response may frighten or confuse him without yielding a clear answer. At this early stage of your relationship, you may have to resign yourself to some indirectness and uncertainty.

Q: If my girlfriend and I argue, does that mean we're not suited for each other?

A: Not necessarily. Some couples are happy together despite arguments, or even partly because of them. Arguing may be how they let off steam, liven things up, even show their affection.

On the other hand, bitter arguments may express serious incompatibility and leave lasting wounds. So if you and your girlfriend have gone beyond squabbling and are really at each other's throats, then you do have a problem.

Q: How can we stop arguing?

A: The first thing you need is your girlfriend's cooperation. It takes two to fight, and it takes two to stop fighting. She also has to agree to tackle this problem.

The key to curbing arguments is improved communication. True, coded messages are common early in a relationship, when you're getting to know each other. Later on, however, direct communications are a must, particularly concerning specific grievances. Both of you need to express your needs and respect the others' needs in order to put an end to the discord.

Here are communication tips:

- **Be assertive.** Express wishes and concerns directly and promptly, before you reach the exploding point.
- **Stick to the matter at hand.** Don't throw in side issues.
- **Refrain from personal attacks.** "I wish you would spend more time with me" is fine. "You're selfish for not spending time with me" is not.
- **Refrain from assigning blame.** Whenever you're tempted to say, "It's your fault" or "It all started when you . . . ," bite your tongue. Even if you think you're right—and what arguer does not?—acknowledge responsibility on both sides.
- **Listen to your partner.** Nothing escalates an argument faster than two people simultaneously lecturing each other. Saying "Yes, I see what you mean" can defuse tensions immediately.
- **Pay attention to your discussion style.** Do you tend to fall apart emotionally, crying and yelling? Do you become cold and hyperrational, all reason and no emotion? Do you make threats to leave the relationship? Do you give the silent treatment after a disagreement? Whatever you're doing now is obviously not working, so it's

time to try something new. Experiment with a different approach and see if that brings better results.

Q: We've gotten nowhere in our efforts to stop arguing, so now we're thinking of going to a counselor. But which one of us should go?

A: Generally speaking, a couple's difficulties, like Caesar's Gaul, can be divided into three parts: the first partner's personal problems, the second partner's personal problems and the couple's interactional problems. So in theory, the relationship could improve if either of you gets help alone or if both of you go together. We recommend starting with an evaluation as a couple, and then discuss with the professional the merits of individual counseling and/or couples counseling.

Q: What should I do if my boyfriend always teases me and finds little ways to put me down?

A: This is a good question that will take some explaining to answer. When two people become romantically involved, they often slip into complementary roles. For example, one may call the shots while the other submits. One may be the talker, the other the listener. And one may tease, and the other gets teased. These roles tend to replay early family interactions. People behave with partners based on what they learned as children observing and dealing with parents and siblings.

While some role-playing is inevitable, obviously it can get out of hand. It's no fun to be teased and put down all the time, nor is it any consolation knowing your boyfriend ridicules you because of his early family experiences. Quite properly, you want to break out of the role you're playing.

As a first step, clearly tell your boyfriend to cool it. Since his behavior may be ingrained, once won't be enough. Remind him often. Say "Please don't tease me" or "You're doing it again" every time he teases. If he's at all sympathetic, he should soon start catching himself before he zaps you.

Second, weed out your own behaviors that set you up for the victim's role. Do you habitually say "I'm sorry" or "I'm so stupid" or words to that effect? Do you make fun of yourself and belittle your own efforts? If in these ways you put yourself down, then no wonder he puts you down too. Act with self-respect, and he's more likely to treat you with respect.

If neither suggestion pans out and you're serious about your relationship, talk to a counselor about this problem, either alone or with your boyfriend.

Q: Should I tell my new girlfriend about personal problems?

A: That's a tricky one. We know it's tempting when you meet someone new to let it all hang out. You feel close, you want her to know you, you want to prove your interest by entrusting her with secrets and vulnerabilities. The trouble is, you don't really know her yet. You can't know if she'll understand and accept what you tell her, or will judge you and think less of you. Today you may feel exactly on the same wavelength. Next week you may think, "She's not who I thought. Why did I ever tell her all that stuff?"

Our recommendation with self-disclosure is to risk smaller revelations first and if that goes well, save the most personal matters for later. Also, take turns disclosing, so both of you reveal yourselves at roughly the same pace. That way trust and understanding can develop, and you learn through experience whether or not opening up is safe.

Q: My boyfriend loves to analyze my problems and explain what's wrong with me. It really annoys me. What should I tell him?

A: Tell him to cut it out. It's fine if he gives you support and offers occasional advice. You should do the same for him. But when he starts acting like your counselor, spouting lines like "You're an anal-retentive personality because of your relationship with your mother," then he's gone too far. For one thing, his psychologizing treats you like an inferior—it's demeaning. For another, your boyfriend is not a professional and can't possibly see you objectively because he's involved with you.

So ask Dr. Freud to go off duty and just stick to being your boyfriend. And for your own part, try not to relate to him in the subordinate role of patient. If you really need the assistance of a counselor, schedule an appointment with a professional.

Q: My boyfriend is insanely jealous. If I just look at another man he's upset all night, and he doesn't want me to see my male friends anymore. What should I do?

A: First, ask yourself whether he has any reason for his insecurities. Have you ever cheated on him? Do you flirt with your male friends? Do you often stare at men or talk about them in a jealousy-inducing way? If any of the answers is yes, then to earn his trust you must change your own behavior.

Assuming he's jealous without cause, try offering a healthy diet of reassurance. All of us need reassurance from time to time; jealous people need it more than most. Reassure him that he's mistaken in his suspicions, and especially reassure him that you really care. With luck, he'll then be less afraid of losing you and correspondingly less jealous.

At the same time, assert your own rights. You have the right to look at anyone you please (though preferably not seductively). You have the right to have male friends. You have the right not to be grilled for your actions.

These efforts may not work. Jealousy can be fairly mild, in which case reason and reassurance have an effect, or it can be pathological, in which case nothing you say gets through. If your boyfriend is pathologically jealous, you have two options: to convince him to get professional help or to consider leaving him for your own peace of mind.

Q: I'm the jealous type myself. Why do I feel this way and act like a jerk sometimes with my boyfriend?

A: One source of jealousy is insecurity. You may believe (perhaps unconsciously) no one can love you, so you doubt your partner's love and look for signs that he prefers someone else. Jealousy can also spring from your own wandering eye. If you yourself are tempted to be unfaithful, you may attribute that same motive to your partner. This is called projection: suspecting someone of something that's really on your own mind.

Whatever's going on, it sounds as if you're motivated to change and could benefit from talking to a professional counselor.

Q: My boyfriend transferred to another college and I only see him on Christmas and during summer vacations. Do you think it would be okay to start seeing some guys here on campus?

A: That depends. For one thing, you haven't indicated if you plan to tell him. Perhaps you think you can safely date other guys without your boyfriend knowing, but this is risky. He may pick up clues and figure out what's happening, or you may feel guilty and confess, and the upshot can be the end of your relationship. Even if your boyfriend never catches on, what kind of relationship are you left with? If he can't trust you, how involved are you, really? Such are the dangers of sneaking around.

If everything's out in the open and you both agree to see other people, then you're certainly entitled to do so. Going out with others may even be desirable if you and your boyfriend aren't ready yet for a serious commitment. On the other hand, be aware of the risk. The people each of you meets on your own campuses have a strong geographical advantage over the partner who's not around. Dating some guys locally may spell the demise of your current relationship.

Q: My boyfriend always wants to hang around with his friends. I say we love each other and should spend our time together. Who's right?

A: Both of you, up to a point. We agree with you that a healthy relationship requires exclusive, just-you-and-me time. Unless you spend time together you can't come to know each other and develop genuine intimacy. But in fairness to your boyfriend, too much time spent as a twosome can be stunting and stifling. Neither of you by yourself can possibly meet all of the other's needs for companionship and stimulation. Besides, the richer your social experiences when you're apart, the more you have to share when you're together.

Let us add a few words about dependency. Some college students are intimidated by people or frightened to be alone, and so attach themselves to a boyfriend or girlfriend, who makes them feel safe. Needless to say, this is not a sound basis for healthy living or healthy relating. Dependency on a partner is as limiting as depending too much on Mom and Dad.

Q: My parents don't want me to go out with my boyfriend anymore because he's from a different race. What should I do?

A: This is a frequent concern, voiced by students from every race as well as every religion and ethnic background. Whatever group you belong to, there's a good chance your parents don't want you mixing with other groups. "Keep to your own kind" is a universal parent refrain.

How you handle this dilemma depends on several factors. Let's start with your boyfriend. Do you really feel strongly about him? Is he truly someone special? If so, you don't want to give him up lightly; but if not, preserving the relationship may not be worth a family brawl. Also, be honest about whether you deliberately chose someone from a different racial group to assert your independence, or even to force a confrontation with your parents. Obviously, this isn't a solid foundation on which to build a relationship. Give careful thought to your motives. Time and reflection will be necessary to sort out your feelings for your boyfriend and to decide how important it is to stay with him.

Now let's consider your parents. Possibly they're adamant and won't listen to your side of things. They may threaten to disown you or pull you out of school unless you end the relationship. But sometimes students are too quick to give up on dialogue with their parents. Have you tried to explain your feelings about your boyfriend and also listened to their reservations? Have you invited them to meet him? It's at least possible that with patience and good communications their stance may soften.

Q: My boyfriend sometimes hits me when he's angry. How can I make him stop?

A: Possibly you can't. If he's done it more than once, his physical aggression may be a deep-seated reaction that you are powerless to prevent.

Q: But why would he act aggressively toward someone he loves?

A: Your boyfriend may act violently because he experienced violence in his own family. He also may not know constructive ways to cope with feelings of jealousy, anger, rejection or stress. Feeling powerless in these situations, he resorts to the only power he knows: brute force.

Q: What should I do?

A: If this has continued at all, you should seriously consider ending the relationship. No matter how much you love your boyfriend, it's not good for body or soul to stay in an abusive relationship.

You may also want to consult a counselor to look into why you've stayed with him so far. Is your self-esteem low so you feel you don't deserve better than an abusive boyfriend? Did you pick an abusive boyfriend because this is what you're familiar with in your own family background? Do you seek out abusive people in other aspects of your life? These are important questions deserving of exploration in counseling.

BREAKING UP

Q: My girlfriend just broke up with me. I can't study, I can't sit still, I can't think of anything but her. How will I get through this?

A: You will, but not without difficulty. Breaking up is a wrenching ordeal, particularly on a college campus. Not only are you hit by the shocking force of loss and rejection. Making matters worse, your "ex" is still around, maybe in the same classes or residence hall. You'll keep running into her, and everywhere you go will be a reminder of your loss.

The book *How to Survive the Loss of a Love* describes a three-stage process of mourning or grieving following a breakup. First you react with shock and disbelief, then you become angry and depressed, and finally you achieve understanding and acceptance. In our own experience, these stages progress unevenly, and no two people react quite the same. However, the basic point still holds: You mourn after a breakup, similar to mourning the death of a parent. You feel pain, it takes time, and there's no shortcut to healing.

Here are suggestions to cope with a breakup:

- **Get support from family and friends.** Though no one can replace your girlfriend (it's her company you want most), still it's consoling in times of grief to have people on your side. If you're concerned about burning out one or two friends, spread out your requests by using several sources of support.
- **Expect to be shaken.** Don't blame yourself for feeling sad or angry or for having trouble sleeping or concentrating: It's normal.
- **Try to carry out your usual responsibilities and routines—** going to class, studying, showing up at work, going to the gym,

even doing the laundry. These mundane duties continue to be necessary, of course. More important, accomplishing them makes you feel purposeful and good about yourself, and that's what you need after a blow of this magnitude.

- **Consider visiting your college counseling center.** Not only have you lost someone central in your life, but it wouldn't be surprising if you're questioning your self-worth and feeling depressed. A counselor can give you support and help you retain perspective during this difficult time.

Q: My ex-girlfriend and I haven't been speaking to each other for weeks, but I'd really like to see her just to talk. What do you think?

A: One of the cruel ironies of breaking up is that the person who was once your main support is now the source of your pain. You've lost your best friend as well as your girlfriend. So it's understandable you want to speak to her. You also may hope there's a chance of reconciliation, or perhaps you have questions about why she broke up with you.

But before you visit, first make sure she agrees. If not, you have to respect her wishes; she has the right to break off communications. Doing so doesn't mean she's lost all feelings for you. She may well feel strongly, but that can be confusing and make it hard for her to abide by her decision. Later, once passions have cooled on both sides, possibly the two of you can be friendly or even become friends.

Assuming she says yes, you still must decide if seeing her is in your best interest. Will a visit lift your spirits or cause sharper pain? Are you harboring false hopes about what will happen, setting yourself up for further disappointment? Unless you are confident about your own reactions and realistic about the meeting, the safest course is to stay away for a while.

Q: First my ex-boyfriend suddenly stops seeing me three weeks ago, telling me he's not ready for a relationship. Now he's going out with somebody on his hall. I'm furious, and I want to know what I can do about it.

A: Not much, we're afraid. You can tell him off, if you'd like, but that won't change anything. Neither will any other strategy you employ. You've lost your influence over your ex-boyfriend, which is one of the bitter fruits of breaking up.

Your only constructive course of action is to continue with your own healing and get on with your life. If it's any consolation, consider that the worst has now occurred, and you survived. This guy broke up with you, he lied about his reason and started seeing someone else, and now there's nothing left he can do to you.

Q: I broke up with someone about a month ago after a two-year relationship. Now someone new has been asking me out. If I start seeing him, will it just be on the rebound and prove a mistake?

A: It all depends. Are you still, as one would expect after only a month, preoccupied with your ex-boyfriend? Are you still angry, still hurt, confused and sad? Are you feeling vulnerable, as if one more blow would push you over the edge? These factors would suggest you're not yet ready to throw yourself into a new relationship.

Dating someone new also depends on how you feel about him, of course. Are you sure you really like this guy? Are you sure he's more than a stand-in for your ex, more than a distraction to take your mind off your loss? Unless you really are drawn to him, the relationship will surely fizzle somewhere down the line.

Whether you should date someone new depends on if you feel emotionally available and he seems genuinely interesting. If these conditions hold, then go ahead, but take it slow.

Q: Since my breakup I've been eating like a pig and have gained 15 pounds. What's going on here?

A: What's going on is you're in pain and have turned, under-standably, to a painkiller. Overeating can momentarily numb suffering; so can alcohol, drugs, compulsive shopping or indiscriminate sex. Of course, all these remedies eventually backfire. Overeating and other self-destructive behaviors end up making you feel worse than ever.

By definition, compulsive behaviors—overeating is one—are difficult to resist. Considering your difficulties following the breakup, we urge you to consult a counselor. In the meantime, try to use healthy coping devices during this vulnerable time. Options include friendships, physical exercise, studies, clubs, creative outlets, journal writing, religious faith, meditation and volunteer work.

Q: Why am I still thinking about my ex-girlfriend three years after we broke up?

A: There's no precise timetable for getting over a loss. If you love someone deeply, some of those feelings last a lifetime. You still think about the person because she meant so much to you.

At the same time, you also may dwell on a past relationship if present relationships pale by comparison. Like nature, the heart abhors a vacuum, so of course you hark back to the last person who deeply mattered. Once you find someone new, thoughts about your ex-girlfriend won't vanish but should recede into the background.

Q: I hurt so bad when my last relationship ended. How can I know my next relationship will succeed?

A: You can't. In fact, the odds are stacked against you. The majority of love relationships break off sooner or later, and when they do, usually one or both partners feels horrible about it.

So why try again? The answer is that anything worthwhile is achieved in spite of the risk. When you learned to ride a bicycle, you fell off sometimes and scraped your knee. When you started off at kindergarten—and years later at college—you dared to leave home and face the unknown of teachers and classmates. And so it is with romance. Achieving the goal of intimacy requires a determination to keep going even though there's the likelihood of getting hurt along the way.

Meanwhile, consider the alternative. You can play it safe and steer clear of potential involvements. You can avoid dating seriously or at all, and that way you won't get hurt. The cost, however, is leading a restricted existence, like an agoraphobic who's afraid to leave the house. You'll be secure, but confined.

Let us be clear. We're not saying you must have a romantic partner to be happy. That kind of thinking makes you desperate for love, and that's not healthy. What we *are* saying is that it's a pity to narrow your experience unnecessarily. Why not participate fully and take your chances on romance, as does everyone else?

MARRIAGE

Q: I'm 20 years old and in college. Does that seem too young to marry my girlfriend?

A: Only in the last 50 years or so would this question even be asked. Before this time, marriage was considered perfectly appropriate at your age, or younger; Shakespeare's Juliet was all of 13 when she pledged herself to Romeo. But nowadays we tend to think of persons your age, particularly college students, as somewhere in a fuzzy middle zone: no longer quite adolescents, not yet fully adults. The usual assumption is that 20-year-old students aren't ready to marry.

Is that fair? Certainly you may be capable of loving and making a commitment, and in that sense you're ready to marry. On the other hand, neither you nor your girlfriend is finished with emotional and intellectual development. As you continue to grow up, you may find yourselves growing apart. And then there are finances to consider. You and your girlfriend may need money from your parents while you're still in college, and that may affect your sense of yourselves as married. Right after college, it may be difficult to assume the full responsibilities of marriage. Bear in mind, too, that as college students you face important unknowns, such as what jobs you will find after college and where you will be located. Getting married now puts constraints on the opportunities you can pursue.

Since marrying during college is fairly unusual and goes against the norm, you also should examine your motives. Are you marrying to escape domineering parents? Are you deliberately defying them, marrying mainly because they're opposed? Are you running away from the pressures of college social life? Are you trying to compensate for an unhappy childhood?

This consequential decision deserves full examination. You and your girlfriend should seek out objective third parties, and perhaps a counselor, to gain perspective on what's best for you.

FOR FURTHER READING

Melba Colgrove, Harold Bloomfield, and Peter McWilliams, *How to Survive the Loss of a Love.* Los Angeles: Prelude Press, 1993.

Barbara DeAngelis, *Are You the One for Me? Knowing Who's Right and Avoiding Who's Wrong.* New York: Dell, 1994.

Erich Fromm, *The Art of Loving.* New York: HarperCollins, 1989.

Willard Gaylin, *Rediscovering Love.* New York: Penguin, 1986.

Judith Sills, *A Fine Romance.* New York: Ballantine, 1993.

Philip Zimbardo, *Shyness.* Reading, Mass.: Addison-Wesley, 1990.

SEX

Rare is the college student who has no worries about sex. This may come as a surprise. College students love to talk about sex but not about sexual anxieties, and therefore it's easy to assume that other students don't have any. Everyone else besides you must be confident, knowledgeable, certain about sexual matters—and, of course, totally "normal."

In reality, you're in good company if "doing what comes naturally" doesn't feel so very natural. One reason for this is inexperience. Many students entering college have had few or no sexual contacts, and even those with extensive sexual histories are still just learning about themselves and other people. Sex is not simply an inborn drive. Comfort with sexuality depends on sexual experience, life experience and personal growth. Sex gets better as you mature.

Another source of anxiety is questions about normality. Many students falsely believe that there are only a few normal feelings, normal fantasies, normal "moves," normal physical responses. Comparing themselves to these supposed norms, they conclude there's something disturbingly wrong about themselves. While it's true that some sexual behavior *is* unhealthy, often students frighten themselves needlessly. In fact, some worry themselves into a sexual problem where none originally existed.

In this chapter you will notice frequent references to nonsexual issues. That's because self-esteem, assertiveness and ability to communicate, to name three such issues, have an enormous impact on sexuality. To work on sexual concerns, it may not be enough to learn new sexual information or try out new sexual behaviors. You may also have to take a close look at what makes you tick and how you relate to others.

TOO LITTLE OR TOO MUCH?

Q: I'm a college senior who's never had sexual intercourse. Am I the last inexperienced 21-year-old alive?

A: Not at all. According to one survey, roughly 20% of both men and women are still virgins in college.[1]

Actually, there are many reasons why you might delay having sexual intercourse, or any sexual experiences. Your religious convictions or family teachings may persuade you to wait. You may feel sex is wrong unless you're in love. You simply may not feel ready; sexual closeness is more than you can handle emotionally at this time. The threat of AIDS, other sexually transmitted diseases (STDs) and pregnancy is also a compelling reason to think carefully before hopping into bed with someone.

Abstinence is a valid choice, whether or not you've had sex before. You can choose to have some sexual contact but draw the line at sexual intercourse, or choose to refrain from sexual activity altogether. What matters is whether abstinence feels right to you.

Q: But in my case, I *want* to have sex. What's wrong with me?

A: Several possibilities come to mind. Are you approaching people the wrong way and scaring them off (see page 14 for tips on social skills). Or is it *you* who's scared—perhaps that you won't "perform" properly, or will get shot down if you express interest in someone, or will get too emotionally close if you have sex, or will end up with a disease or unwanted pregnancy?

If fear is holding you back, then you are working at cross-purposes, both approaching and avoiding sexual intimacy. See if you can identify what is frightening you. Sometimes recognizing a fear exposes it as exaggerated or irrational and relaxes its hold over you. Even if the concern is valid—disease or unwanted pregnancy—you can take measures to substantially reduce the risk and permit you to have sexual experiences.

Some fears are stubborn and deep seated. If you have trouble identifying or overcoming fears about sex, consider discussing the matter at your college's counseling center.

Q: If I'm still inexperienced at 21, haven't I fallen too far behind my classmates?

A: Sexual experience isn't a race. Though sexual maturity does take time, you'll eventually learn about lovemaking regardless of when you start.

Q: What about techniques? Aren't there certain things I need to learn to become a good lover?

A: Sure there are. Possibly when you're ready to have sex you'll find an experienced partner to teach you. If not, you and your partner can learn together through trial and error (which isn't so bad either).

But sexual techniques count for only a small fraction of lovemaking. Much more important is good communication. Good lovers let each other know what they want and don't want, communicating both in words and through actions. Good lovemaking also depends on learning about your own body, so you can communicate your desires to your partner. Another ingredient is a commitment to shared pleasure. Selfish people who are insensitive to their partners' pleasure aren't good lovers, and neither are self-denying people who disregard their own pleasure. Good lovers strive for a mutual experience in which both partners give and receive.

Q: I've had sex with lots of people. Sometimes I wonder if that's wrong.

A: The real issue isn't how many partners you've had, but the reasons you've had sex and your feelings about it. Some people have sex with many partners and feel genuinely fulfilled. They like the sex, they like the closeness, and afterward they feel fine; they haven't violated their own principles. They also don't exploit their partners or feel exploited by them. For them, casual sex is a natural, healthy expression of tender and sexual feelings, although of course having many partners does increase the risk of disease or pregnancy. (For safer sex practices, see the "Protection" section later in this chapter.)

But people have sex for all kinds of reasons, not all of them healthy. If you've had many partners and are concerned about it, you need to ask yourself some tough questions:

- Do you have sex because you are afraid the person won't want you otherwise?
- Are you simply afraid to say no?
- Do you have sex when what you really want, but can't ask for, is to be close to somebody?

- Do you have sex to escape feelings of loneliness, anxiety or depression, or to express anger, to get back at someone?
- Do you sometimes have sex against your better judgment, even with people you don't really like?
- Do you have sex because you are drunk or high—and regret it afterward?
- After lovemaking do you end up feeling hurt, used, guilty or angry?
- Do you have sex to prove that you're lovable? Do you have sex to compensate for low self-esteem?

Please consider these questions carefully. If you answered yes even once, then you may not be having sex for healthy reasons. At this point, a sensible response might be to take a break until you feel confident about your motives. And if you can't seem to stop yourself despite sensing casual sex is wrong for you, take up this issue with a counselor.

Q: I'm dating a tease. She starts to get physical with me, and then when I want to have intercourse she makes me stop.

A: Slow down a minute. Just because a woman likes physical contact but draws the line at intercourse doesn't make her a tease. Women have a right to say no at any point of lovemaking—men do too. Make sure you respect your partner's limits regarding sex. Otherwise you run the risk of committing date rape (see Chapter 8).

On the other hand, there *are* some people, men as well as women, who promise sex or romance and then back away when you get interested. They act seductively because turning you on feeds their self-esteem (in men this is called the "Don Juan" complex). It's not *you* they really want; they want the excitement of the chase. If you suspect your girlfriend of this kind of "teasing" (and it's often done unconsciously), directly ask her what she wants from you. Open questions may put an end to the game-playing, allowing you to find out where you stand. If this approach doesn't clarify her wishes, you may want to reevauate the relationship and move on to someone else.

Q: I've been seeing my boyfriend for a while, and our relationship is somewhat physical, but I just don't want to go all the way. What worries me is that everyone else seems to be doing it. What do you think?

A: What matters is not what everyone else may or may not be doing but what feels right to you. If you don't want sexual intercourse because of your personal values, the health risks or simply a sense of not being ready, then you are acting wisely by setting a limit to the lovemaking. Just make sure that you and your partner are open with each other about your sexual expectations.

Q: This guy I just met says he wants to make love. I'd like to have sex with him, but how do I know when I'm ready?

A: The answer depends on your personal values and expectations. Assuming you want more than a casual experience, we suggest waiting at least until you sense the budding of a real relationship. For sexual intercourse—or any physical contact, for that matter—isn't only an experience, it's also a deepening of involvement. Sex draws you closer, implies that something is happening between you. But many people upon first meeting don't feel ready to plunge into a relationship. Because sex makes things so serious so fast, one or the other party may get scared and run away before the relationship can get started.

   If you have hopes for this new person, we suggest postponing lovemaking until your feelings and his feelings clearly point toward a relationship.

COUPLES' PROBLEMS

Q: My boyfriend never wants to have sex anymore. I know infatuation dies after a few months, but this is ridiculous: We've become like brother and sister. What should we do?

A: Once again, we stress the importance of good communication, not just about sex but your entire relationship. Share your concern about your dormant sex life, and then ask what's going on with him. Have his romantic feelings died? Does he like someone else? Is he angry at you? Is he so worried about school or the future that his mind isn't on romance? Does he feel *you* don't care about him or want to make love?

People in relationships often feel uncomfortable speaking their minds. What they can't put into words, they may convey through sexual behavior. Hurt, anger, insecurity or lack of interest may be expressed through avoiding sex, demanding sex, acting physically cold or showing extra physical tenderness. You need to talk openly with your partner about the underlying problem, whatever it may be. If you can work out whatever's troubling him—a big "if"—the sexual spark may return.

Q: Every time I get ready to have intercourse I lose my erection. Why is this happening to me?

A: It's possible, though unlikely, you have a medical problem, and therefore you may want to consult a doctor. (Doctors can also prescribe medicine for impotence, but that's usually for old codgers, not college-age males.) However, if you can maintain an erection during masturbation, most likely the problem isn't physical. Some psychological problem or feelings of discomfort are interfering with your sexual performance.

We realize the idea of a psychological impediment may be uncomfortable for you. If you're like most young males, you want to be like those smooth characters portrayed in the movies—always ready to perform, under all conditions. Sorry, human beings don't work that way. If for some reason you are troubled, if psychologically you don't feel ready, then you won't be able to have sex—your mind will make your penis go soft. This problem is hardly rare. Perhaps half the male population has experienced at least temporary difficulties with erection, usually for nonmedical reasons. Women's inability to become aroused or have an orgasm is of course similarly affected by negative feelings.

Why might your mind turn off to sex? The cause could be stress (perhaps more than you realize) or depression; reduced "libido" is a classic sign of depression. You also could feel angry or distant toward your partner, in which case impotence is sending a message that you haven't wanted to deliver directly. You also may be worried about possible sexual disease or pregnancy.

Another possible culprit is worry about the sex act itself. When you fret about how good a lover you are or whether you can sustain an erection, your attention is on your worry rather than the pleasure of lovemaking. You're too preoccupied to be excited. The more you dwell on performing, the less likely you'll be able to perform.

Q: What can I do about this problem?

A: The wisest course is to seek help from a professional counselor who specializes in sexual performance difficulties. (And yes, these difficulties usually can be helped.) In the meantime, do what you can to take the pressure out of lovemaking. Specifically, choose a partner who is understanding and makes you feel comfortable. Don't act like a stud or pretend to more experience than you have; trying to live up to a "cool" image only increases the pressure. And let yourself enjoy *all* of lovemaking—kissing, touching, closeness—without putting undue emphasis on intercourse.

One method recommended by sex therapists is to postpone intercourse and slowly build up to it, as you learn to find sex pleasurable again. The idea is to advance toward more intimate sexual acts one comfortable step at a time. First, you and your partner might only caress. Later, you might freely explore each other's bodies, but without touching the genitals. Later still, you might incorporate genital contact, but without attempting intercourse. Finally, after a period of weeks or even months, you would feel ready to resume sexual intercourse. This approach depends on feeling comfortable at each step and working with an understanding partner, and it has the best chance of success if you're also seeing a professional.

One warning: Don't calm your fears through alcohol or other drugs. Getting high can depress sexual performance and leave you more discouraged than ever.

Q: What can I do if I come too quickly?

A: This is a common problem for young males, especially the sexually inexperienced. Since anxiety can be the cause, we again recommend reducing the pressure by choosing an understanding sexual partner and not overemphasizing intercourse. Orgasm is not the goal of sex, just part of the process. Also, try not to overreact when you ejaculate—or come—quickly. If you do, so be it. To reduce sexual urgency, you might try masturbating before lovemaking, or having sex a second time after you've already come once.

You can also try this exercise while you masturbate: First, stop stimulating yourself just before ejaculation, then start again when your excitement has subsided, then stop again, and so forth. Through this masturbation exercise, you learn to recognize your pre-ejaculation sensations, which helps you control your level of sexual arousal and so control when you ejaculate.

Q: My ex-boyfriend kept losing his erection, and now my current boyfriend comes too soon. Is it my fault?

A: No. You can't cause someone to lose his erection or ejaculate prematurely. Besides, we discourage thinking in terms of fault anyway. An atmosphere of blame, whether self-blame or blaming your partner, heightens the tension and makes matters worse.

Though your boyfriend's problem must be frustrating, as much as possible try to convey support and understanding. Encourage him not to overreact to the problem. Search together for sexual satisfaction apart from intercourse through hugging and kissing, petting, masturbation, oral sex, whatever. Though his problem isn't your fault, your patience, flexibility and good humor create a supportive climate that may help him overcome it.

Q: I love my boyfriend, I'm attracted to him and in my limited experience he seems like a good lover. But I don't enjoy sex. Am I just frigid?

A: Let's begin with the matter of labels. Emotionally loaded words like *frigid* don't shed light on your situation. They only serve to frighten and condemn. The real problem if you don't get pleasure from sex probably has nothing to do with inherent sexual unresponsiveness, which is what frigidity implies. Consider five alternative explanations:

1. You were taught when you were young that sex is dirty and wrong. Although your conscious views may have changed since then, early teachings have an insidious staying power. On some level, sexually letting yourself go may mean betraying your ideals and letting down the people you care about.
2. You lack sexual assertiveness. In bed, you devote yourself totally to pleasing your partner, discounting your own sexual needs and pleasures. Naturally, sex isn't much fun.
3. You're not relaxed when making love; you're too worried about doing it right. Similar to men who have erection difficulties, you

worry about being a good lover, having an orgasm, feeling the right feelings or possessing the right kind of body. Such worries squelch sexual feelings.

4. You haven't discovered your full sexuality. You're not yet responding sexually because you haven't yet learned how. This is especially likely if you don't masturbate and have little overall sexual experience.

5. Fear of pregnancy or contracting an STD hampers your desire.

Q: So if I'm not "frigid," what should I do to get pleasure from sex?

A: You can try various approaches depending on the source of the problem. For example, you can practice sexual assertiveness, asking for what you want in bed and letting yourself be "selfish" and feel pleasure. You can reduce sexual pressure by deemphasizing or taking a vacation from intercourse, and by encouraging yourself to relax while making love. You can assuage fears about pregnancy or disease by making sure you use protection. You can explore your sexuality through masturbation.

But don't be alarmed if nothing much happens for a while. You may just be a slow sexual developer who needs time to reach full responsiveness. Given our culture's confusing messages about women's sexuality, a gradual discovery of sexual fulfillment is not at all unusual.

Q: I have orgasms when I masturbate, but never with my boyfriend. What should I do?

A: Many women don't have orgasms during intercourse. If your boyfriend doesn't stimulate your clitoris and vulva in the right way, you can ask him to do this and show him how you'd like it done. If he's entering you before you're ready, speak up and let him know you want more sexual play, and also let him know if you can come to orgasm in ways other than intercourse. The only way he can learn what gives you pleasure is if you tell him.

Remember, though, that enjoying sex doesn't depend on having an orgasm. If lovemaking with your partner brings you close and lets you share pleasure, then maybe it satisfies enough of your needs. Sex shouldn't be a goal-directed activity where success is measured by whether you climax.

Q: Sometimes sex is fantastic and sometimes it's just so-so. Is that normal?

A: Yes. However, you may enter the fantastic zone more often if you and your partner openly communicate about what you like and want.

Q: My boyfriend always gets on top of me and has intercourse in the standard "missionary position." I'd like to try other ways to make love and maybe have oral sex. How do I bring this up?

A: Your boyfriend may be sexually shy and inexperienced, or he may be a slave to sex-role expectations and feel unmanly unless he assumes a dominant position. We recommend simply telling him or showing him what you'd like to try. Make clear that you're not criticizing him; you just want to experiment. With luck, he'll be delighted to try something new now that he knows you approve.

Each of you should respect the other's limits, however. If there's something either one of you doesn't want to do—some people don't like oral sex, for example—then don't do it.

Q: Right after we make love my boyfriend turns over and goes to sleep. Why are guys like that?

A: Partly it's a question of biology. Males and females have some inborn differences in sexual responsiveness. Younger males tend to be innately aroused more quickly than females, and after orgasm their sexual excitement subsides more quickly (and they can grow sleepy). Women can have multiple orgasms, while men for a while after ejaculation (the refractory period) can't have an erection or ejaculate again.

Other differences between the sexes depend at least partly on conditioning, or learning. Traditionally in our society, males are taught to be sexual pursuers and aggressors, while women are taught to let themselves be pursued, play a passive role in bed and express tender emotions. Males are taught to dissociate sex from love, while females learn to link the two. Males learn to value independence and competitive striving; females are taught to emphasize relatedness and cooperation.

But none of these differences are hard-and-fast rules. In recent years traditional sex roles have blurred so that more women feel comfortable being assertive in and out of the bedroom, and more men are comfortable acknowledging tender emotions and dependency needs. Even back in the days when traditional sex roles were accepted without question, plenty of women and men didn't conform to feminine and masculine stereotypes.

Your boyfriend, then, may fall asleep partly for a biological reason—after ejaculation he *is* sleepy—and partly for the sociocultural reason that as a male he isn't comfortable expressing tender, nonsexual feelings. Then again, his behavior isn't chiseled in stone. Have you tried asking him to stay awake? Perhaps in spite of biology and cultural expectations he'd be happy to cuddle with you once you make your wishes known.

Q: My boyfriend is pretty clumsy in bed, but I'm crazy about him anyway and frankly it's not a big deal. Is our relationship okay?

A: Satisfaction is entirely a personal matter. Society bombards us with sexual images on TV and in the movies and magazines so that it's easy to lose perspective about sex. But there are many important aspects to a relationship besides sex. If on balance your relationship truly pleases you, then you've answered your own question and you've got a good thing going.

MASTURBATION AND FANTASIES

Q: Shouldn't people stop masturbating by college?

A: They should? Many men and women masturbate their whole lives, even after they're in long-term relationships. Provided you have privacy—which isn't easy to find in college—and provided your religious and ethical beliefs permit, there's no reason why you have to stop masturbating.

Q: But suppose I masturbate too often?

A: What's "too often"? Do you masturbate instead of going to class, studying, spending time with friends? That certainly would be too often; we would say the same thing if you overdid physical exercise or snacking. The issue isn't how frequently you masturbate but whether it interferes with important activities in your life.

Masturbation won't hurt you physically or mentally. (Guys, it won't use up your sperm, diminish your fertility or leave you physically weakened.) Masturbation won't prevent you from making love with a partner. In fact, many lovers incorporate masturbation into their lovemaking.

Some college students who are ashamed of masturbation come from authoritarian or perfectionistic households, with rather rigid standards of right and wrong. Other students have qualms about masturbation because of religious teachings. If you feel in conflict between your desires and your teachings, we recommend getting perspective on the issue by talking to a counselor.

Q: Sometimes I have odd sexual daydreams, like making a woman my slave. Should I be worried?

A: Probably not. All of us have diverse sexual wishes that come out in fantasies and dreams. Heterosexual men, it's been found, may have occasional fantasies about sexual dominance, making love to two women, watching women make love together or having sex with other men—and lots more besides. Heterosexual women may have occasional fantasies about being viewed naked, having sex with young boys or with other women, even being forced to have sex—and, again, many other themes. Gay males and lesbians similarly may fantasize about all sorts of things—including having sex with the opposite gender.

The point to remember is that fantasies and dreams fall into a separate category from actions and behavior. Just because something excites you in imagination doesn't mean at all that you'd actually want to do it. (No one *really* wants to be raped.) As long as you can enjoy sex without acting out harmful fantasies—as long as you don't hurt yourself or someone else in reality—then your fantasies are probably nothing to worry about. It's only when your fantasies are disturbing to you, perhaps because they're violent, or you feel compelled to act out harmful fantasies in reality that you would be wise to seek professional assistance.

Q: What does it mean if I think about other people when I'm having intercourse with my partner?

A: Here again we are talking about fantasies. Most people do have occasional wandering thoughts during lovemaking. It's not uncommon to think of other places, other acts or other persons.

On the other hand, if during lovemaking you mostly feel apart from your partner, something may be amiss. Possibly you don't feel sexually or romantically attracted to the person, which raises the question of why you stay in the relationship. Maybe you mentally withdraw because something about emotional closeness or the sex act itself makes you uncomfortable. You don't fully like or approve of what you're doing, and that's why your attention wanders to other people.

One commonsense tactic worth a try is focusing on the here and now. Concentrate on touching and being touched, on what you hear and see and smell, right at the moment. Whenever your attention wanders, gently bring yourself back to the immediate moment. This simple exercise may enable you to refocus your attention and truly be with your partner.

Q: Sometimes at night I stand outside windows, hoping to find a woman undressing. What's wrong with me?

A: Your problem is called "voyeurism": getting sexual pleasure from watching unsuspecting people who are naked or disrobing. It's part of a group of sexual problems that includes exhibitionism (publicly exposing your genitals), sadism (getting sexual pleasure from hurting your partner), masochism (getting sexual pleasure from your own suffering) and fetishism (getting pleasure from objects or non-sexual body parts).

All these themes are common and of no concern—so long as they remain just fantasies. There's no harm in imagining a woman taking her clothes off; most heterosexual men do. There's also nothing wrong if you and a partner consent to act out a fantasy where no one actually gets hurt. But that's not what's happening in your case. You are peeking at women without their permission. You are violating their rights and also breaking the law.

Why are you doing this? Shyness and a sense of inadequacy may play a part. It may seem safer to sneak a look at women than to approach them and risk rejection. Whatever the reason, don't wait to get caught before you seek assistance. We urge you to go into counseling without delay.

PROTECTION

Q: My boyfriend and I are ready to start making love. What's the best protection to use?

A: For vaginal, oral or anal penetration, at the very least use latex condoms ("rubbers"), and for extra protection use condoms with a contraceptive jelly, cream, film or foam containing nonoxynol-9, which kills sperm. If either of you is allergic to latex, polyurethane condoms are recommended. Condoms and spermicides, though not foolproof, are an effective means of contraception (birth control) and are the best protection other than abstinence against HIV and other sexually transmitted diseases (STDs). The only exception to condom and spermicide use is if you and your partner are totally monogamous (though unwanted pregnancy would still be an issue), and you're both certain that you don't carry the AIDS virus or have another STD. But please note: Even lab tests can't rule out all STDs.

Condoms are available without prescription at drugstores and most likely at your college's health service. Thin rubber sheaths placed over the erect penis before intercourse, they collect sperm and prevent it from entering the vagina. They must be put on as soon as the penis is erect to prevent sperm or pre-ejaculation fluid (pre-come) from touching the vulva since pre-come can transmit infection and sperm. Do not reuse condoms; a new one is necessary every time you have intercourse. Also available in recent years is the female condom, which covers the inside of the vagina. More expensive and less popular than regular condoms, female condoms have the advantage of protecting women when their partners are unwilling to use condoms.

Condoms are equally necessary for gay male couples and heterosexual couples.

Q: I'm a heterosexual woman concerned about pregnancy. What other forms of birth control should I consider besides condoms?

A: First, let us emphasize that there's no substitute for condoms to prevent the spread of STDs. Since condoms alone are also 90% effective in preventing pregnancy,[2] other methods should be used strictly as an extra form of birth control. For each method, a woman should follow a health care professional's instruction and read the product instructions carefully.

The most popular contraceptive method for college women is *the pill.* Prescribed by a doctor or nurse practitioner, the pill prevents ovulation, the monthly release of an egg from the ovary for possible fertilization. Birth control pills are more than 99.9% effective in preventing pregnancy if used properly. However, some women forget to take them, reducing their effectiveness. Health concerns are also an issue, although the jury is still out about the long-term consequences of taking the pill. Possible side effects include nausea and breast tenderness.

Norplant capsules, a new method, are tiny sticks containing the hormone progestin that are implanted by a doctor into the inside of the upper arm. Progestin, the same hormone found in birth control pills, is gradually released for a period up to five years. Norplant's health risks are presumably the same as for the pill, though menstrual irregularities are common with this method.

Depo-Provera, a drug also containing the hormone progestin, is administered every three months through an injection into the muscle of the upper arm. Like the pill and Norplant, Depo-Provera is highly effective in preventing pregnancy but also leads to menstrual irregularities.

Diaphragms are shallow rubber bowl-shaped objects placed in the vagina to stop the man's sperm from entering the cervix, the opening of the uterus. They are used with a cream or jelly spermicide, which must be applied each time you have intercourse. Prescribed and fitted by a medical practitioner, diaphragms and spermicides have no dangerous side effects and are effective in preventing pregnancy—if used properly. With typical use, however, the effectiveness of diaphragms decreases. Diaphragms require insertion before intercourse and must be left in for six hours after intercourse.

A smaller version of the diaphragm is the *cervical cap.* Attached to the cervix by suction, cervical caps prevent sperm from entering the uterus and are used with a spermicide. Available by prescription, they are inserted before intercourse and require time to learn to use correctly. They have no serious side effects and are about as effective as the diaphragm.

Foams, creams, film and *jellies* contain spermicides and are placed in the vagina before intrecourse. Typically they're only 70–80% effective in preventing pregnancies, because women don't always follow the instructions carefully. To be safe with these methods one should also use condoms, which greatly increases their effectiveness.

Intrauterine devices, or *IUDs,* are placed by a specialist into the uterus, with the intention of preventing the egg from implanting. They are quite effective in preventing pregnancy and require no further action after being inserted. But because they increase the risk of pelvic inflammatory disease and can cause infertility, IUDs are not recommended for college-age women.

The *fertility awareness method* teaches women to observe signs of fertility. She and her partner then either abstain from intercourse around those times or use an alternative form of contraception. This method is not recommended for college students, who because of stress may ovulate at different times of the month. Checking calendar dates to calculate times of ovulation—*the rhythm method*—is also unreliable, especially if the woman has irregular periods.

The least complicated birth control method is *withdrawal.* No expense, no complicated methods, no medical practitioners: The man simply withdraws his penis from the vagina just before ejaculation. But withdrawal is not a reliable method. The man may not withdraw in time, and even if he does pull out before ejaculation, a small amount of pre-ejaculation fluid may be released into the vagina— enough to fertilize an egg or transmit disease. The best that can be said about withdrawal is that it's better than nothing if a couple starts making love without using other protection.

This brief summary of birth control methods in no way exhausts the issues involved with each method. Before making any decisions about which method is right for you, speak to a medical practitioner at your college's health service or a birth control clinic. Also, make sure to discuss the matter with your partner, if you have one. The risk of an unplanned pregnancy and sexually transmitted disease affects both of you.

Q: But what if my partner doesn't like to put on a condom?

A: He isn't the only one. Studies show that the majority of college students fail to use condoms on a consistent basis.[3] They may know (or think they know) about sexually transmitted diseases, but their knowledge isn't translated into safe behavior.

Your partner may think that:

- **"Nothing can happen if we only take an occasional risk."** But this simply isn't true. As one student said, "It's like playing Russian roulette with your dick."[4] Just one time of unprotected sex may infect you with the AIDS virus or another sexually transmitted disease.
- **"People our age don't get infected with AIDS."** Wrong again. True, you personally may not know of any classmates who have AIDS, but that's because AIDS takes years to develop after infection with the HIV virus. Chances are someone you know, now perfectly healthy, will develop AIDS some time in the future. As for other STDs, people your age get infected with alarming frequency.
- **"Straight people don't get AIDS."** Yes, they do. The rate of AIDS is growing faster among heterosexuals, especially heterosexual women, than among homosexuals. Getting other STDs, of course, has nothing to do with being straight or gay either.
- **"We don't have to use condoms because we're monogamous."** Monogamy only protects you if neither of you is already infected with HIV or other STDs. And even lab tests can't guarantee that you're disease-free, as we explain below. As for monogamy, going from one relationship to another (serial monogamy) still puts you into contact with multiple partners, and any one of them might have been infected.
- **"But my partner assures me he doesn't have an STD."** People can be mistaken about having an STD. People also lie to have sex.
- **"I don't want to ruin the mood by discussing protection and putting on a condom."** Okay, so don't wait until the last minute to discuss protection. Talk about condoms well before intercourse becomes a possibility. As for putting on a condom, practice makes the process easy. (Men can practice privately in the bathroom; women may also want to practice by putting condoms on a broom handle or a banana). Putting on a condom doesn't have to spoil the fun. It can become part of the lovemaking, both partners joining in the unrolling process.
- **"Sex doesn't feel as good with condoms."** Possibly, but the problem may be more in your attitude than in loss of sensation. When you focus on what does feel good, the annoyance of the condom diminishes.

Q: But if my partner still doesn't want to use condoms, what should I do?

A: Then you need to assert your rights. Here are some suggestions:

- **Take STDs seriously.** Pledge to yourself that a condom, and preferably a spermicide too, will be used every single time you have sex. Be firm in your resolve.
- **Discuss protection with your partner before you make love.** Be assertive. Insist that a condom and spermicide be used prior to vaginal or anal intercourse. Stick to your position if he or she raises objections or downplays the importance of these protections.
- **Stick to your guns.** If once the action starts your partner gets all hot and bothered and wants to race into intercourse, call a time-out (we know it's difficult) and insist on protection. If he or she protests, say you won't have sex otherwise. If you're still not getting through, then leave or tell him or her to leave. The bottom line is, you have to take responsibility for your own health. You can't leave it up to your partner.
- **Avoid excessive drinking or taking any drugs before you have sex.** Getting high impairs judgment and makes it likely you'll forget about protection.

Q: But suppose I have trouble bringing up the topic of protection?

A: We realize this can be a problem. Shy people can be embarrassed to talk about condoms. Unassertive people tend to let their partners call the shots. People who don't like to be rejected—and that's just about everyone—don't want to turn off their partner by making a big deal about condom use.

Consider, though, that we're talking here about your health and *your life.* Whatever your hesitations, you can't afford to remain silent. So if it's hard to speak up about condoms and such, rehearse beforehand. Role-play with a close friend, if that will help, or consult a counselor to build up your assertive skills. One way or another, learn to overcome your inhibitions and communicate assertively about protection.

Q: I'm terrified about getting AIDS. Is that irrational?

A: It depends. If you have the wrong idea about AIDS transmission, then yes, your fear may be irrational. Some students believe the AIDS virus (HIV) can be transmitted through tears, saliva, food, casual contact with an infected person or even association with a gay classmate! All these are untrue. The AIDS virus can only be transmitted when: 1) semen, pre-come or vaginal secretions of an infected person, either straight or gay, enters your body during sex; 2) an infected person's blood enters your blood during sharing of needles for intravenous drug use; 3) an infected person's blood is transmitted to you during a blood transfusion (thanks to blood testing, this is very rare); or 4) an infected person's blood is transferred from his or her open wound to your wound (again, this is rare). You cannot get AIDS in any other way.

Fear can also get out of hand if you confuse AIDS with other issues. One male student told his counselor he was terrified about contracting AIDS based on having had sex a year earlier with a man. The fear had no medical basis—he and his partner had used condoms and he'd recently tested negative for HIV—but he couldn't be reassured. He was obsessed with the disease because it represented the punishment he felt he deserved for responding to homosexual urges.

Although fear of AIDS can be blown out of proportion, obviously it's not crazy to be concerned about a life-threatening disease. Although new treatments are prolonging the lives of persons infected with the virus, AIDS remains incurable and it does still kill. So maybe it's just as well if AIDS makes you wary. That way you'll practice safer sex methods.

Q: What should I know about STDs?

A: One thing to know is they are common. If you're sexually active, the risk of contracting some disease, especially chlamydia, herpes, genital warts or crabs, runs from 10–25%.[5] Another point is that you don't always know if you have them. Persons infected may or may not have symptoms. Fortunately, you can considerably cut down your risk of catching these diseases by practicing safer sex techniques. Here are thumbnail sketches of the most prevalent STDs:

- **Chlamydia** is treatable with antibiotics. Many infected people, especially women, lack the usual symptoms (burning during urination or unusual discharge) and don't know they have chlamydia. If unchecked, it can cause women to have pelvic inflammatory disease, resulting in infertility.

- **Genital warts,** caused by the human papilloma virus (HPV), can show up in flat or raised bumps around the vagina, cervix, penis or scrotum. But women may not notice symptoms. In that case, the only way to detect genital warts is from an abnormal Pap smear. Treatment involves eradicating the warts; the virus itself has to run its course. If left untreated, certain strains of HPV can cause cervical cancer.
- **Herpes,** also caused by a virus, produces outbreaks of painful sores or blisters on the genitals. Again, many persons are unaware of having the disease. Although there is no cure, drugs can reduce the severity and frequency of outbreaks. Since herpes can be transmitted orally as well as genitally, it's wise to ask partners if they ever get cold sores.
- **Crabs,** or pubic lice, cause itching in the pubic area. They can be cured by applying special shampoos.
- **Gonorrhea** (the "clap") sometimes but not always causes symptoms (abdominal pain, thick discharge, burning during urination). It is treated with antibiotics.
- **Syphilis,** rarer on campus than the others but hardly unknown, is treatable at any time by antibiotics. It can be detected early by a painless sore on the genitals and at a later stage by rashes on the body and aching joints. If left untreated, syphilis many years later can cause blindness and death.

For more information about STDs, including AIDS, contact the organizations listed in Appendix 2.

Q: How should I protect myself against AIDS and STDs if I want to be sexually active?

A: The main rule bears repeating: Use latex condoms and spermicides containing nonoxynol-9 whenever you have vaginal or anal intercourse. In addition, here are other precautions:

- **Get tested periodically if you're sexually active, especially if you're not conscientious about using protection.** Granted, you can't test for all STDs; HPV and herpes can only be tested if you have lesions. Still, it's good idea to have periodic STD testing, even if you have no symptoms. Not only are STDs dangerous in their own right, but if you have unprotected penetrative intercourse, they may facilitate the transmission of the AIDS virus.

- **Wait three months after possible exposure to get tested for HIV.** The HIV test can't detect antibodies to the virus until three months after infection.
- **Choose your partners carefully.** Ask about past and current sexual partners, history of STDs and history of needle use. Ask when they've had sex and when they've been tested.
- **Don't have sex in the dark.** You want to see your partner's genitalia to check for bumps, lesions, etc.
- **Think it over if you have more than one partner.** The more partners you have, the greater the risk of catching something.
- **Take precautions with anal sex.** Condoms are a must, and use lubrication to minimize the risks of tearing the condom or the skin.
- **Take precautions with oral sex.** A nonlubricated condom should be used when giving or receiving fellatio (oral sex on a man), and a dental dam should be spread over the vulva and vaginal opening when giving or receiving cunnilingus (oral sex on a woman).
- **Be cautious with alcohol and drugs.** When intoxicated or high, your judgment is impaired and you're much more likely to have unprotected sex.

UNWANTED PREGNANCY

Q: I just found out I'm pregnant. I'm not sure if I want to have an abortion, but if I keep the baby my life is ruined. What do I do?

A: We recognize how overwhelming all this must now seem. This is a decision you weren't expecting, and now that it's here you don't have much time to make it. You have to consider many factors in making your decision, factors that may pull at you in different directions.

What are these factors? There are your principles and personal beliefs, which may or may not be accepting of abortion. There is your relationship, close or casual, with the man involved; if you're committed to each other, pregnancy raises the issue of marriage. There are the probable reactions of family and friends, assuming you choose to tell them. There are your college education, career plans and future goals, all of which are affected by the choice you make.

Some women in your position choose to have and raise the child. Although sometimes they can find a way to continue in school, more often keeping the child postpones college and derails plans for the future. If you are considering this option, you need to think through the consequences for both of you. Will your own life, though radically changed, be fulfilling? Will you have the financial and emotional resources to adequately provide for a child and be a good mother?

Another option is to give the baby up for adoption. Before taking this step, you need to assess how you'll feel about the decision in the future. On a practical level, this option requires finding a reputable agency and working out medical arrangements.

The third option, abortion, is least disruptive to your educational opportunity and future plans. However, abortion sometimes causes guilt even in women who consider themselves pro-choice, and it can stir up surprising disappointment at missing out on motherhood. If you elect to have an abortion, you must promptly arrange for the procedure, find a way to pay for it and prepare yourself for the experience. Someone you trust should accompany you during the day of the procedure and remain with you the entire time.

As complicated and distressing as an unwanted pregnancy can be, bear in mind that the decision is hardest at the beginning, when the shock of being pregnant clouds your thinking. After the shock subsides, you'll be able to think more clearly. Although unwanted pregnancy isn't a small matter, remember that thousands of college women have faced, and come through, the same predicament.

To help you cope during this difficult time, turn to others you trust, especially your parents if they're likely to be supportive. (Some parents are initially upset but soon calm down and are tremendously helpful). If at all possible, include the man in the process. Not only does he share responsibility, but he has feelings of his own concerning the pregnancy and the various options. The college health service can also help; if you decide on an abortion, they can refer you to a clinic. We also recommend counseling sessions to help you sort out complex feelings and make a decision that's right for you.

SEXUAL ORIENTATION

Q: How can I know if I'm heterosexual or homosexual?

A: The predominant pattern of your sexual, emotional and romantic interests is what decides sexual orientation. If you *primarily* focus on persons from the opposite sex when you have sexual or romantic daydreams, fall in love or fantasize, then you're probably heterosexual. If you *primarily* are aroused sexually, romantically and emotionally by the same sex, chances are you have a homosexual orientation. And if you're equally turned on by both males and females, then your sexual orientation is probably bisexual.

We stress the word primarily because although some persons are exclusively heterosexual or homosexual, many straight people, gays and lesbians have at least some potential for bisexual feelings. If you're mostly heterosexual, then, you still may feel attracted sometimes to your roommate's body or have the urge to hug a same-sex friend. You may even have sexual contact at some point with someone from the same sex. Similarly for gays and lesbians, you sometimes may feel physically and emotionally drawn to the opposite sex, and perhaps you've actually had heterosexual sexual experiences. These exceptions don't call into question your basic sexual orientation. They simply illustrate that human desire tends to be complex and unpredictable, that it's normal to have various feelings and reactions to others around you, both men and women. Being basically heterosexual or homosexual doesn't mean your every moment of arousal must fit into a tidy box labeled "straight" or "gay."

Again, it's the overall pattern of yearnings, not the exceptions, that decides your sexual orientation.

Q: But I'm not sure yet about my overall pattern of sexual and romantic feelings. Is it weird if I don't know whether I'm gay or straight?

A: Not really. Some college students recall being aware of their homosexuality from a very young age, although they may not have had a name for or fully understood their feelings. Many heterosexuals "know" their sexuality just as early. But other college students are still unsure at age 18 or even 21, still trying to discover what they feel, and for whom. If you're one of these undecideds, you may be tempted to end uncertainty by prematurely assigning yourself an identity—homosexual, heterosexual or bisexual. We think that's unfortunate. A better course is to forgo labels until you've sorted out your feelings and desires. Be alert to your attractions. Be open to what you feel. There'll be plenty of time later, once you're certain of your sexual leanings, to declare your sexual orientation.

Q: Could I think I'm gay and be wrong?

A: Absolutely. This mistake can occur because you don't fit certain societal sex role stereotypes. You may be a sensitive, shy male who doesn't like football and beer or have large muscles. You may be an assertive, large-framed female, and not particularly interested now in finding the right man, getting married and starting a family. Male or female, you may not be comfortable with the opposite sex or go out on dates, or you may not be particularly attracted to the sex acts or the body parts that your friends say turn them on. You may be afraid of dating, afraid of being rejected, afraid of not performing well in bed. Because in any of these ways you don't fit the masculine or feminine stereotype, you may wonder whether you're gay, lesbian or bisexual.

Remember, conforming to sex role stereotypes isn't what determines sexual orientation. What matters is which sex primarily turns you on.

Q: Could I be gay without really knowing it?

A: Yes, this can happen too. Again, societal stereotypes can be a source of confusion. You may think you can't be gay and like football or be lesbian and want to get all dolled up. But sexual orientation isn't defined by preferences for football or nice clothes or by any of the other stereotypes associated with gays and lesbians. Sexual orientation simply has to do with the preponderance of your sexual and erotic desires.

If because of society's negative messages you are ashamed of homosexuality, you also may misread your sexuality by denying what you really feel. You may explain away homosexual experiences ("I was drunk") or lack of heterosexual desire ("I haven't met the right person"; "I'm not interested in a relationship right now.") You may tell yourself that attraction for the same sex is just a phase, something you'll outgrow, or a weakness you can work on. Here again you may mistake your sexuality.

Denying your sexual orientation makes you a stranger to yourself and prevents you from making informed choices about sex and relationships. If you're gay or lesbian, it's important to work on any shame you may feel (counseling can help with this) in order to be honest about your feelings and decide on the best life for you.

Q: Isn't there something psychologically wrong with me if I'm gay or a lesbian?

A: No more so than if you were straight. Today the American Psychological Association and the American Psychiatric Association view homosexuality as a valid expression of human sexuality, not a psychological disturbance. Being homosexual is as normal as being heterosexual.

While homosexuality isn't "wrong," it's true that living as a homosexual in our society can be stressful. One reason is society's "homophobia"—its fear and intolerance of homosexuality. Even on a college campus, where overt gay-bashing is relatively rare, homophobia does exist. Some heterosexual classmates may subtly treat you as different and inferior or make hostile comments about gays and lesbians. These incidents hurt and are demoralizing.

Even worse, being gay or lesbian can cause internal conflict. Since society has traditionally been intolerant of homosexuality, many gays and lesbians have internalized society's worst views and become intolerant of themselves—in effect, homophobic. They fear and hate their own desires, which is tantamount to fearing and hating themselves. If this describes you, then something is psychologically "wrong," but it's not your sexual orientation. It's societally conditioned self-rejection.

Q: Why am I homosexual?

A: This is a debatable question. There is some scientific evidence, at least for males, pointing to a biological predisposition to homosexuality.[6] An older theory suggests, again for males, that distant fathers and overprotective mothers tend to produce homosexuals; by no means, however, does every gay male come from such a family. A third theory holds that homosexuality is learned based on early life experiences.

On balance, the biological explanation is currently considered the most promising theory, but all the data aren't in. It seems likely that different factors account for homosexuality in different individuals.

Q: If I'm homosexual, can I change?

A: Probably not. Sexual orientation is too integral a part of the personality to be reversed. Over the years, various mental health professionals have tried behavior therapy, psychoanalysis and other forms of treatment to change homosexuality, but most therapists today (there are a few dissenters) see these efforts as a waste of time. You can't change a homosexual orientation any more than you can "cure" a heterosexual.

But if therapy can't change sexual orientation, it can certainly change attitudes. Counseling can ease the guilt, self-hatred and fear that haunt some gay men and lesbians and help them move from cursing their sexual orientation to embracing it. Counseling can also help persons explore their options for living with a homosexual orientation.

Q: How can I become comfortable being homosexual?

A: This is a lifelong process. The best way is to talk to other students who are gay, lesbian or questioning. They may accept your sexuality in ways that others have not, which makes it easier to be self-accepting. And since many of these students wrestle with the same concerns you have, you'll learn from one another how to deal with society's homophobia and achieve self-acceptance. It's a powerful, uplifting, self-affirming experience to air your concerns in a community that understands.

To find other students, consider attending discussion or support groups for gay, lesbian, bisexual and questioning students. These may be sponsored by a student organization, the counseling center or a professional office dedicated to gay/lesbian concerns.

In addition to reaching out to others, you can independently work toward self-acceptance by examining your worries about being homosexual. Your reasoning, you may find, is flawed and unduly pessimistic. Are you concerned about family attitudes or friends' opinions? Gays and lesbians often discover after they come out that their heterosexual friends and even their parents are surprisingly understanding. (There are exceptions, of course.) Are you troubled by the religious or moral implications? Many religious authorities are fully accepting of homosexuality—some are openly homosexual themselves. Do you condemn yourself for being "abnormal"? Remember, the major psychology and psychiatry organizations have emphatically affirmed that homosexuality and bisexuality are valid sexual orientations. Do you fear that a homosexual life condemns you to unhappiness? Look carefully around you. You'll notice there are happy gays and lesbians and miserable gays and lesbians—just like everyone else.

In suggesting self-analysis, we are not trying to minimize the problems homosexuals face. Homophobia is real. Self-acceptance is a struggle. What we are saying is, Don't exaggerate the problems— don't catastrophize. To become comfortable being homosexual it's imperative to view opportunities and challenges realistically. If this seems hard to do on your own, consider speaking with an accepting minister, priest or rabbi, or a professional at your counseling center.

Q: I think I can accept being homosexual. What I can't stand is the idea of living the gay lifestyle.

A: To begin with, gays aren't confined to one lifestyle any more than heterosexuals are. And since you're in charge of your life, it's up to you which lifestyle you adopt. So you can choose to express homosexual yearnings or choose not to. If you do have homosexual relations, you can try to find one partner or experiment getting to know various people. You can choose whether to come out and to whom, whether to involve yourself in gay and lesbian political causes, and whether the party, bar and club scenes are to your liking. You can have a long-term committed relationship and explore options to have and raise children.

Being homosexual means you have certain feelings and desires, but it doesn't determine how you conduct your life. Ultimately, it's you, not your sexual feelings, in control of your actions.

Q: I'm a heterosexual woman who likes to think of herself as a tolerant person, yet I find myself inwardly uncomfortable around certain gay people. Does that make me a hypocrite?

A: No, it doesn't. All of us have varying inner reactions to different people we come across, and we all are infected by society's prejudices. It would be unrealistic to expect to feel the same bland acceptance for everyone who crosses our path.

However you inwardly feel around certain gay people, the important thing is how you behave. If you treat all people with respect and strive to be open minded in your dealings, then you can fairly call yourself tolerant. You also may discover after closer contacts with gay people that your inner reactions evolve. Phobias thrive on unfamiliarity. The very persons who once made you feel uncomfortable may turn into welcome companions after you get to know them better.

Q: I'm gay, and I've been thinking about coming out. Do you think that's a good idea?

A: We can't give a blanket answer. Telling your best friend privately and confidentially may be relatively safe, provided this person is trustworthy and accepting. But announcing your sexuality to a wide audience or to relative strangers is a much riskier proposition.

Some in the gay/lesbian community advise against coming out publicly during the college years. In their view, other students may reject you because fitting in and being "normal" is so valued in college. Keep in mind, too, that you can't take it back once you let the cat out of the bag. Once you've identified yourself as gay or lesbian, you'll have to live with the consequences for the rest of your college career.

That's the cautious view. According to another school of thought, hiding your sexuality makes it seem there's something secret and shameful about you, and so you demean yourself. Others don't get to know the real you, which leaves you feeling alienated, possibly depressed. Further, college is not really such a bad time to come out. By and large your classmates are a tolerant bunch, as accepting or more so than the people you'll encounter later in life.

As you can see, you can build a good case either way. You need to think carefully before deciding this issue. Here are some other points to consider:[7]

- **Trust your own instincts.** Come out only if you're ready and are sure it's right for you. If you feel pressured into coming out, are unsure about your sexuality or are uncomfortable being gay or lesbian, then you're probably not ready.
- **Study your motives.** Do it in the spirit of enhancing mutual understanding. Don't come out because you're angry, or want attention.
- **Don't come out to someone who can't handle the news.** You shouldn't come out to someone who's sure to reject you.

Q: When I did tell my roommate I was a lesbian, I thought she'd be understanding. Instead she hardly said anything and she's been distant around me. What should I do now?

A: Possibly she just needs time to digest the news, and soon she'll accept you as before. It's also possible that she's troubled by some aspect of your disclosure. Perhaps she's afraid that you're going to talk more than she wants to hear about your personal life, or that you'll bring female lovers into the room—or even that you'll come on to her. Whatever may be her fears, having another talk may allow you to correct any misconceptions.

If talking doesn't help and she remains estranged from you, there is one small consolation. You can tell yourself that the friendship wasn't worth much if it couldn't survive an infusion of honesty. You're better off seeking friendships that allow both of you to be genuinely yourself.

Q: I want to tell my parents, but I'm scared. How do most parents take it when their children come out?

A: Every parent is different, of course, but there are some general trends. At first, you can expect shock and denial. Don't be surprised if they try to talk you out of being gay or lesbian and insist you see a therapist, or if they are guilt-ridden and focus on themselves: "Where did we go wrong?" Later on, after the initial impact has subsided, their reaction can be predicted from their usual behavior. If they've been supportive and caring up to now, chances are they'll continue that way in the future. If support and caring aren't their style, then they may never accept your homosexuality. They may even refuse to discuss it again, as if it didn't exist.

You'll need to be patient with your parents. This is a big pill for them to swallow, and it may take months or even years for them to grow comfortable with this new image of you. Giving them reading material may help them make the adjustment. (See the suggestions at the end of this chapter.)

With some parents you can predict disastrous results. If your parents will probably stop speaking to you or paying for your college education, it may be wise to duck the issue or at least wait until graduation before breaking the news.

Q: What do I do if someone attacks me because I'm gay? There have been some ugly incidents of gay-bashing on my campus.

A: Harassment of gays and lesbians is no less serious than harassment of women, blacks or Jews. Any incidents on your campus are undoubtedly a violation of your college's code of conduct and carry disciplinary penalties. We recommend reporting them to college authorities. If you are ever assaulted, the proper step would be to report the incident to the police. On the other hand, with subtle forms of harassment it may be futile to lodge a complaint. Hostile looks snide comments and the like, you may just have to accept as the shortcomings of others.

Colleges are moving—some would say too slowly—to eliminate bias against gays and lesbians. Many colleges have written policies banning discrimination on the basis of sexual orientation. Become familiar with the policies on your own campus. If they seem inadequate, this may be a good opportunity to get involved and work toward changing them.

FOR FURTHER READING

Ellen Bass and Kate Kaufman, *Free Your Mind: The Book for Gay, Lesbian and Bisexual Youth—and Their Allies.* New York: HarperCollins, 1996.

Boston Women's Health Collective, *Our Bodies, Ourselves for the New Century.* New York: Touchstone, 1998.

Don Clark, *Loving Someone Gay III.* Berkeley, Calif.: Celestial Arts, 1997.

Leland Elliot and Cynthia Brantley, *Sex on Campus.* New York: Random House, 1997.

Richard Isay, *Becoming Gay: The Journey to Self-Acceptance.* New York: Holt, 1996.

Eric W. Johanson, *Love and Sex in Plain Language.* Toronto: Bantam, 1988.

Sue Johanson, *Sex, Sex and More Sex: 101 Questions and Answers.* Upland, Penn.: Diane Publishing, 1998.

Ruth K. Westheimer, *Dr. Ruth's Guide to Good Sex.* New York: Warner Books, 1984.

SEXUAL HARASSMENT
AND RAPE

Many students, and not a few faculty and staff, are unclear about the limits of acceptable sexual and romantic behavior. In order to protect yourself from harassment and rape, you need a clear understanding of these offenses. In this chapter we clarify the terms, explain precautions you can take and discuss the aftermath of rape: how victims react, cope and can recover.

Q: My English professor invited me into his office to talk about my term paper. While we talked, he put his arm around my shoulder, and I felt uncomfortable. Was this wrong for him to do?

A: This is a very gray area. Your professor's gesture may have been innocent, but maybe not. Regardless of his intentions we recommend trusting your feelings of discomfort. Don't meet him again alone in his office.

Professors have influence over students. They command respect, assign grades, write letters of reference. The vast majority use their influence constructively. But occasionally a professor (usually a male) exploits his influence to get sexual favors from a student. This is sexual harassment, and it should be reported to the appropriate authorities on campus—the dean of students, the campus security office or the affirmative action office.

Sexual harassment may also be perpetrated by teaching assistants, staff members or classmates. It can take various forms: unnecessary touching and fondling, sexual comments, leering at your body, or lewd phone calls or letters. If something like this happens to you, you can talk to the harasser and strongly denounce the behavior, simply avoid the person (if possible) or notify him or her in writing that you will contact university authorities if the harassment continues.

And if the harassment does continue, by all means alert someone in authority—your campus security office, a dean, a department chair, the ombudsman's office or the affirmative action office.

Q: Do I really have to worry about rape at college?

A: Unfortunately, you do. Understand, however, that the greatest danger comes from persons you know—dates and acquaintances—rather than strangers, and that rape can occur because of threats, intimidation, pressure and persistence as well as physical force.

The popular image of rape—a stranger jumping out from the bushes and brandishing a knife or a gun—may happen infrequently in your college community. But date and acquaintance rape are threats on every campus.

Q: What you're describing sounds unfortunate but it's not what I'd call rape.

A: Rape is defined as sexual penetration performed against someone's will or without the person's consent. When this happens, it's rape, even if the rapist knows the victim and doesn't use violence, and even if he acts conciliatory after the assault and tries to convince the woman that what happened wasn't rape.

Q: Can I protect myself against rape?

A: Yes, here are safety measures you can take:

- **Know your rights.** You have the right to say no if someone asks you out. If you do go out, you have the right to refuse physical relations; no one but you should decide who touches your body. If you do want physical relations, you have the right to set limits—you can refuse sexual intercourse. It also doesn't matter if a man is sexually aroused, says he loves you, has spent money on you or even has regularly slept with you before. You have the right in *every* instance to say no to sex.
- **Avoid secluded places.** Whether you're alone or with a new date or male acquaintance, stick to public places, with lots of other people around. If you're alone at night and need to return to your room, call your college's escort service to have somebody accompany you.

Make sure your roommate is within earshot if you invite a new male friend to your dorm room, and take along a friend on visits to fraternities.

- **Attend to uncomfortable feelings.** If you're uneasy because a casual friend sits too close at the cafeteria or a new date's hands wander during a slow dance, trust your instincts and tell him to stop. If he doesn't, leave.
- **Decide about physical relations beforehand.** Before going out on a date, decide whether you want physical contact, and if so, what you want to do. Perhaps this seems unspontaneous, but determining your limits beforehand makes it easier to resist pressure during the date.
- **When physical contact is about to start, clearly express what you want.** Announcing your wishes may sound unromantic, but clear messages can spare major misunderstandings. Be consistent in your messages. Psychologist Diana Pace gives an example: "Don't engage in petting, then say you don't want to go any further, then return to petting."[1]
- **Communicate about physical relations before either of you takes a drink.** Better yet, don't drink at all, or at least not much, if physical relations are possible. Staying sober is the surest way to retain good judgment and clearly communicate your intentions.
- **If you do drink, make the drink yourself.** It's unclear how prevalent the so-called date-rape drug, Rohypnol, actually is. It reportedly has been slipped into the drinks of women so they'll pass out and can be raped. Take no chances. Don't accept drinks from people you don't know well.
- **If you are uncomfortable during petting, speak up.** Clearly stating "I don't want you to do that!" may stop him in his tracks.
- **If you feel in danger or are attacked, try to leave at once.** Don't reason with the person or hope he'll come to his senses.

Q: After a party last week, this guy who's sort of a friend invited me into his bedroom. I thought he just wanted to talk, but instead he forced me to have sex. I'm very upset about the whole thing, but I really don't want to report it. Do you think I should?

A: A tough decision. We can understand why you'd hesitate to report a rape. You may feel guilty or responsible for what happened (even though it's not your fault). You may not want to accuse your attacker publicly, or you may fear that he'll retaliate somehow and hurt you. You may want to spare yourself the ordeal of questioning by police and lawyers. You may worry about your friends' or parents' disapproval, or fear they'll want you to leave college when they find out what happened.

Given these considerations, no one has the right to tell you to report a rape. Taking that step is not a routine matter. Still, consider that this man committed a crime and deserves to be held accountable. Unless he's caught, he may strike again. So do give careful thought to reporting the incident, or at least discuss the pros and cons of doing so with a professional counselor.

Q: If I report a rape to the campus authorities, what happens?

A: If you report the rape right away, you will be encouraged to go to the emergency room to be physically examined and treated. The doctors will check for possible internal injuries, test you for sexually transmitted diseases and evaluate the possibility of pregnancy. They will also gather physical evidence—semen samples, hair, etc.—which will be used if you choose to report the crime to the police. Probably, a rape crisis counselor will be called in to provide emotional support and information.

The decision to notify the police is yours. If you go ahead, the police will ask for specific details about the rape and may ask you to identify your attacker. Being accompanied by a friend or rape crisis counselor will help during this potentially difficult process. If there is enough evidence and you choose to pursue it, the case may then be brought to trial. There you will face your attacker in open court, tell your story, listen to contradictory evidence and undergo cross-examination by a defense attorney who may argue that you consented to have sex. "Shield laws" are meant to protect you, although there's the possibility that you will be questioned about your prior sexual history and that your identity will be revealed in the media. All of this will be emotionally trying, of course, but reporting a rape can be an important and empowering experience as well.

You also can choose to report the crime to your college's disciplinary system by notifying the dean of students, the affirmative action office, or the judicial administrator. This route may be less disturbing than hiring a lawyer and pressing legal charges, and sometimes charges that will not stand up in court do result in college disciplinary sanctions against the attacker. Of course, the college's sanctions against the attacker are also probably less severe than legal penalties.

Q: Since I was raped last month, I don't want my boyfriend to touch me and I've been having nightmares. Is this normal?

A: Yes, it is. Initially after a rape, the tendency is to experience emotional shock and confused thinking. Later a return to normal life is usually possible, but typically there are psychological aftereffects, such as fear, anger, depression, intrusive memories and sleep difficulties. You may feel dirty and defiled, numb and detached, or ashamed and guilty, as if you were to blame. You may feel less safe in the world and start to question your own perceptions and judgments. Other common reactions include social withdrawal, mistrust of men and a lack of interest in, or even revulsion to, sex. So the responses you describe are perfectly understandable.

But everyone is different. A few women cope rather well considering the trauma they've endured. Other women *appear* to be doing fine. They go on with their lives as if nothing happened, only to have the pain and emotional distress emerge later. Sometimes they come into counseling with puzzling symptoms, which are then traced back to the rape they suffered years earlier.

Q: Aren't I partly to blame for the rape, since I invited the guy into my room?

A: No, you're not. Perhaps with the benefit of hindsight you can identify things you would have done differently, but that doesn't mean you invited the rape or are in any sense responsible for it. Other men in the same situation wouldn't have raped you. There's only one person to blame in a rape: the rapist.

Q: I was raped some time ago and thought I had dealt with it, but I've been having a rough time lately. What should I do?

A: Get help! Many colleges have special counselors, sometimes at the counseling center, trained to handle sexual assaults. These professionals can help you with medical, legal and psychological issues associated with rape. If help is not available on campus, utilize the medical, legal and counseling resources in the college community. Talking to a trusted friend, family member or clergyperson can also help.

Rape is a traumatic event, a severe psychological shock. The passage of time may help, but time alone is seldom enough. You need to talk through the experience with a professional for healing to take place.

Q: My girlfriend was raped by her ex-boyfriend more than two years ago. It gets hard to take sometimes when she acts as if I'm like him, an abuser too. I've always treated her with respect. What should I do?

A: Be patient with her. She has been traumatized. It takes time, sometimes a long time, to get over the fears, mistrust and sense of violation. If you really are respectful of her, most likely she'll eventually relax around you, particularly if she's working with a professional counselor.

At the same time, make sure you are sizing up your own behavior accurately. Do you get irritated with your girlfriend because of her ongoing difficulties with the rape? Are you subtly disrespectful of her in other ways? You may not be overtly abusive yet still unintentionally convey hurtful messages.

That having been said, let us emphasize that you shouldn't let yourself be unjustly accused. Certainly try to be understanding about your girlfriend's rape and open to her feedback about you and your relationship. But at the same time, inform her that it hurts to be unfairly cast as an abuser, and point out examples where she is misreading your intentions. Another option is for you and your girlfriend to go for couples counseling.

Q: My best friend was raped last week. How do I help her?

A: Let her talk about it. The opportunity to air feelings to a trusted friend can be a great comfort. At the same time, don't force her to talk about the rape if she doesn't want to. Be accepting of her moods and feelings, and make sure she knows you're not judging or blaming her and don't think less of her.

Finally, strongly encourage her to seek counseling. As a friend you have a lot to offer, but a professional is also indispensable during this crisis.

Q: I'm a male student. What about me? Can I be raped too?

A: It's possible. Occasionally a man rapes another man, or a woman uses threats or intimidation to force sex on a man. When this occurs, the male victim may suffer intensely, just as female victims do, and he may be even more reluctant than a woman to report the crime for fear of being laughed at or viewed as weak.

However, the overwhelming majority of college rape cases are a man assaulting a woman. So as a male you're not at great risk.

Q: How likely am I as a male to be *accused* of rape? I know someone who was charged with date rape and he seemed like a regular guy to me. Could the same thing happen to me?

A: You sound worried that you'll be falsely accused of rape, but this is unlikely. It's rare that a woman would report a rape frivolously, and in almost all cases she won't mistake the identity of the rapist because she already knows him fairly well. Of course, you should get legal counsel immediately if you're ever accused of rape.

Of much greater danger to you than false accusations is the possibility that you will actually rape someone. This may sound absurd if you think of all rapists as psychotics or psychopaths, as people fundamentally different from you. But many males who commit date or acquaintance rape aren't disturbed or usually considered malicious. Otherwise "normal," they may force a woman into sex because they misinterpret what she wants, they think it's the man's role to overcome the woman's resistance, they feel peer pressure to "score," or their judgment is clouded by alcohol or other drugs. Afterward they may be shocked to discover that what they've done isn't simply harmless fun or a regrettable incident. They have committed rape.

To avoid this grievous mistake, take the following precautions:

- **Communicate beforehand if the evening promises to turn sexual.** Make sure you and your date explicitly discuss the extent of lovemaking both of you want.
- **Respect the woman's limits.** Don't bully, cajole, force or threaten her into going farther than she wants.
- **Don't interpret "no" as "yes."** For that matter, don't take silence, "I don't know," "maybe" or "I'm not ready" as consent either. And

don't assume that sexy clothes, a flirtatious smile, a touch or even a kiss is an invitation to sex. Make sure she's expressly told you her wishes regarding sex.

- **Be cautious with alcohol.** It only takes two drinks to impair judgment and the ability to communicate. So discuss sexual intentions before you and your partner take a drink.

FOR FURTHER READING

Susan Brownmiller, *Against Our Will: Men, Women and Rape.* New York: Fawcett Books, 1993.

Linda E. Ledry, *Recovering from Rape.* New York: Owlet, 1994.

Barrie Levy, ed., *Dating Violence.* Seattle: Seal Press, 1998.

Robin Warshaw, *I Never Called It Rape.* New York: Harper Perennial, 1994.

ALCOHOL AND
OTHER TEMPTATIONS

At college, you'll hear competing points of view about alcohol and other drugs. College officials and some students will argue against them, bombarding you with information about the health hazards of alcohol and drug abuse. They'll stress the legal angle too: Underage persons (which usually means under 21) cannot legally buy or be served alcoholic beverages. Driving under the influence of alcohol is illegal—and dangerous. So-called street drugs—marijuana, cocaine and the rest—are of course illegal too.

But these aren't the only messages you'll hear. In private, some classmates will casually dismiss all the fuss about alcohol and drugs and urge you to experiment, to have fun, to get trashed. Others may make it seem that either you drink heavily and take drugs or else forget about fitting in. Usually they won't even bother making their case; they'll just assume you intend to "party."

In the end, it's left squarely up to you to decide what to do. No one can force you to take alcohol and drugs, but no one can shield you from them either. How you react when a mystery punch is served at a party or a joint is passed in a dormitory room depends on your ability to be your own person, to consider all the arguments and then think and act for yourself. The material in this chapter is intended to help you make sensible decisions. We also take up other temptations of modern life: tobacco, gambling, computers and TV.

DRINKING

Q: When I'm out on a date, I like to drink. Any problems with this?

A: That depends. In moderation, alcohol has its selling points, making the conversation seem livelier, the jokes funnier and the atmosphere lighter. Not everyone likes or approves of these effects, but obviously many people do. Having wine or beer on an evening out is a popular pastime throughout the world.

Go overboard on the stuff, however, and good fun can degenerate into bad judgment and awful decisions. One danger is saying things that you later regret. While drunk you may share intimate details of your life or make hostile or even loving comments, which in the sober light of the following day, you wish had never escaped your lips. Worse, you may have sex that leaves you feeling guilty or ashamed and perhaps involved in a relationship you didn't really intend to develop. A greater danger still is one person's initiating sex without the other's consent (see Chapter 8) or having sex without using safer sex and contraception techniques. What college male can, or wants to, put on a condom when he's plastered? What college female can insist on the man's using a condom when she's in the same condition?

If you plan to drink on a date, stay clearheaded enough to assure your judgment stays intact.

Q: I get buzzed faster than my boyfriend. Is that common?

A: Yes. Serve a woman and a man the same amount of alcohol, and typically it's the woman who feels it more quickly. Previously it was thought that this difference is because women are usually smaller than men, and smaller people need less alcohol to get drunk than larger people do. However, recent studies have found that women compared to men have less of an enzyme that breaks down alcohol in the stomach. If you and your boyfriend each take two drinks, you will be affected more, even if you're the same size.

Q: I hold my liquor better than my friends and never get a hangover. Does that mean I can safely drink more than they can?

A: Sorry, no. True, high tolerance protects you from some of the immediate penalties of drinking, such as blackouts, hangovers and vomiting. But being able to drink large amounts without paying the price sets you up for drinking to excess. You may find yourself drinking more and more to get the same effects from alcohol; your tolerance may continue to go up. Over time this can develop into alcoholism.

If you've got a high tolerance, you need to keep close tabs on your drinking.

Q: Is everyone around here a big drinker?

A: No they're not, though you're not alone in thinking so. Recent research shows that college students consistently overestimate how much other students drink, how frequently they take drugs and how often they engage in hazardous drinking practices.[1] Though it may surprise you, more than half of college students have no more than a single drink per week, and about one in six don't drink at all.[2]

Yet while the majority hardly drinks at all, a sizable minority does go overboard while drinking. According to recent studies, approximately two in five students drink four, five or more drinks in a row at least once every two weeks, and half of them drink this much at least three times every two weeks.[3] That's a lot of uncontrolled drinking on college campuses—and a serious problem for many students.

Q: I don't feel comfortable on this campus with all the drinking and drug use around here. Should I just switch to another school?

A: Alcohol and drug use go on just about everywhere, even on so-called dry campuses. Chances are wherever you transfer, the majority of students will drink, even if sparingly, and some will use drugs.

Are you sure you've given your college a fair shake? On any campus the drinkers and drug takers tend to make a lot of noise, drowning out the nonusers and occasional drinkers who quietly go about their business. Maybe if you search harder you'll find the sort of people and events you prefer.

Have you also considered making a difference on your campus? Almost every college has a committee of students, faculty and administrators responsible for programs and policy regarding substance abuse. Opportunities for action may also exist through the student government, the campus health service or peer counseling programs. Not only can you improve your campus, but you'll meet like-minded students.

Q: How can I drink sensibly?

A: Good question. Here's a "survival kit" for staying out of trouble with alcohol:

- **Avoid drinking games.** They usually make you drink more than you intended.
- **Don't drink mystery punches.** They may contain huge amounts of alcohol.
- **Watch out for mixed drinks.** If necessary, dilute them with soda or water. Remember that a "double" mixed drink equals two drinks.
- **Be as cautious with beer and wine as with hard liquor.** A can of beer or a glass of wine has as much alcohol as one shot of hard liquor, so monitor your trips to the keg.
- **Plan beforehand.** Before going out, set a limit to what you'll drink. Then keep track to stick to the goal. In choosing a limit, consider that the liver can eliminate roughly one drink per hour. If you take three drinks the first hour, you'll have two left in your system an hour later, and one left, two hours later. One possible goal is never to have more than one drink in your system (i.e., one drink per hour).
- **To keep to your limit, pace yourself.** Drink slowly. If necessary, alternate alcoholic drinks with nonalcoholic beverages.
- **When you've had enough, stop!** If someone insists you have another, be assertive and decline. If saying no doesn't work, change the subject, say "I'll get one later" or make any other excuse ("I don't feel well") that lets you turn down an unwanted drink.
- **Never drink and drive.** You've heard this admonition a thousand times, and even so on almost every campus some students still end up dead after driving under the influence or riding with someone who did. Even small amounts of alcohol impair driving ability. If you drink off campus, make sure to go back with a designated driver who doesn't drink at all that night.
- **Promptly get medical help in emergencies.** If someone's in bad physical or emotional shape from drinking, head immediately to a hospital emergency room or the college health service. Do this even if you're unsure. Alcohol can be dangerous. Though it's legal (for those over 21) and comes in liquid form, it's still a drug, in particular a depressant that slows down the central nervous system. As with any drug, you can overdose or even die from a single episode of excessive use.
- **Ask for help.** If you think you or someone else has a problem, get a professional opinion.

Q: If there's a party on the weekend I have maybe a six-pack of beer at most. Is that too much to drink?

A: Possibly. We can appreciate that you'd like an exact limit, but there is no such number. "Too much" is whatever amount causes a problem, either immediately (an acute physical reaction) or over the long term (chronic difficulties). However, as suggested above, you may want to experiment with a maximum of one drink per hour to see if that pace works for you.

Q: How do I know if I have a drinking problem?

A: Look for any of the following signs:

- **Medical problems:** accidents and injuries, nausea and vomiting, hangovers, blackouts (you can't remember the next day what happened while you were drinking) or passing out (you became unconscious).
- **Academic problems:** missed classes due to hangovers; low or failing grades due to drinking; procrastination on assignments.
- **Sexual problems:** sexual activities that you regret later, including taking advantage of someone or someone taking advantage of you; failure to use birth control or safer sex techniques; impotence in males.
- **Habits:** inability to drink moderately or cut down on drinking; concern from others about your drinking; drinking alone.
- **Motives:** drinking to feel confident or to stop feeling anxious, depressed, bored or lonely.
- **Consequences:** arguments and fights; property damage; social isolation; driving while under the influence.

Q: But my friends drink more than I do. And besides, I only drink on weekends.

A: Maybe your friends do drink more than you, but that really has no bearing on you. And just because you drink only on weekends doesn't get you off the hook either. All that matters is whether you show any of the signs of problems listed above. If you do, then you may have a drinking problem.

Q: But what does it mean if I have some of those signs?

A: At the very least, you have misused alcohol, even if you do not yet have a full-fledged drinking problem. But possibly you *do* have a drinking problem, especially if you checked off several symptoms and they happen often. It's even possible that you're addicted to alcohol. Though a professional can help you make these judgments, the bottom line is that it's time to take a serious look at your drinking.

Q: You mean I could be an alcoholic?

A: Yes. Most alcoholics are not how we picture them: bedraggled lost souls lying in the gutter. Most look surprisingly normal and lead surprisingly normal lives. Some of them, in fact, are your classmates; approximately 10% of college-age people qualify as alcoholics.

What does it mean to be an alcoholic? Basically, you abuse alcohol, meaning you suffer various negative consequences from drinking. You also need more and more alcohol to get high (tolerance), have withdrawal reactions, drink more than you intend, are unsuccessful at stopping or reducing drinking, spend inordinate time getting drinks or recovering from drinking, continue drinking despite health effects and allow drinking to interfere with important activities. You don't need all these symptoms to be considered alcoholic. Having as few as three of these characteristics places you in the alcoholic category.

But don't get caught up in the question of whether or not you're an alcoholic. The more important issue is whether you have a problem when you drink. If some of the signs in the previous questions apply to you, the answer is yes.

Q: Where can I get help?

A: Many campuses have substance abuse specialists at the counseling center or health service or even entire offices devoted to students' alcohol and drug problems. These specialists provide substance abuse education and evaluation, shedding light on the extent of your problem. If your campus lacks these resources, look in the telephone book for off-campus specialists. See also the hot line numbers listed in Appendix 2.

What you do next depends on the evaluation. If you've misused alcohol but your problem falls short of alcoholism, a realistic goal may be learning controlled, responsible drinking. Accomplishing that goal involves adopting the drinking methods found in the "survival kit" (see page 167). Also necessary may be professional therapy from a substance abuse specialist to address coping skills, relationship difficulties, depression and anxiety, low self-esteem or other issues that fuel problem drinking. Drinking problems seldom exist in isolation. You have to get a handle on what led you to abuse alcohol in the first place. Another task is making life adjustments, since moderating drinking habits sometimes requires ditching drinking partners and finding new places of entertainment or living arrangements.

Although controlled drinking is a realistic goal for most alcohol abusers, for others the only realistic solution is abstinence. We realize this is a hard decision for a young person to make, but sometimes there is no realistic alternative; the drinking is too entrenched and harmful for halfway measures. Achieving abstinence may call for a course of counseling, an intensive outpatient program or even a stay in a hospital or rehabilitation facility—it all depends on the seriousness of the problem. There's no shame in taking these steps. The only shame is denying the problem and depriving yourself of the assistance to solve it.

Another resource often recommended in combination with counseling is Alcoholics Anonymous (AA). (The equivalent for drug problems is Narcotics Anonymous [NA].) Listed in the phone book and perhaps found on your own campus, AA offers group meetings providing information and support. AA can seem a bit overwhelming at first. If you're considering trying it, go with a friend and attend at least half a dozen meetings before making up your mind about continuing. You don't have to talk if you don't want to; just listening while others speak can be an eye-opener. Since meetings cater to different groups—young people, smokers, nonsmokers, gay people—look around for one where you feel comfortable. As an alternative, check out other self-help groups whose philosophies differ from AA, such as Rational Recovery and Women for Sobriety.

HELPING OTHERS WHO HAVE A DRINKING PROBLEM

Q: I think my roommate is drinking too much. I want to speak to him, but I'm afraid of saying the wrong thing. What should I do?

A: By all means do speak up. A real friend is honest about these things, even at the risk of upsetting the other person. We suggest you start by pointing out that you care, and that's why you want to talk. Then cite specific facts and events regarding his drinking: "You missed your class again this morning because you were drinking last night. That's the third time this week. And I could hear you throwing up in the bathroom—again." Convey your personal feelings about his behavior: "I get scared for you when I see this happening again and again." This approach stands the best chance of being heard. Your roommate can dismiss your judgments and opinions, but it's harder to argue with the facts and your feelings.

The next step is to specify what you want him to do. Since he obviously has a problem, ask him to talk to a counselor to evaluate his drinking and meantime to reduce or stop his alcohol consumption.

Q: I've tried that before, but he blew up at me and said I was exaggerating everything. Now what?

A: His reaction isn't unusual. Alcohol (or drug) abusers often get angry when confronted, partly to discourage the confrontation. Typically, they also deny or explain away their problem: "I can stop drinking whenever I want." "I only drink on weekends." "Lots of people drink more than me." "My low grades have nothing to do with my drinking." As a general rule, the worse their problem is, the stronger the anger and denial.

If you think about it, there's nothing surprising about this. Who among us likes to admit having a huge personal problem? If you bear in mind that anger and denial are understandable reactions and that denial is at least partly unconscious (problem drinkers fool themselves with their explanations), you may feel less frustrated dealing with your roommate. Also realize that he heard you, despite the protests. At some future time he may face up to his problem thanks in part to your words.

Since he reacted as he did, your next step should be to consult a professional. The professional may recommend backing off for the time being since your roommate isn't ready to face his problem. The professional may suggest asking someone else—a friend, family member, professor or member of the clergy—to speak to your roommate and reinforce your message. A third, even more powerful technique, an intervention, would involve several of you confronting your roommate together. Interventions can be dramatically effective. They also are trying and emotionally upsetting for all concerned, and for this reason the professional would need to coach you through the process.

Q: My friend got drunk last night and was really hung over this morning. I told her professor she couldn't take the test today because she was sick. Did I do the right thing?

A: What you did is called "enabling"—sparing her the negative consequences of substance abuse. Though you meant well, enabling makes matters worse because she can keep on abusing alcohol without facing the music. Other examples of enabling would be typing her papers because she's too hung over to finish them herself, or lending her money because she's spent her own on alcohol or drugs.

If you really want to help your friend, don't bail her out.

Q: But I'm really worried about her. I lose sleep over her problem. Can't I help somehow?

A: You can help by avoiding enabling behaviors, confronting her about her problem, speaking to a counselor and possibly persuading others to join you in confronting her. But beyond these measures, we urge you not to get too wrapped up in her problem. It's better for both of you if you maintain a certain detachment or distance.

If it's hard to achieve the proper amount of detachment or you're slipping into the role of enabler, consider talking to a counselor—not for your friend, but for yourself. Also, check out the support group called Al-Anon. A companion group to Alcoholics Anonymous, Al-Anon is designed for the friends and family members of alcohol abusers. Similarly, Nar-Anon is the companion group to Narcotics Anonymous.

Q: My father has been a problem drinker on and off ever since I was a child. Now he's "on" again. How do I handle him?

A: The same basic options apply: You can confront him with the facts you've observed and your personal feelings about his drinking;

you can urge other family members, either individually or in a group, to join you in confronting him; or you can leave him alone and wait until the time is right. The same basic cautions apply too. You should expect anger and denial; watch out for enabling behavior; and try to maintain objectivity.

Of course, maintaining objectivity is no mean feat when the substance abuser is your own parent. Therefore we strongly advise consulting a professional and/or attending Adult Children of Alcoholics (ACOA) meetings. Though it may not seem this way, the issue isn't so much helping him (though that would be desirable) as it is addressing the effects of his drinking on you.

DRUGS

Q: I think the laws against marijuana use are absurd, like banning alcohol during Prohibition. Lots of people smoke pot, and I can't see that it causes them any harm.

A: Without getting into the politics, we do want to give you some facts you may not want to hear. It's simply not true that pot causes no harm. Occasionally, marijuana induces acute anxiety, disorientation or paranoia. Some long-term users lose their motivation and stop studying and going to class. A few develop an outright addiction, adopting what can only be termed a drug lifestyle: a chaotic sleep-wake pattern, disrupted eating habits, suspension of physical exercise and general neglect of daily living activities. Studies also suggest that long-term use may cause physical damage to lungs and other organs, lower male sex hormones and cause changes in women's menstrual cycles and possible birth defects.[4]

You may like pot, enjoy its effects and fervently believe it should be legalized. Please understand, however, that it's not harmless.

Q: I've never taken other drugs but I'm thinking about it. What do they do?

A: We can't pretend to be neutral here. Although some students obviously like getting high, the risks of experimentation are considerable.

Cocaine is a stimulant. People take it to get a rush and a sense of confidence and well-being. But since these effects are short lived and are typically followed by a "crash"—a period of extreme depression—

there's a strong pull to take more cocaine to feel good again. In short, cocaine's extremely addictive; once you get started, it's very difficult to stop. Cocaine also poses grave physical risks: heart attacks, strokes, and coma or death from an overdose. One student we know tried it and landed in the hospital emergency room with an acute cardiac arrhythmia, or irregular heartbeat. He never tried it again.

Amphetamines (speed) are stimulants, like cocaine. They can boost energy and alertness and are sometimes used for late-night studying. They also can have some nasty effects, like anxiety, rage, addiction, psychotic reactions, even seizures and death.

Psychedelic drugs, or *hallucinogens*, include LSD (acid), mushrooms and mescaline. Their appeal is vivid perceptual effects and flights of imagination. Their chief downside is the risk of a "bad trip"—acute panic and paranoia—or even a psychotic reaction requiring hospitalization.

MDMA (ecstasy), chemically similar to amphetamines, was originally touted as safe and enlightening, a mind expander, truth serum and a libido booster. Later returns haven't been so upbeat. Ecstasy is now known to have potentially irreversible effects on the brain and addictive potential.

Narcotics, such as heroin, have enjoyed a dismaying revival in recent years. A decade ago it was unheard of for college students to inject or snort heroin; today some students do try it. Believe us when we tell you this is a dumb idea. Heroin has considerable addictive potential. Once hooked on it, you need a detox program and intensive treatment to set yourself free. Injecting heroin also runs the risk of contracting HIV or hepatitis from a contaminated needle.

Anabolic steroids are taken by some campus athletes to build up muscle tissue and enhance performance. This of course is illegal. Steroids can also cause serious emotional disorders and lasting bodily damage, even death.

Heard enough about drugs' dangers? Well, there's more. With alcohol, for all its risks, it's at least clear what you're ingesting (excepting of course mystery concoctions). Not so with street drugs. The marijuana you smoke may be tainted with paraquat, a herbicide, and what you think is LSD may actually be PCP (angel dust), which can lead to wild, violent behavior. The Food and Drug Administration does not provide quality control on illegal drugs.

Q: I've heard all about the dangers of drugs, but I've taken them and have never had any problems.

A: There may not be any warning signs. Since cocaine, amphetamines, LSD and other street drugs can be dangerous even if taken only once, you may have been fine with them before and still have a disastrous experience next time around. One student we know took LSD with a group of her friends. Twice before she'd experimented with this drug without any trouble, but this time she suddenly went berserk, started shouting incoherently and tried to climb out the 10th-floor window. Her terrified friends barely restrained her until the police carted her off to the hospital.

As for signs of an ongoing problem, consult the checklist for alcohol-related problems on page 168, because this list also applies for drugs. If you have some of the problems listed there, that would indicate you've got a drug problem.

Q: What do I say if my friends insist that I try cocaine? I know they'll tell me I should experience it and judge for myself, or else I'm being narrow minded.

A: You know how mothers always say, "Would you jump off a cliff because your friends did it?" Well, we're with Mom on this one. Why should you try cocaine just because your friends do it? Tell them you *have* judged for yourself—and you don't want to do it.

Peer pressure is a given when it comes to drinking and drugs. There will always be friends who urge you to experiment, to get wasted, to get as drunk or high as you can. Despite this, most classmates will respect you for refusing to take drugs. They may even respect you more for staying true to your convictions rather than caving in to pressure.

But if your friends aren't understanding and won't take no for an answer—or if you can't say no and make it stick—perhaps you should plan to see them when drinking or drugs won't be involved, or even reconsider your choice of friends. Look around, and you'll find other students who respect your point of view and whose idea of a good time isn't getting high or stoned. Many campuses have even set up substance-free living areas where you can live in a totally alcohol- and drug-free residence.

Q: Sometimes I pop a few pills and then have a couple of beers. Is it okay if I take moderate amounts of each?

A: Don't do it. Mixing alcohol and drugs, or mixing any combination of drugs together, can be dangerous. This holds true even if one of the drugs is prescribed by a doctor. Combining alcohol and a tranquilizer, for example, can cause extreme side effects, even death.

TOBACCO

Q: I've tried to stop smoking, but without any luck. What do you recommend?

A: Stopping smoking is hard; nicotine is highly addictive. But given the grave health risks of lung cancer, bronchitis, emphysema and heart disease, you're wise to keep trying. Experts recommend several steps to stop smoking:

- **Hide or give away ashtrays, matches, and other smoking paraphernalia.**
- **Chew sugarless gum** if you miss having something in your mouth.
- **Identify high-risk situations.** Do you smoke in a particular friend's room, or in bars or clubs? Do you buy cigarettes at a particular store? If possible, bypass these places.
- **Use coping skills.** If you can't avoid a high-risk situation, find ways to deal with the temptation. Take deep breaths to relax, reach for a stick of gum, assertively refuse when offered a smoke or inwardly coach yourself to keep to your pledge.
- **Reduce stress levels.** Since people often smoke when they feel stressed, the stress reduction techniques in Chapter 4 will support your effort to stop smoking. And since some people smoke to self-medicate for depression, counseling is advisable if smoking cessation seems to stir up emotional distress.
- **Reduce damage from slips.** If you slip up and have one or two cigarettes, take steps to prevent a full-fledged relapse: Leave the scene immediately, call a friend and renew your commitment to stop smoking.
- **Don't get discouraged.** After a slip, don't conclude that you can't stop smoking. Instead, treat a slip as a learning experience that illustrates traps to avoid in the future. And if you've tried to stop before but couldn't make it stick, remember that very few people stop smoking on their first attempt. Most who beat the habit do so after a series of sincere efforts.

- **Get support from family and friends.** A formal smoking cessation program may help too, although quitting the habit is ultimately accomplished through your own effort.
- **Talk to your physician about the advisability of nicotine patches or gum.**

Q: I chew tobacco. How safe is that compared to smoking?

A: Nicotine is an addictive drug, whether you smoke it or chew it. Even more importantly, the chewing of tobacco can lead to deterioration of teeth and gums and has been associated with cancers of the tongue, mouth, throat and larynx. Anyone who's seen photographs of ex-professional baseball players who got one of these cancers will want to spit out the chaw once and for all.

GAMBLING

Q: I keep betting on sports and now I'm several thousand dollars in debt.

A: Pathological gambling is on the rise in society, affecting perhaps 5% of the general population,[5] and college students are no exception. Signs of a problem include preoccupation with gambling, a need to bet larger amounts to feel excited and an inability to cut back or stop the behavior—even after losses and damage to relationships or studies. Also, pathological gamblers tend to gamble to escape from problems or to relieve anxiety or depression.[6] Your continuing to bet despite a large debt is reason enough to assume you have a problem.

People gamble for different reasons. For some, the motive is to escape from problems or negative feelings, while for others it's the urge for competition and excitement. Easily bored, these latter action-hungry individuals love the thrill of the wager. Often, like alcohol abusers, they deny the extent of their problem until their habit spirals out of control.

Whatever your own motives, paying off debts is obviously an immediate concern, but the ultimate goal must be coming to grips with the gambling. This will require learning to avoid situations and places where you gamble, learning coping methods when you're tempted to gamble, identifying and correcting distorted thinking ("I know I can win if I keep betting") and dealing with associated problems such as anxiety or depression. Battling a gambling problem is a tall order, difficult to achieve on your own. We recommend working with a professional counselor or attending meetings at Gamblers Anonymous, a community-based program modeled after Alcoholics Anonymous.

COMPUTERS AND TELEVISION

Q: I spend most of my waking hours at the computer. Is that bad?

A: You tell us. Do you concentrate on computer games for hours but give up on textbooks after 10 minutes? Do you surf the web until 4 A.M. and then blow off your morning classes? Do you speak more with strangers in a chat room than with your suitemates and supposed friends? Have you forgotten what it's like to get physical exercise, see a live band, read the paper or take a walk in the park? If you answered these questions affirmatively, then yes, we would say that's bad. Man doth not live by PCs alone.

As a college student, you obviously have to use a computer, so the goal has to be moderation of use, not abstinence. Perhaps you can achieve this goal simply by setting a limit, for example, no more than one hour of computer time per day devoted to nonschool activities. Sticking to the limit may not prove easy, however, if you retreat to the computer for psychological reasons. If you can't seem to control your computer use, tear yourself away from the screen for an hour and talk to a counselor.

Q: Sometimes I look at pornographic websites. Is there something wrong with me?

A: Interest in sexual matters is normal enough. Males in particular are often drawn to arousing visual stimuli. In past decades, the popular heterosexual male ritual, generally considered harmless, was passing around copies of *Playboy* and *Penthouse*. Getting your jollies from a computer monitor doesn't strike us as inherently worse than ogling a glossy magazine.

A few words of caution, however. Visiting pornographic websites isn't healthy if you overdo it and take time or money away from other activities—this is the issue of balance again. Visiting these websites is particularly unfortunate if doing so becomes a substitute for real relationships. If you're on the college's mainframe, visiting these sites raises the potential risk of being discovered by others (schools have different policies and practices regarding browsers' protection from outside inspection). Visiting these sites is also unhealthy if you feel deeply guilty and ashamed, or if doing so runs counter to your moral or religious values. Lastly, visiting these sites is unhealthy if you want to cut down or stop but can't. With any activity an inability to control use is a sign of becoming dependent, or addicted.

If these cautions suggest your activity is unhealthy, try to curb it on your own. If that doesn't work, seek the assistance of a counselor.

Q: I watch television eight hours a day.

A: Then you've got a problem. By now it must be clear that, drugs and tobacco aside, it matters less what activities you choose than whether the activities affect you adversely. You can drink moderately (and legally too, we hope), and no problem. You can safely make a friendly bet with a friend or spend profitable time surfing the Web. But when these pursuits start shoving aside other necessary activities, warning bells should go off. And that certainly applies to TV as well.

Television addiction is not a trendy cause. You won't find a Television Cessation Day on your campus or TV Addicts Anonymous groups in your community. Still, quite a few students miss out on social activities and clubs because they're holed up watching *Gilligan's Island* reruns, and many students' grades are inversely related to the time spent staring at the small screen. For shy or depressed or stressed students, TV is an easy escape—too easy. So we suggest you take your viewing habits as seriously as you'd take any other problem. Set a reasonable daily viewing limit, and make up your mind to stick to it. If you are unsuccessful, consider counseling.

FOR FURTHER READING

James Cocores, *The 800-Cocaine Book of Drug and Alcohol Recovery*. New York: Villard, 1990.

Mark S. Gold, *800-Cocaine*. Toronto: Bantam, 1984.

Cynthia Kuhn, Jeremy Foster and Leigh Heather Wilson, *Buzzed: The Straight Facts about the Most Used and Abused Drugs from Alcohol to Ecstasy*. New York: W.W. Norton, 1998.

Alan G. Marlatt and Judith R. Gordon, *Relapse Prevention: Maintenance Strategies in the Treatment of Addictive Behavior*. New York: Guilford Press, 1985.

EATING ISSUES

Ideally, eating is a worry-free activity. You eat when you're hungry, enjoy meals for the food and company and don't give much thought to the subject otherwise. But for many college students, eating is the worry hot zone. They agonize about food and calories and are obsessed with weight and slight or imaginary physical flaws. Often they unhealthily restrict their eating or develop bingeing or purging patterns, sometimes to the dangerous extent of a full-fledged eating disorder. This chapter provides a perspective on these troublesome topics, stresses the damage unhealthy diets cause and offers a way out of the hot zone with suggestions for healthy eating and a positive body image.

RECOGNIZING A PROBLEM

Q: What does it mean to have an eating problem?

A: There are three main eating disorders. *Anorexia,* or anorexia nervosa, is defined as pronounced weight loss caused by self-starvation and often excessive exercise. Anorexics intensely fear gaining weight and, incredibly to others, believe they're fat despite being dangerously underweight. *Bulimia,* or bulimia nervosa, is the binge-purge syndrome. During binges bulimics consume huge amounts of food and feel out of control of their eating. Afterward they purge by making themselves vomit or by using laxatives or diuretics (which induce urination), or they compensate for the binge by strenuous exercise or going on a diet. *Binge-eating disorder* consists of the binges without the purges. The person feels distressed about bingeing and during the episodes may feel disgusted, depressed or guilty.

To qualify for one of these disorders, you have to meet certain criteria. The symptoms of bulimia and binge-eating disorder, for example, must occur at least twice per week and have lasted for months.

But you don't have to have a full-fledged disorder to have an eating problem. Even if your weight is normal, you have a problem if you unduly restrict eating. Even if you don't binge as frequently as twice per week, you have a problem if you do binge, particularly if doing so causes you distress. (It's estimated that 40% of college women binge at least once a month.[1]) And even if you don't restrict or binge, you have a problem if you're excessively anxious about body image or food.

BODY IMAGE

Q: Why am I so worried about my body?

A: In our society it's difficult to escape some concern about body image. Women in particular, who naturally have more body fat than men, often see themselves as fat even if they're normal weight or even underweight. And if they don't feel fat, they often worry about the size and shape of their hips or breasts or the amount of hair on their body. Men worry too. In the privacy of counselors' offices, male students confess that they feel too short, scrawny or pudgy, that their hairline is receding or their penis is too small.

Much of the blame for these feelings of inferiority rests squarely with our image-laden culture. Movies, television and magazines flaunt stunning, lean physical specimens, suggesting that's the way everyone's supposed to look. Implausibly thin female dancers, skaters, models and gymnasts add to the unrealistic expectations. The societal pressure to be slender, especially for women, is enormous.

Q: Is it superficial to care about my looks?

A: Not really. Although our society goes overboard on appearance, wanting to look good is a natural human desire. Feeling attractive is an expression of healthy self-esteem. So it's normal to inspect yourself in the mirror sometimes, and it's good if you like what you see.

However, being *obsessed* with your appearance is something else. Excessive preoccupation with looks may be a sign of low self-esteem or other psychological problems. A distorted body image also often goes along with an eating disorder.

Q: How can I learn to accept my body?

A: First, make the most of what you've got. Exercise regularly—but not excessively—and eat properly to keep your body in good condition. Stand up straight, carry yourself with pride and learn to smile. Wear flattering clothing and hairstyles, choose attractive glasses, or switch, if you prefer, to contact lenses.

However, nice clothes and the treadmill can only take you so far. Since you can't remold your basic bone structure, the real key to accepting your appearance is to view yourself positively. And to do that you must rid yourself of negative ways of thinking and substitute constructive thoughts. Check if you're psyching yourself out in these ways:

Dwelling on the negative—focusing only on your supposed weak spots. Try instead to see yourself as others see you—a total person ("Sure, my rear end is a little big, but overall I'm pretty attractive.").

Overassuming—taking for granted that someone is turned off by your face or body. If so, remind yourself that tastes vary. In someone else's smitten eyes, your big nose or stocky legs may be your most charming feature.

Thinking in all-or-nothing terms—concluding that you're fat when you're really only a little plump, or ugly when you're actually average looking. If so, work on accurate self-assessments: "I'm a few pounds overweight, and it's no big deal."

Catastrophizing—thinking that it's disastrous to look the way you do and you might as well join a nunnery or monastery. Instead, place your concerns in perspective. "I'm not the most gorgeous creature on campus, but I'm sure some people find me attractive, and I've got a lot going for me besides my looks."

Your feelings about your face and body are a reflection of your deepest attitudes about yourself. There are physically striking college students who think they're ugly and rather plain students who feel incredibly attractive. The difference lies in their basic feelings about themselves. So your body isn't the main issue here; it's your capacity to view yourself approvingly. Consider too that your opinion about your looks has an influence on other people, as psychiatrist Willard Gaylin has observed: "Think of yourself as ugly and eventually you will be so considered. Think of yourself as beautiful and it is extraordinary to what degree people will treat you as a beauty."[2]

For help in gaining perspective and accepting your appearance, see if your campus has a women's group—males, look for a men's group. Individual counseling can also help you work on the poor self-esteem that underlies dissatisfaction with appearance.

Q: I'm proud of myself for losing 30 pounds. So why am I still so unhappy?

A: Perhaps you had unrealistic expectations about the consequences of losing weight. You assumed that once you became thin you'd be beautiful and irresistible, the object of everyone's attention. Now you are discovering that life's not that simple. You can be thin yet still feel dissatisfied with your looks, reach your ideal weight yet still feel lonely or shy.

Another possibility is that you've always been hesitant about dating, romance and sex. Now that you've dropped the pounds there are no more excuses to stay on the sidelines, and you're frightened.

Becoming thinner requires a psychological adjustment. Any change, even a positive one, is stressful. Be patient with yourself as you gradually grow used to life at your new weight.

DIETING VS. HEALTHY EATING

Q: I'm 20 pounds overweight. Why do I do this to myself?

A: At one time, this would have been a perfectly valid question. It was taken as a given that overweight people gained weight because they overate and they overate because they had an "overweight personality" or other problems.

Today the topic of weight is understood differently. Yes, some people do overeat, but studies show that most overweight people don't actually consume an inordinate amount of food. Usually, the reason they're heavy is because they're genetically programmed to be that way. Their bodies are quicker than normal to convert calories into fat, and therefore their natural "setpoint"—the weight they gravitate toward—is higher than normal. In short, psychological problems or even bad eating habits may have very little to do with your scale readings. You may eat a normal diet and still never be slender.

Q: So how can I lose weight? Should I go on a diet?

A: That depends on what you mean by diet. If you're talking about learning healthy eating habits, then by all means go ahead. Healthy habits won't take off pounds *below* your body's natural weight, but they will help you stay *at* that weight—the weight nature intends you to maintain.

But if by diet you mean starting some sort of quick weight-reduction program or taking diet pills, we strongly advise against it. It's true crash diets and pills often succeed in producing dramatic weight loss. But afterward the lost weight almost always returns—and sometimes more for good measure. And so frustrated dieters tend to repeatedly lose and regain pounds, the so-called yo-yo syndrome. Not only is this discouraging and embarrassing, but the up-and-down weight cycle is physically hazardous, arguably more so than staying overweight. Dieting is also a prime cause of bulimia and binge-eating disorder, as we shall see. In the strong words of psychologist Martin Seligman, "Dieting is a cruel hoax, and it is time for Congress to intervene."[3]

Crash diets fail for several reasons. First, they slow down your metabolism (remember, the body tries to protect its fat stores and remain at its natural weight). At the end of the diet, the combination of a still slowed metabolism and a return to normal eating can jack up your weight in a hurry. Second, crash diets don't teach proper eating habits. You learn how to avoid food while dieting; you don't learn how to deal with food when the diet ends. Third, crash diets—or brief fasts—create a feeling of deprivation. You can only stint yourself for so long. Sooner or later, the urge to eat becomes irresistible, and then the tendency is to go overboard and truly gorge yourself.

Q: Suppose instead of following a diet I just skip some meals?

A: That won't work either. It doesn't matter whether you restrict food by eating much less than normal, as in a diet, or by eating less often than normal. Either way, the body is starved of necessary nutrients and the probable aftermath is a binge. Equally counterproductive is eliminating certain types of food, such as fats and carbohydrates. Your body then craves these foods, and you're again primed to pig out.

Any restriction in normal eating encourages overeating.

Q: What does it mean to eat healthfully?

A: Experts advise the following:

- **Plan permanent changes in eating habits, not temporary sacrifices.** Changes should be incorporated into your way of life. Make a commitment to carry them out.
- **Set realistic goals.** Plan small eating changes rather than drastic revisions. With realistic goals you're less likely to get discouraged and give up.
- **Eat when you're hungry.** If you're hungry, eat. If you're full, stop eating. To recognize the sensation of fullness, stop during a meal and ask yourself if you're still hungry. If not, end the meal (there's no law saying you must finish everything on your plate). Also, eat slowly to help you gauge how you feel. These methods will help if you tend to overeat.
- **Consult a nutritionist or read a nutrition book.** It's important to have information about nutritionally balanced and healthful meals. Generally, it's good practice to cut down on—but not eliminate—foods high in fats and simple sugars: red meats, butter, mayonnaise, whole milk dairy products, candy bars, ice cream, cookies, pies and potato chips. Good substitutes are low-cholesterol, low-sodium and high-fiber foods: pasta, poultry, fish, bread, skim milk, low-fat frozen yogurt, fruits, vegetables, cereal, unbuttered popcorn, bagels and pretzels. But exercise moderation when eating these foods as well, since calories still add up and some (for example, pasta and bagels) are high in carbohydrates.
- **But don't be rigid about eating categories.** If you make rigid rules, you're apt to break them and then feel discouraged and out of control. So don't make any foods taboo. Have hamburgers and pizza once in a while if you want. Just cut back on the frequency and size of the portions.

Along with healthy eating practices, regular exercise is a foundation of good health. Exercise burns up calories both during the workout and for hours afterward, while your metabolism rate is still high. Exercise also instills confidence, a sense of well-being and motivation to eat right.

An exercise program should consist of at least three or four 20–30 minute sessions per week doing activities that raise the heart rate. Like eating, exercise ought to be fun and interesting; that way you'll keep at it. Experiment to see what you like: aerobic classes, running, fast walking, tennis, dance, swimming, biking. Varying activities and doing them with a friend can help maintain your interest.

Some people have the best intentions to follow an exercise program but soon give it up because they feel too tired or would rather watch TV. But you can't base an exercise program on always being in the right mood. What's needed is to build exercise into your schedule and make it a routine, like brushing your teeth or going to class: Then, rather than debating "Should I work out today?" you'll go to the gym automatically.

Regular exercise is healthy, but excessive exercise can be dangerous. If you suspect you have anorexia or bulimia or if you have any other medical condition, consult a doctor before starting an exercise program.

BULIMIA AND BINGE EATING

Q: My roommate sneaks into the bathroom after we go to dinner. And sometimes I notice a cake or a quart of ice cream missing from the refrigerator. Could she be bulimic?

A: Very possibly. Her going to the bathroom may be to purge, most likely by vomiting. And the missing cake and ice cream are suggestive too; bulimics often binge on such "forbidden" foods. Because bulimics are often ashamed of their problem, they tend to binge and purge on the sly. That would explain why the food's missing but you don't see her eating it.

It's hard to be sure about your roommate, though. Not only haven't you directly observed her bingeing or purging, but you can't necessarily tell by looking at her whether she's bulimic. Unlike anorexics, most bulimics are approximately their normal weight, though sometimes their weight fluctuates.

Other signs you might look for are expressions of concern about eating and weight and indications that she feels out of control with eating or is depressed.

Q: If I suspect she's bulimic but am not sure, should I do anything?

A: Definitely. Bulimia is a serious condition associated with both psychological problems (depression, mood swings, low self-esteem) and medical consequences (fluid and electrolyte abnormalities, digestive tract disorder, erosion of tooth enamel, possible cardiac damage). The possibility your roommate has a problem is too serious to ignore.

One way to proceed is to state your concerns directly to a residence hall staff member, dean, college physician or counselor, who will then either speak to her or advise you how to proceed. The other way is first to approach her yourself. Tell her exactly what you've observed (the bathroom visits, the missing food), say you're concerned and ask her to explain. Your next move depends on her response:

- **If her explanation convinces you that she's fine,** you needn't do anything further.
- **If she admits to a problem,** ask her to consult a college counselor, physician or nurse—and strongly encourage her to follow through.
- **If she offers vague, unconvincing explanations** ("There's nothing wrong with me"), then you're in a tricky position. Maybe nothing *is* wrong, but on the other hand she may be in denial, which is typical for eating disorders. Perhaps the wisest course is to suggest she at least go for a physical and blood work to rule out health problems. Then bide your time and give her opportunity to reflect. If she continues to avoid treatment and you continue to see worrisome signs, at some point report your concerns to a residence hall staff member, dean, physician or counselor.

Q: Is it my family's fault that I'm bulimic?

A: That's difficult to answer. Certainly, how you were raised may predispose you to bulimia—as it can to many conditions. It's thought that some women with eating problems come from families unduly focused on food and weight, while others grow up in cold and uninvolved families, prompting them to soothe themselves with food as compensation.[4]

But not everybody from such families develops an eating disorder, nor does everyone who has an eating disorder come from such families. Your upbringing, if it was troubled, is at most part of the story.

Q: Then why else might I be bulimic?

A: A primary cause of bulimia and also binge-eating disorder is failure to eat enough to achieve satiety. Fats and carbohydrates trigger

feelings of satisfaction—they turn your appetite off. If you don't get enough of these foods, your body develops a powerful urge to eat. The result can be out-of-control bingeing and, in the case of bulimia, compensatory purging. Here lies the great irony of diets and fasting. Their purpose is to cut back on eating, but instead the deprivation they cause prompts excessive eating.[5]

Emotional factors can set off binge eating too. From time to time, all of us visit the refrigerator when we're feeling bored, lonely or sad. There's no great harm in doing this—from time to time. But if food becomes your habitual response to negative feelings, problem eating is the result. Guided by emotional need rather than sensations of hunger, you lose a sense of control over food.

Societal pressures to be thin are also implicated in bulimia, encouraging the diets and fasts that so often spark the bingeing-and-purging cycle. Not only do women feel these pressures; male wrestlers and crew team coxswains also may feel obliged to go below their normal weights. Sometimes students start vomiting or using laxatives by following the example of a peer. "That's cool," one woman student remembers thinking, when a high school friend taught her to vomit after eating. The aftereffects turned out not to be so cool.

Q: If I think I'm bulimic, how can I stop myself?

A: First things first: If you really are bulimic or have binge-eating disorder, you should get professional help. Once caught in a web of binge eating and purging, you will find it very difficult to extricate yourself without assistance; binge-eating disorder can be similarly intractable. Both your college's counseling center and health service have dealt with many students who share your problem. These offices can offer individual counseling, medical monitoring, nutritional consultations and a referral to an off-campus eating disorders clinic if that's called for.

Many colleges also have on-campus groups for students who have eating concerns. In a group, you can overcome your sense of shame, give and receive support, identify feelings, and share experiences.

In conjunction with professional assistance and support groups, here are measures you can try on your own for a bingeing or purging problem:

- **Try to resist purging after a binge.** We realize this is impossible for many bulimics; the impulse to purge is simply too strong to resist. However, try to avoid or cut down on purging if possible. That will help your efforts to avoid overeating.
- **Set realistic goals.** If you're bingeing and purging twice a day now and can't stop, shoot for once daily. If you're trying to eat sensibly, introduce realistic changes into your diet.
- **Try various strategies to reduce bingeing.** Plan to eat regularly: three meals per day plus a couple of snacks. That way you're not restricting yourself unrealistically, and you'll never be so ravenous that you must overeat. Buy cartons of food containing individual, not multiple, servings. Put away leftovers once you fill your plate.
- **Chart your progress.** Accurately record in a notebook binges, purges and all your food intake. Treat any improvement as a step in the right direction.
- **Expect setbacks.** If several good days are followed by a relapse, get back to your goals. It's the overall progress that counts, not occasional lapses.
- **If possible, control the damage during a slipup.** If you've already scarfed down half a pint of ice cream or a bag of potato chips, stop right there. Bulimics and binge-eaters sometimes defeat themselves through all-or-nothing thinking: "Either I follow my eating plan to the letter, or I've failed miserably." "I've blown it already, so the rest of the day (or week) is shot." Such rigid reasoning can turn a small unplanned snack or a minor episode of overeating into a full-scale binge or series of binges. Instead, say to yourself, "Okay, I went too far, but I can stop now."
- **Look for new coping strategies when you're upset.** Search for ways besides bingeing to cope with strong feelings: Call a friend, play an instrument, read, assertively express your needs when you're frustrated. Chart your success by keeping a written record of situations that arouse strong feelings and how you deal with them.
- **Identify self-defeating and irrational beliefs.** Psychologist Randolph Lee lists several irrational thoughts typical of college students with eating disorders: "I am either fat or I am thin." "My weight is the best measure of my self-worth." "I must be perfect or no one will like me."[6] When you recognize such thoughts, replace them with realistic substitutes: "I may be a bit overweight, but I'm hardly fat," and "I'm still attractive, whatever the scale says."
- **Work at accepting yourself as you are.** This includes accepting your body.

ANOREXIA AND FOOD RESTRICTION

Q: A friend of mine is very thin and keeps on getting thinner. How can I tell if she's anorexic?

A: Weight loss alone doesn't add up to anorexia, just as occasional bingeing and purging, though still a problem, doesn't necessarily mean bulimia. An anorexic is someone, usually a woman, who starves him- or herself and exercises compulsively until he or she is at least 15% underweight. An anorexic is intensely afraid of gaining weight, irrationally feels fat despite emaciation and—if female—has skipped her menstrual period at least three times consecutively. A professional is needed to make this diagnosis.

Even if your friend doesn't meet all the conditions of anorexia, a pattern of intentionally restricting food still qualifies as a problem.

Q: How does anorexia compare with bulimia?

A: In certain respects they are similar. Both anorexics and bulimics are obsessed with diet and weight and are afraid of becoming fat. Both conditions increasingly take over the person's existence, crowding out social life and academics. Both (but particularly anorexia) endanger health; anorexia can seriously damage the digestive system, muscles, bones and major organs and occasionally causes heart arrhythmia leading to death. Persons who are anorexics sometimes later develop bulimia.

The two conditions also have significant differences. Anorexics don't binge. Anorexia is much more visible than bulimia; the skeletal young woman who jogs for hours around campus is hard to miss. Anorexia is also rarer than bulimia. Though estimates vary, maybe one in several hundred women is anorexic, while perhaps one in 20 is bulimic.[7] The rates for men are significantly lower.

Q: What should I do about a friend who may be anorexic?

A: Follow the same procedures outlined above for bulimia. If you speak directly to her first rather than alerting someone in authority, be prepared for denial. Although anorexics tend to be well behaved, perfectionist and "good," typically they're also proud of their ability to control weight and are unlikely to concede anything's wrong. But overcoming denial and persuading her that she has a problem isn't your goal. Your purpose is simply to find out if she's already in treatment or at least has been evaluated by a professional. If she hasn't seen a professional, then discuss your concerns with a residence hall staff member, health service physician or counseling center professional, who can follow through to have her evaluated.

Q: I know the charts say I'm too thin, but I hated it when I was 15 pounds heavier. I like myself better now because I have the willpower to control my weight.

A: The issue is at what cost you keep your weight down. Are you devoting valuable time and energy to thinking about food and your body? Is your concern about food and body image preempting other activities and social relationships? Do you too often feel anxious about eating or guilty and ashamed afterward? Are you jeopardizing your health because of malnourishment?

If you restrict food intake, you owe it to yourself to consider the consequences. There's a big world out there waiting for you, but you won't appreciate it if you're preoccupied with counting calories.

Q: How can I get help if I'm anorexic?

A: Anorexia is a serious condition requiring professional attention from medical doctors, therapists and dietitians. The first step is to restore you to normal weight. Doing so will be hard for you and rouse anxiety; you lost the weight in the first place for powerful psychological reasons. Then comes a lengthy process of therapy to correct irrational beliefs about yourself, food and exercise and about other's reactions to you. Undoubtedly therapy will also explore your attitudes about perfectionism, growing up and—if you're female—womanhood. Therapy will delve into family issues, and family sessions may also be called for.

Treatment for anorexia can be a long struggle. But if you want help and recognize that there's a problem, you've already taken an important step toward recovery.

FOR FURTHER READING

Marlene Boskind-White and William C. White, *Bulimarexia: The Binge/Purge Cycle*. New York: W.W. Norton, 1991.

Jane Brody, *Jane Brody's Nutrition Book*. New York: Bantam, 1989.

Hilde Bruch, *The Golden Cage: The Enigma of Anorexia Nervosa*. Cambridge, Mass.: Harvard University Press, 1978.

Christopher Fairburn, *Overcoming Binge Eating*. New York: Guilford, 1995.

Paul Haskew and Cynthia H. Adams, *When Food Is a Four-Letter Word*. Englewood Cliffs, N.J.: Prentice-Hall, 1984.

Susie Orbach, *Fat Is a Feminist Issue II*. New York: Berkeley, 1991.

Janet Treasure, *Anorexia Nervosa: A Survival Guide for Families, Friends and Sufferers*. East Sussex, England: Psychology Press, 1997.

IS COUNSELING
FOR YOU?

You've seen the suggestion to "consult a counselor" sprinkled throughout this book. But what happens when you see a counselor or therapist? How is talking supposed to help? Is it best to see a Freudian psychologist or a Jungian psychiatrist or a cognitive-behavioral social worker? In this chapter we clear up these and other mysteries of the counseling process.

Q: I've been thinking of going into counseling. But what is it, exactly?

A: Counseling is a general term for professional guidance to help a person (the client or patient) solve problems. The counseling practiced at your college's counseling center is specifically geared toward students and their issues—fitting in, depression, anxiety, relationships, substance abuse—the issues discussed in this book.

Q: What happens at the counseling center?

A: Usually you can either call in or stop by the office to schedule an appointment. On the day of your appointment, you may be asked to fill out some confidential forms providing information for your counselor. You then are directed to the counselor's office, where you sit facing each other in comfortable chairs (no Freudian couches here). If you are like most first-time clients, your heart is now pounding and you half want to bolt out the door.

Typically at the start of the session, the counselor asks you why you've come in for help. Though he or she then asks follow-up questions, offers some feedback and may explain some ground rules about counseling, usually from this point on it's you who does most of the talking. Opening up about personal concerns will feel strange at first, especially since you don't know this person. But after a while you start feeling comfortable, and a sense of relief comes over you. It's good, you realize, to get these problems out at last.

Toward the end of the 45- to 50-minute session, you and the counselor decide if more visits would be helpful. If so, the counselor explains who will work with you (you may continue with this counselor or be assigned to another). Together you may agree on tentative goals for the sessions. Then you leave the office to schedule another appointment—and to mull over what has happened.

Q: What then happens next session and in the weeks to follow?

A: That depends largely on you and your concerns. True, the counselor will no doubt inquire about certain areas—your family, your friendships and love life, your academic progress. He or she will ask questions, make observations, venture opinions. But the heart of counseling consists of you speaking your mind freely, bringing up what's important at that moment, and therefore the discussions won't follow a predetermined course. The talk may shift from one problem to another, from seemingly trivial events to deeply disturbing matters, from current happenings to childhood memories to future plans. Even your feelings about counseling and the counselor are fair game for discussion. You and the counselor deal with topics as they arise, and you both continue to make discoveries as you go along.

Q: But how does all this talking help?

A: That's a complicated issue, and by no means is every counselor in full agreement on the answer. Here is a very brief, partial explanation.

First, counseling helps because you make discoveries through talking—in a sense, you discover yourself. When you struggle to put experiences into words and to express them to another human being, you clarify your thinking and realize your true wishes and feelings. Talking to the counselor also encourages taking your thoughts seriously. On your own you may make discoveries yet dismiss them, but you give weight to things you say in counseling.

Second, you learn from the counselor. He or she won't feed you all the answers or tell you what to do, but his or her questions and observations may open up possibilities you hadn't previously considered.

Third, the relationship with the counselor can boost your self-esteem and morale. You realize you're not crazy, not immoral, not radically different from everyone else, but a person worth listening to and respecting. Ideally, the sense of acceptance the counselor conveys becomes generalized, and you start feeling acceptable in the eyes of other people as well.

Lastly, going to a counselor can inspire you to make positive changes. With support from the counselor, you may feel motivated to start studying, start speaking honestly to friends, start eating healthfully. And once you get moving in the right direction, it's easier to keep up the constructive momentum.

Q: But if counseling is just talking and support, why can't I get help from my friends?

A: Up to a point you can. But very few people have friendships that allow them to reveal everything. In most friendships, people slant what they say and leave things out for fear that their friends will disapprove, be bored or won't understand. With a counselor, you can tell all—you're *encouraged* to—and you're accepted and well understood whatever you say.

In counseling, all the attention is on you; you don't have to share. No other relationship presents this opportunity to focus entirely on self-understanding. And though friends may be wise and well meaning, they're not objective about you, nor are they professionally trained. A counselor is able to see you with fewer distortions.

Q: Why should I talk to someone who's doing it as a job? That's not a real relationship.

A: Is the counselor-student relationship real? It's certainly *different:* exactly 45 or 50 minutes per week, always situated in an office, with the spotlight only on the student and the conversation mostly about the student's problems. Yet we would argue that this unusual relationship is more genuine than most. Both persons are talking honestly, without putting on facades, about matters of substance. How many relationships are this real?

Q: You keep saying counseling, but what you're describing sounds like psychotherapy to me. Are they the same thing?

A: Although many professionals draw a distinction between counseling and psychotherapy, we're using the terms synonymously. We refer to counseling and counselors in these pages, but we could as easily say psychotherapy and psychotherapists, or therapy and therapists.

Q: Do you have to be crazy to see a counselor?

A: Not at all. In fact, truly crazy people often can't see anything is wrong and balk at getting help. Basically healthy people are more able to recognize a problem and take constructive action to correct it.

Did you know that approximately 5–10% of your classmates visit the college counseling center in any one year? As for the rest, many currently see private counselors, or have in the past, or will in the future. So not only aren't you crazy for going to a counselor, you're also in good company.

Q: Lots of people have worse problems than I do. Why should I go into counseling?

A: It depends on your own sense of need. The fact that somebody else is worse off is beside the point. If you are troubled about a problem, especially if you've been unable to handle it on your own, then the matter isn't trivial—we're talking about your life, after all—and you have every right to avail yourself of the counseling center.

Q: But I want to solve problems on my own. Isn't it a sign of weakness to depend on a counselor?

A: No. It takes courage to face up to a problem and ask for help. It takes courage to engage in self-examination and struggle to make personal changes. The "weaker" approach—it's called denial—is to sweep problems under the carpet and hope they don't reappear.

Mind you, we respect your desire to solve your own problems. Self-reliance is a valuable personal asset. But even self-reliant people have to take their cars to the mechanic and consult doctors when they're sick. Likewise, it's only sensible to ask for help when you can't solve a personal problem on your own.

Q: How much will counseling cost?

A: Most counseling centers offer students free services. Even if your college does impose a charge, it will probably be quite low.

Private counseling or psychotherapy is another matter. Depending on the region of the country and the credentials of the professional, the fees per session may range from $60 to a hefty $175 or more.

How then can you afford private psychotherapy if you want it? Your parents will have to help (if they can), you'll have to get a part-time job, or you'll need to be reimbursed for psychotherapy under your parents' or your college's health insurance policy. With regard to insurance policies, be sure to read the fine print or ask the right person to find out exactly how much, if anything, you'll be reimbursed.

Fortunately, some private practitioners and most community mental health centers operate on a "sliding fee scale"—the fee depends on your ability to pay. So by doing some investigating you may find quite affordable psychotherapy. Your college counseling center can give you leads on where to look.

Q: I've been hesitating about counseling because I don't want to damage my college record.

A: There's no need to worry. Your appointments at the college counseling center are confidential; what you discuss is not disclosed outside the office. No information about your sessions, not even the fact that you're in counseling, is passed on to deans, parents, faculty or anyone else outside the counseling center. Nor does your counseling experience show up on your official college record. So freely discuss anything you want; your disclosures will be safeguarded.

A few more points about confidentiality. To assist in understanding you, your counselor will write some notes and keep them in a locked file (no one else will see them), and he or she may discuss your case with another counselor on staff. These are standard practices in the field, meant to help your counselor help you, and do not compromise confidentiality. Also, a circumstance might arise where you'd *want* your counselor to communicate with a professor, dean, parent or a private therapist. If this comes up, your counselor would do so only after discussing it with you and receiving your permission.

Are there exceptions to confidentiality? Yes, a few. According to the law in many states, your counselor has a duty to warn the appropriate parties if somebody's life is in danger, must report incidents of child abuse and must respond to court orders. But these exceptions come up very rarely and should not discourage you from getting help.

Q: When is the best time to go into counseling?

A: The sooner the better—but it's never too late. Sooner is usually better because tackling a small problem is easier than a problem that has grown big and complicated. So if you need counseling, go now rather than wait until you're really in hot water. On the other hand, it's never too late; long-standing, seemingly desperate problems can be helped too. Just because you've hesitated doesn't mean things are hopeless now.

Here's a tip. College counselors' schedules tend to get filled up by the time of midterms. So if you have a choice, schedule your first appointment early in the term.

Q: My counselor has recommended group therapy, but I don't feel comfortable in groups.

A: That's exactly why group therapy may be wise for you. Here is a safe opportunity to practice group interactions, with the support of the leader behind you and the knowledge that every other member probably feels much as you do. Chances are in a few weeks you'll feel surprisingly comfortable with these people. You'll talk with newfound freedom and look forward to the weekly meetings.

Some counseling groups are organized around a theme, such as eating disorders, sexual identity or substance abuse. In these groups you discover that you're not alone with your problem; others have had experiences and feelings like your own. Sometimes students attend one of these groups in conjunction with individual counseling; each counseling experience reinforces the other.

Q: Should I see a psychologist or a psychiatrist?

A: If you want or need medication (most students in counseling do not), then you have to see a psychiatrist, who is a medical doctor. For counseling, though, it doesn't really matter which professional you see. Both psychologists and psychiatrists are very well trained, and both do essentially the same kind of counseling. Also well trained and offering quality counseling are clinical social workers and master's level counselors, the other main professions represented at college counseling centers.

Are these professions different at all? Yes, in certain ways. Psychiatrists specialize in prescribing medication, psychologists are specialists in psychological testing, and social workers are most familiar with community resources. But when it comes to talking to clients, these professions have much more in common than setting them apart. Good counseling is good counseling, whatever the counselor's profession.

Q: Should I see a Freudian or a cognitive therapist?

A: Here again, the difference may matter less than you think. Sure, there are important differences among various therapy approaches. Freudian psychoanalysis digs deep into your past and uncovers your unconscious conflicts. Cognitive therapy pays closest attention to thinking patterns, behavior therapy to the ways you act, gestalt therapy to unexpressed feelings and interpersonal approaches to personal relationships. There are literally hundreds of therapy orientations—Jungian therapy, object relations, hypnotherapy and on and on—each with a different slant, each, it seems, claiming to be the best.

But although these approaches sound dissimilar in theory, good counselors tend to pick up on the same issues no matter what their philosophy. And many counselors consider themselves "eclectic," which means they draw on a variety of approaches. So a counselor's theoretical orientation, while not unimportant, still may not indicate how well he or she will work with you.

Q: Then are you saying it doesn't matter who my counselor is?

A: Not at all. Your counselor matters a great deal. But the profession of your counselor counts far less than his or her personal qualities and the chemistry between you. By chemistry, we don't mean that your feelings for the counselor must be 100% positive. In fact, negative feelings are important information that may shed light on your relationships with other people. On balance, though, you should feel positive about the counselor and his or her way of working.

If your counseling relationship passes the following tests, then your counselor is probably right for you:

- You generally feel that the counselor understands you.
- You generally feel accepted.
- You feel encouraged to speak candidly, to reveal yourself in depth.
- The counselor strikes you as a competent professional who knows what he or she is doing.
- The counselor seems genuine and caring.
- On balance, you like and respect this person.

Q: I don't feel comfortable talking to a male counselor. If I ask, will the counseling center assign me to a woman?

A: Most counseling centers will try to satisfy your request. They'll also do their best to match you up with, say, an African-American counselor, a young counselor, a gay counselor or a particular counselor a friend recommended. But bear in mind that your college's clinic may not have exactly the type of person you want. And even if that person exists, scheduling problems may make it difficult to match the two of you.

We appreciate that you may not like the thought of confiding in a male. Going into counseling can seem daunting enough without being assigned an intimidating-seeming counselor. But sometimes you can benefit precisely because your counselor is the "wrong" gender, ethnicity or age. Much can be gained from learning to relate to people whom ordinarily you would keep at arm's length.

Q: I don't feel comfortable with my counselor. Now what?

A: This happens sometimes. Counseling is a highly personal activity—it's a *relationship*—and sometimes the combination of personalities just doesn't click. However, before you give up on the counselor, try talking to him or her about your feelings, since your reaction may be rooted in your personal issues. If you can discover why you feel uncomfortable with this person, you may gain valuable insight into yourself. You may even start to feel differently and find that you can work with the counselor after all.

But after the discussion, you still may not want to continue working with the counselor. That's okay; he or she will understand. Set up an appointment with somebody else. With luck, your second counseling relationship will work out fine.

Q: I sometimes feel worse after my sessions. Does that often happen?

A: Sometimes that happens. Counseling involves getting in touch with truths that you have pushed out of awareness. For example, you may finally admit to yourself that your childhood was unhappy, that you don't really love your boyfriend or girlfriend, or that you are unhappy with your current career path. Such realizations are disturbing. The pain they cause is the price you pay for authentic self-awareness.

But over the long haul, counseling should make you feel better, not worse—freer, not more burdened. If you continue to feel worse with no letup in sight, or if you sense you're not making any progress at all toward your counseling goals, you need to discuss this problem with your counselor.

Q: I've been working on some difficult problems in counseling, but I'm feeling okay today and recently nothing bad has happened. Should I cancel my appointment?

A: It's probably best to keep it. Having a good week doesn't mean long-term problems have evaporated. And even though you lack an immediate concern to bring up, you may be surprised at what you unearth during the session. Quiet times, when there's no crisis to resolve, often afford the best opportunity for self-exploration and reflection.

For counseling to be effective, it's necessary to maintain a certain continuity. Keeping appointments only when you feel upset is no more productive than taking an exercise class only when the mood strikes you.

Q: How will I know when I'm finished with counseling?

A: That depends on your goals, and these may change as you go along. Initially, you may be concerned about symptoms like anxiety attacks, whereas later, after the symptoms have abated, you may want to explore underlying issues like relationship fear. You never get to the endpoint of self-understanding. This is not to say you should be in counseling forever. The point is simply that you need to examine and reexamine your counseling goals. If there is important work still to do, then continue. If not, then maybe it's time to stop.

Q: My counseling center only offers short-term counseling. Should I see a counselor in the community? Won't it be hard to start all over again?

A: A decision about long-term counseling is best made in consultation with your current counselor. It depends on your unfinished counseling goals and your motivation for continued work.

Starting in with a new counselor can be awkward at first. You need to explain things all over again and adjust to the new counselor's style. But the time spent in explanation is never a waste; each time you go over the material you learn from the telling. And no matter how helpful your initial counselor was, it's always enlightening to work with someone new, who has fresh insights and a fresh perspective.

Q: What if I never go into counseling?

A: That's fine. Unless you have a problem that's too much for you, you certainly don't have to see a professional. All we suggest is that you be honest with yourself about your difficulties and open minded about getting help in case you need it again.

FOR FURTHER READING

Francine Roberts, *The Therapy Sourcebook*. Los Angeles: Lowell House, 1998.

Judi Striano, *How to Find a Good Psychotherapist: A Consumer Guide*. Santa Barbara, Calif.: Professional SBcA, 1987.

IS THERE LIFE
AFTER COLLEGE?

The final challenge of college is to learn how to leave it behind. Finishing up is not a simple matter of completing course requirements, putting on a cap and gown and sitting through the commencement ceremony. It is, like starting college, a major transition, a passage into the next developmental stage. Though you may be eager to move on, more likely you anticipate the change with some uneasiness, a wistful looking back and an apprehensive looking ahead. It's not a small matter to pull up stakes and embark on a new phase of life.

In this chapter we focus on career issues and other concerns you may have about graduating. Yes, there *is* life after college, but it's not surprising if you feel ambivalent about getting there.

Q: I'm only a sophomore, and I'm worried because I don't know what I'll do when I graduate. How do I go about choosing a career?

A: Slow down a bit. You don't have to map out your entire life by the second year of college. Some of your classmates already do know their life's work, or think they do, and that may work fine for them. But most undergraduates, especially those enrolled in liberal arts programs, need more time and experience to pick a career direction. Many still have not made a career decision even at graduation, and sometimes for several years afterward.

Choosing a career should come about naturally. It's far better to select wisely and when you're ready than to force a premature career choice.

Q: Then is sophomore year too early to think about careers?

A: No, it isn't. Now is a good time to pursue interests, preferences and abilities that may lead to a career. Here's what you can do:

- **Pursue summer jobs, internships, work-study positions, student activities and volunteer work.** These experiences give a taste of what it's like to work in various fields.
- **Sample widely from your college's course offerings.** In time, a pattern may emerge pointing in a given career direction. Do you enjoy and excel in political science, history and international relations courses? Then you may want to consider a career in law or the foreign service. Are visual studies and fine arts courses your thing? Then a future might follow in museum curatorship, architecture, commercial photography or computer graphics.
- **Bear in mind, however, that people enter careers from widely differing academic backgrounds:** Your major doesn't commit you to any particular profession. Provided you fulfill the course requirements, you can major in biology and go to law school, or major in political science and enroll in medical school.
- **Be sensitive to your own reactions.** Be aware of jobs, activities and courses that really suit you rather than talking yourself into ones that don't fit. One student, for example, decided early on to become a doctor based on her supposed interest in natural sciences. This plan comforted her; it felt good to be certain about her future and to impress family and friends that she'd be an M.D. some day. Trouble is, she didn't especially enjoy or do well in college-level biology and chemistry, and meanwhile she found deep satisfaction working part-time at a neighborhood day-care center. Only after repeatedly beating her head against the wall of premed courses did she finally admit to herself that elementary education suited her much better than medicine.
- **Talk to professionals in the fields you are considering.** Your college's career counseling office may have a list of alumni or participants in a mentor program who can tell you about their jobs.
- **Read "insider" guides.** They tell about careers, jobs and job searches.
- **Take advantage of your college's career development office.**

Q: In a few months I'll be graduating and getting a job, but somehow I don't feel ready to enter the work world. Why is that?

A: Many possibilities come to mind. One is lack of confidence in your abilities. Think back to when you took on previous challenges, such as entering college or starting a part-time job. Did you question yourself then? If so, it's not surprising that you're feeling uneasy again at the prospect of this new challenge.

Probably, too, you can't quite picture yourself as an adult professional. After all, your main job in life has been to be a student, not an employee. The idea of entering the work world is understandably strange, scary and different. This feeling can last even into the first few years on the job. Many young professionals feel at work as if they're acting somehow, like children pretending to be grown-ups. They're not *really* accountants or salespersons or architects; those are just the roles they're playing. If you are feeling this way—if, understandably, your professional identity hasn't consolidated yet—then you may feel unready to enter the work world.

Family issues can also give you pause. If your career path has been staked out by your parents, now at the moment of truth you may not want to go forward. Or you may hesitate to start a career that has you outdoing your parents or that falls below their high standards.

Finally, you may feel that you haven't fully taken advantage of college or haven't sampled enough of life. You don't want to get started on a career until you've fulfilled these other goals.

Q: Then if I don't feel ready to work, what should I do?

A: That depends on the strength of your ambivalence. You don't have to feel 100% positive about working to make a successful entry into the work world; almost everyone has some qualms at the beginning. But if your resistance is strong, then we suggest consulting a counselor to uncover the reasons and discuss sensible options such as volunteer work, temporary employment or travel. A professional can help you explore whether or not getting a job is now in your best interests.

Q: I'm afraid I won't get the right job after graduation.

A: Your first position doesn't have to be your dream job. To take the pressure off, sometimes it makes sense to find work that's just interesting or fun or that simply pays the bills. This way you're already doing something while you're exploring opportunities closer to your long-term goals.

Q: After the freedom and stimulation of college, I dread the idea of a nine-to-five routine and the same thing each day. How can a free spirit like me ever be happy with the same old grind?

A: Fortunately, the work world is a lot more varied than you imagine. Yes, there are many highly structured jobs, and many people who prefer them that way, but there are also looser company environments, freer careers, creative jobs and the possibility of self-employment, where you set your own rules. Your college's career development office can give you leads on job and career opportunities where you'll enjoy freedom and variety.

No job will fit your needs to the letter. But just as some romantic partners are a good match for you, certain jobs will be well suited to your personality type. Rather than dismissing the work world as alien, be open minded about working and look for a career compatible with your needs.

Q: But I can't imagine limiting myself to one profession and giving up other possibilities.

A: You're right, up to a point—pursuing a career does mean giving up options. You can't become, say, a nurse, while simultaneously pursuing full-time careers in teaching, administration and acting. But you can either look at this negatively, as a terrible limitation, or positively, as a chance to specialize. For while it's true that in choosing a career you give up the unlimited horizons of childhood, where any future seems possible, now comes the exciting opportunity to really know one area, to become an expert.

But let's not overstate the point about closing off options. Careers, after all, are multidimensional; they let you express different sides of yourself. So if you do go into nursing, you can still end up teaching nursing, being a hospital administrator or being a health educator who draws on acting skills. You grow in careers too; your duties change as you gain experience and expertise. Also, don't forget that you can pursue interests in your free time. If you have a glorious tenor voice that must be muzzled at the office, nobody can stop you from belting out arias once you clock out at five.

Bear in mind, too, that a career decision isn't a lifetime sentence. If you want to try a new field in two, five or even 20 years, then you can switch careers, as millions have done.

Q: Can my college get me a job?

A: Getting a job will be your doing, but your college's career development office can equip you with skills to find jobs. This office can show you how to prepare a résumé and find literature about professions and particular companies, can help with computerized employment searches (many offices have sophisticated job search systems) and can improve your interviewing skills. Many career development offices also invite representatives from major corporations and nonprofit organizations onto campus to interview students for jobs.

Q: I'm terrified of job interviews. How can I cope with them?

A: They can be intimidating, at least at the beginning. Here are several ideas that may help:

- **Attend career development office workshops on interviewing skills.** There you can often role-play interviews and get used to fielding typical interview questions. Another option is having a friend simulate an interviewer while you practice giving answers.
- **Interview for several jobs.** Experience at interviewing may increase your confidence.
- **Consider several job possibilities rather than becoming fixated on one.** An open-minded attitude about jobs reduces the pressure you'll feel on any one interview. Make sure, however, that you have some focus in your search and convey your sincere interest and knowledge about each position.
- **Remember that interviewing isn't an exact science.** Interviewers disagree on candidates, and the best candidate does not always land the job. So hone your interviewing skills, but don't torment yourself worrying about perfect answers, since you can never be sure how your answers will be perceived.

- **Think of interviews as a conversation.** You are talking to another person, not to an impersonal interview machine.
- **Be prepared with successes and accomplishments you're proud of.** That way you're in a confident frame of mind and can portray yourself positively during the interview.
- **Review your performance.** While you shouldn't overdo second-guessing, it's a good idea after each interview to analyze what went well and what needs improving. A career counselor or a friend can help you objectively review your performance.
- **After a rejection, ask for feedback.** That way you take advantage of the experience. And remember that sometimes organizations later recruit runners-up for other positions.

Q: How do I find out about graduate schools?

A: Your college's career development office has catalogs and other information about programs. For the inside scoop on particular programs, consider visiting the schools and seeking out officials and enrolled students. Professors at your own college are another resource who can provide information about graduate training and professional opportunities.

If you plan to go to graduate school, you'll need to start about a year in advance to learn about different programs, write to schools for applications, request letters of recommendation and apply. Application forms and required standardized tests must be completed by certain deadlines. The entire process is involved, but no more so than the steps that got you into college.

Once you've applied, be prepared to wait. Often graduate schools don't mail out notifications until mid-April. To ease your anxiety and increase your chances, it pays to apply to several programs rather than putting your fate in the hands of one or two admissions committees.

Q: There are two months left until I graduate. All my classmates have plans except me. Help!

A: It's not unusual for college seniors to be undecided about their careers. Since time is short, we recommend postponing ultimate career decisions anyway. Much more important now is to make some immediate plans. Consider your options: Is it best to look for a job, find volunteer work, help out in a family enterprise or take time off to travel? Should you live alone, find a roommate or move in with your parents? How will you pay for your room and board?

The sooner you make short-range plans, even if only for a few months or so, the better you'll feel about yourself and the future.

Q: My plans after graduation are to move back home and get a job until I save enough for my own place. But how will I manage living with my parents again?

A: Granted, the arrangement can be touchy, even if you generally get along well with them. Though different problems can arise, the most predictable are battles over privacy and control. You'll want to be treated as an independent adult, free to come and go and do as you please, while they may ask you where you're going at night, tell you to be home by midnight and remind you to drive carefully. If you protest that they're treating you like a child, they can retort with the two classic parental arguments: "We're still your parents" and "When you're in our house, you follow our rules."

One remedy for power struggles is to come to an early agreement about ground rules. Discuss with your parents when you may come and leave, when you will and will not report your whereabouts, how often you may have visitors and how much you will tell them about job hunting and social life. For best results, present your side calmly and work toward compromise. You may not get all the privacy and freedom you want, but at least you and your parents will know where matters stand, and the atmosphere can stay cordial.

Some college graduates who move back with their parents pay rent or earn their keep by doing household chores. Paying your own way lets you feel less dependent on your parents while encouraging them to treat you like an adult.

Q: I'm looking forward to starting my new job and having an apartment when I graduate next month, yet I still feel anxious. Why?

A: Chances are you're more upset about moving on than you realize. Like any other major transition, graduation from college involves an ending and a beginning. Both aspects can pack an emotional wallop.

Stop and consider how much of your life is coming to a close. You must say good-bye to classmates and professors, to classes, activities and social events; to places you've known; to the entire undergraduate lifestyle. Perhaps you have a boyfriend or girlfriend you won't see as easily now, or perhaps you haven't had a good college romance—and now you realize you never will. Symbolically, you also bid farewell to the idea of being a student, or at least a college student. You leave behind, once and for all, the status of childhood. All this is a lot to give up, and it's no wonder if a part of you is grieving the losses.

Now consider what lies ahead of you. Starting next month, you embark on a new job. Even though your position may sound desirable, it's only natural to have doubts and fears about the work world. Soon you'll also be looking for new friends, getting used to a new place to live and handling new living expenses. You can't fall back on old routines or your college reputation; on all these fronts you have to establish yourself anew. And then, the flip side of giving up childhood is adjusting to adult status. Thoughts like these are not unusual: "Now I'm supposed to be grown-up, but I don't feel grown-up. My life is real, not a preparation anymore, but I don't feel ready."

In Chapter 1, we counseled being patient with yourself in getting used to college. Now we echo that advice regarding the transition out of college. Be patient if you have misgivings and apprehensions, if you have questions about yourself and what life has to offer. These are the normal reactions of any reflective human being to times of great change.

At the same time, remind yourself of your coping capacities. You made a successful entry into college, and now you can successfully navigate your way out. Remind yourself, too, that change is invigorating, the impetus to growth. Life is different after college, but it is, in its own way, every bit as rewarding.

Q: I burst into tears whenever I see one of my friends or think of leaving this place, and I feel totally overwhelmed. What can I do?

A: Though graduation is inherently stressful, your reaction sounds unusually intense. You may be upsetting yourself with extreme, unrealistic thoughts, for example: "I'll never have such good friends again." "The best years of my life are over." "I'll hate having a job."

As with any irrational thinking, our advice is to refute these assumptions and replace them with realistic alternatives. For example, you might challenge the first assumption by talking to yourself as follows: "Why can't I make good friends again? After all, I've always made new friends in the past. And besides, I don't have to lose my college friendships. Several of my closest friends will be living near me, and I can e-mail the others." Similar reasoning can be applied to the other faulty assumptions.

If this cognitive strategy fails to bring you relief, then the prudent course is to discuss your situation with a counselor.

Q: The problems of the world seem overwhelming. What difference can I make when I graduate?

A: No question, the newspapers are awash in worrisome headlines. Whether you fix your attention on epidemic diseases or drugs or the homeless, the greenhouse effect or the destruction of animal and plant species, regional strife or ethnic hatred or economic upheavals, the difficulties are immense. There's little that you can do, as one person, to change these global realities.

A middle ground exists, however, between saving the planet and giving up in despair. Single-handedly you can't rescue civilization, but your influence matters through the work you choose and how you perform it, the people you touch, the energy and goodness of your daily actions. Thus you can't stamp out illiteracy, but you can, as a teacher or volunteer tutor, teach a few people to read. As a nurse or doctor, you can treat and bring comfort to the ill. In business or law or the civil service, you can serve your clients ably and ethically; in the arts, you can enlighten and entertain; as a parent, friend, neighbor and citizen, you can affect people positively. As the Jimmy Stewart character discovered in the movie classic *It's a Wonderful Life,* individual actions do add up. The part you play has an impact on the whole.

We would add that there never has been a time when problems were in short supply. Every age has enough bad news and dire predictions to justify pessimism for those who are so inclined. Indeed, how you view the world and your own role in it says more about you than it does about the world. A gloomy and easily discouraged personal philosophy will see that darkness mirrored in the world. But if you acquire a certain faith in yourself, then you will have faith that the world for all its problems is still worth engagement and your own efforts do make a difference.

FOR FURTHER READING

Gary Alpert et al., *The Insider's Guides for Job Seekers,* San Francisco: Wet Feet Press, 1996–98.

Richard Nelson Bolles, *What Color Is Your Parachute?* Berkeley, Calif.: Ten Speed Press, 1997.

Clarke G. Carney and Cinda Field Wells, *Discover the Career Within You,* 4th ed. Belmont, Calif.: Wadsworth, 1995.

Martha P. Leape and Susan M. Vacca, *The Harvard Guide to Careers.* Cambridge, Mass.: Harvard OCS, 1995.

H. Anthony Medley, *Sweaty Palms: The Neglected Art of Being Interviewed.* Berkeley, Calif.: Ten Speed Press, 1992.

Paul Tieger and Barbara Barron-Tieger, *Do What You Are: Discover the Perfect Career for You Through the Secrets of Personality Type.* Boston: Little Brown & Co., 1995.

Martin John Yate, *Resumes That Knock 'Em Dead.* Holbrook, Mass.: Adams, 1997.

APPENDIX 1
SOURCES OF
HELP ON
CAMPUS

Many offices at colleges and universities provide assistance and counseling for problems. Here, in thumbnail descriptions, are 11 sources of help if you run into a difficulty:

1) The *Counseling Center* (sometimes called the Mental Health Office or Personal Development Center) provides counseling for personal problems: anxiety, depression, substance abuse, sexual and relationship issues, family concerns and all the rest. Most counseling centers offer short-term counseling (up to 10 or so sessions). Some also run one-session workshops and ongoing therapy groups. If you want long-term psychotherapy, the counseling center can refer you to private practitioners and community mental health agencies.

2) The *Study Skills Center* (also called the Academic Learning Center) specializes in academic difficulties. Professionals there may give tutoring and other workshops on note-taking, studying techniques, test-taking strategies, reading skills, typing and time management. In addition, some study skills centers assess learning disabilities. There also may be a separate learning disabilities office on your campus.

3) *Academic Advisors.* Do you have questions about your academic program? Then contact an academic advisor, who can explain specific academic requirements ("How many science courses do I need to graduate?") and more broadly, help you find your way with important academic decisions ("Should I major in English or business?"). At many colleges these advisors are faculty members—

called, logically enough, faculty advisors. In addition to your official advisor, other faculty members may also be receptive to offering academic guidance.

4) The *Career Development Office* (also called the Career Advising or Career Counseling Office). This office helps you plan for life after graduation. When you first begin to think about careers, counselors there can help you clarify your values and vocational interests. Later in the process, they can help you secure a job through workshops on résumé writing, interviewing skills and job hunting, and through interviews they set up with company recruiters. Most career development offices have a library with information about career opportunities, graduate schools and short-term internships.

5) The *Financial Aid Office*. The role of this office is to assist you to find ways to pay for college if you and your family lack sufficient resources. The chief options available are scholarships and grants (provided by the government or the college itself), loans, part-time employment (either at the college or off campus) and deferred payment plans.

6) *Deans* and *Student Affairs Personnel* (exact titles depend on your college's administrative structure). These individuals wear many hats: academic advisors, organizers of social programs, informal personal counselors and advisors to student government and activities. Deans also serve as ombudsmen, which is a fancy way of saying they can help you with a problem or complaint. Because they participate in the campus disciplinary process, deans sometimes have an intimidating reputation. However, most deans are decent human beings and caring counselors (they wanted us to tell you that).

7) The *Health Service* provides general medical assistance and possibly special treatment and counseling in areas such as gynecology and nutrition. Many health services have contraceptive clinics as well. Like the counseling center, the health service also makes referrals to facilities and private practitioners off campus.

8) *Campus Clergy*. Do you have religious, ethical or spiritual questions? Then consult your campus clergy members, who on many campuses include representatives from various religions. Campus ministers also lead religious services and promote religious activities on campus.

9) *Residence Life Staff*. These are students, called Resident Assistants (RAs), and professionals, often called Residence Managers or Area Directors, who are in charge of life in the residence halls. At most

colleges, residence life staff do far more than assign rooms and give out keys. They also provide informal counseling and put on social and educational programs, and they are often the first people on the scene during psychological and medical emergencies.

10) *Other Professional Offices.* We include this catchall category because most campuses have additional resources serving special populations. For example, there may be offices that specialize in the needs of female students; African-American, Hispanic and Asian-American students; international students; disabled students; gay and lesbian students; and older, returning students. Check out the offerings at your school.

11) *Peer Counseling.* At many colleges, facilities have been set up for students to counsel students. Sometimes peer counselors specialize in particular areas such as alcohol use or sexuality. So if you want to consult with someone who can identify with the student's perspective, see if there's a peer counseling service on your campus.

APPENDIX 2
NATIONAL SOURCES
OF HELP

In addition to sources of help on campus, national organizations can offer information and referrals for particular problems. Here are a few organizations and the services they provide. Regarding Internet sites, we have provided the most recent addresses; however, given their tendency to change, try a search should the address not work.

AIDS, OTHER SEXUALLY TRANSMITTED DISEASES AND CONTRACEPTION

CDC National AIDS Hotline 800-342-AIDS
http://www.ashastd.org/nah/nah.html

Information about transmission of HIV, safer sex, etc. Referrals for counseling, treatment, testing, financial support and related concerns. Spanish line: 800-344-SIDA; teletypewriter machine (for hearing-impaired callers): 800-AIDS-TTY.

CDC National Sexually Transmitted Disease Hotline 800-227-8922
http://www.ashastd.org/std/stdhotln.html

Basic answers about sexually transmitted diseases, information about other hot lines and free pamphlets on diseases and prevention. Referrals for local testing sites. No diagnoses over the phone.

Planned Parenthood
http://www.plannedparenthood.org/

Resources on sexual and reproductive health, contraception, family planning, abortion and STDs, including HIV. Check in your local telephone directory for phone numbers.

ALCOHOL AND OTHER DRUGS

Alcoholics Anonymous
  http://www.alcoholics-anonymous.org/index.html

  Check in your local telephone directory for phone numbers.

Children of Alcoholics Foundation 800-359-COAF
  http://www.coaf.org

  ACOA meeting referrals and basic information available 24 hours a day.

Narcotics Anonymous
  www.na.org/index.htm

  Check in your local telephone directory for phone numbers.

The National Clearinghouse for Alcohol and Drug Information
  http://www.health.org/

National Cocaine Hotline 800-COCAINE
  Referrals to drug treatment centers and private practitioners throughout the nation.

ANGER MANAGEMENT

American Psychological Association
  http://www.apa.org/pubinfo/anger.html

  An informational web page put out by the national organization.

ANOREXIA, BULIMIA AND OVEREATING

American Anorexia/Bulimia Association 212-575-6200
  http://www.aabainc.org

  Eating disorders information and referrals for support groups, private therapists and treatment centers.

Nidus Information Services
  http://www.noah.cuny.edu/wellconn/eatdisorders.html

  An informational website on anorexia, bulimia and other eating problems.

Overeaters Anonymous
 http://www.overeatersanonymous.org

 Check in your local telephone directory for phone numbers.

ANXIETY AND DEPRESSION

Dr. Ivan's Depression Central
 http://www.psycom.net/depression.central.html

This site bills itself as the "Internet's central clearinghouse for information on all types of depressive disorders and on the most effective treatments for individuals suffering from Major Depression, Manic-Depression (Bipolar Disorder), Cyclothymia, Dysthymia and other mood disorders."

National Institute of Mental Health—Anxiety Disorders Education Program
 http://www.nimh.nih.gov/anxiety/

ATTENTION DEFICIT DISORDER AND LEARNING DISABILITIES

Children and Adults with Attention Deficit Disorder 301-306-7070
 http://www.chadd.org/

Information and referrals for ADD testing.

The International Dyslexia Association 800-ABCD123 (Messages), 410-296-0232 (Voice)
 http://www.interdys.org/

Formerly known as the Orton Dyslexia Society, this organization offers information and referrals for dyslexia testing. Call the number above or write to
 The International Dyslexia Association
 International Office
 8600 LaSalle Road, Chester Building, Suite 382
 Baltimore, MD 21286-2044

GAY AND LESBIAN ISSUES

Parents, Families and Friends of Lesbians and Gays 202-638-0243
http://www.pflag.org

Informational brochures and support for gays, lesbians, their families and friends. Call the number above or write to
Parents FLAG
1101 14th Street NW, Suite 1030
Washington, DC 20005

American Psychological Association
http://www.apa.org/pubinfo/orient.html

Answers to questions about sexual orientation and homosexuality, put out by this national organization.

MEDICATIONS INFORMATION

Internet Mental Health
http://www.mentalhealth.com/fr30.html

SEXUAL ASSAULT

American Psychological Association
http://www.apa.org/pubinfo/mem.html

Questions and answers about memories of childhood abuse, put out by APA.

Sexual Assault Information Page
http://www.cs.utk.edu/~bartley/saInfoPage.html

An informational web page.

STUDENT INFORMATION

American College Health Association 301-963-1100
http://www.acha.org

Informational brochures on a variety of student health concerns, including AIDS, alcohol and sexually transmitted diseases. Call the above number or write to
ACHA
P.O. Box 28937
Baltimore, MD 21240-8937

The Chronicle of Higher Education 800-728-2803
http://www.chronicle.com

A weekly newspaper that publishes news about all aspects of academia—finances, athletics, academics, student affairs, job openings.

National On-Campus Report 608-246-3580
http://www.magnapubs.com

A student-oriented newsletter about happenings on campuses around the United States. Call the number above or write to
National On-Campus Report
Magna Publications, Inc.
2718 Dryden Drive
Madison, WI 53704-3086

SUICIDAL CONCERNS

American Association of Suicidology 202-237-2280
http://www.suicidology.org/

Referrals for self-help groups and counseling services across the nation. The website provides a state-by-state directory of crisis centers and support groups.

Internet Mental Health
http://www.mentalhealth.com/fr00.html

This is another informational website.

Also check your local telephone directory for a chapter of the **Samaritans** or **Contact.** These organizations have 24-hour phone services in which trained volunteers talk to persons who have suicidal concerns.

REFERENCES

We have avoided using excessive notes throughout this volume. The reader should refer to the list of suggested readings at the end of each chapter. Sources for specific quotations and references in the text are noted below, followed by sources of general information.

Chapter 1

[1]S.B. Cotler and J.J. Guerra, *Assertion Training* (Champaign, Ill.: Research Press, 1979).

[2]Karen Horney, *The Neurotic Personality of Our Time* (New York: W.W. Norton & Company, 1937), 89.

See also: J. Asher, "Born to be Shy?" *Psychology Today* (April 1987): 56–64; Jane E. Brody, "Personal Health," *New York Times* (November 16, 1989): B19; "Counseling on Religious Groups Encompasses Some Former Members," *New York Times* (March 11, 1990): 43; J.L. Hopson, "The Unraveling of Insomnia," *Psychology Today* (June 1986): 43–49; M. Machlowitz, "As Millions Toss and Turn, Studies Pursue Secret of Sleep," *New York Times* (April 21, 1981): C1–2; H. Molnar, "Of Dorms and Roommates," *New York Times* (August 5, 1990): 10–11; S. Tifft, "Waging War on the Greeks," *Time* (April 16, 1990): 64–65.

Chapter 2

[1]J.L. Thomas, *Do You Have Attention Deficit Disorder?* (New York: Dell, 1996), 142–144.

[2]E.B. Fiske, "Lesson," *New York Times* (April 11, 1990): B8.

See also: J.B. Burka and L.M. Yuen, "Mind Games Procrastinators Play," *Psychology Today* (January 1982): 32–41; G. Du Chossois, personal communication, May 1, 1990; "Dyslexics Learn to Believe, First, Then to Overcome," *New York Times* (November 11, 1990): A49; J. Gottleib, personal communication, May 2, 1990; E. Kaye and J. Gardner, *College Bound* (The College Board, 1988); W. Knaus,

"Why People Procrastinate: Is There a Cure?" *U.S. News & World Report* (October 24, 1983): 61–62; A. Lakein, *How to Get Control of Your Time and Your Life* (New York: New American Library, 1973); S. Singular, "A Memory for All Seasonings," *Psychology Today* (October 1982): 54–63.

Chapter 3

[1]E.E. Goode, "Beating Depression," *U.S. News & World Report* (March 5, 1990): 48–56.

[2]"Mood Disorders: An Overview—Part I," *The Harvard Mental Health Letter* (December 1997): 2.

[3]M. McKay, M. Davis, and P. Fanning, *Thoughts and Feelings: The Art of Cognitive Stress Intervention* (Richmond, Calif.: New Harbinger Publications, 1981): 17–45; H.B. Braiker, "The Power of Self-Talk," *Psychology Today* (December 1989): 23–27; D.B. Burns, *Feeling Good: The New Mood Therapy* (New York: Morrow, 1980); A. Ellis, *Reason and Emotion in Psychotherapy* (New York: Lyle Stuart and Citadel Press, 1962); A. Ellis and R. Grieger, *Handbook of Rational-Emotive Therapy* (New York: Springer, 1977).

[4]E.H. Erikson, *Identity: Youth and Crisis* (New York: W.W. Norton, 1968): 105.

[5]"Suicide—Part II," *The Harvard Mental Health Letter* (December 1996): 1.

See also: American Psychiatric Association, *The Diagnostic and Statistical Manual of Mental Disorders*, 4th ed. (Washington, D.C., 1994); E.H. Erikson, *Childhood and Society* (New York: W.W. Norton, 1963): 247–269; "Mood Disorders: An Overview—Parts I and II," *The Harvard Mental Health Letter* (December 1997/January 1998); F. Schumer, "Bye-bye Blues," *New York* (December 18, 1989): 46–53; M.E.P. Seligman, *What You Can Change and What You Can't* (New York: Ballantine, 1993); E. Shneidman, "At the Point of No Return," *Psychology Today* (March 1987): 53–58; State Education Department, University of the State of New York, *Suicide Among School Age Youth* (December 1984); "Suicide—Part I," *The Harvard Mental Health Letter* (November 1996).

Chapter 4

[1]"Obsessive-Compulsive Disorder—Part I," *The Harvard Mental Health Letter* (November 1995): 2.

[2]H. Benson and M.Z. Klipper, *The Relaxation Response* (New York: Avon Books, 1975).

See also: American Psychiatric Association, *Diagnostic and Statistical Manual of Mental Disorders*, 4th ed., revised (Washington, D.C., 1994); N. Angier, "If Anger Ruins Your Day, It Can Shrink Your Life," *New York Times* (December 13, 1990): B23; E.A. Charlesworth and R.G. Nathan, *Stress Management* (New York: Ballantine, 1982); D. Goleman, "Doctors Cite Gains in Treating Panic Attacks," *New York Times* (January 30, 1990): C3; ———, "For Stage Fright, Rehearsal Helps," *New York Times* (June 12, 1991): C1, C10; ———, "Study Finds Less Cause for Worry in Nightmares," *New York Times* (March 15, 1990): B7; J.H. Greist, J.W. Jefferson and I.M. Marks, *Anxiety and Its Treatment* (New York: Warner Books, 1987); L.E. Kopolow, "Plain Talk About . . . Handling Stress" (Washington, D.C.: U.S. Government Printing Office, DHHS Publication No. [ADM] 85-502m, 1985); C.J. McCullough and R.W. Mann, *Managing Your Anxiety* (New York: St. Martin's Press, 1985); M. Motlet, "Taking the Terror Out of Talk," *Psychology Today* (January 1988): 46–49; "Obsessive-Compulsive Disorder—Part II," *The Harvard Mental Health Letter* (December 1995); C.L. Otis and R. Goldingay, *Campus Health Guide* (New York: College Entrance Examination Board, 1989); "Panic Attacks and Panic Disorder—Parts I and II," *The Harvard Mental Health Letter* (April/May 1996); F.R. Schneier, "Panic Disorder and Social Phobia Can Be Treated with Drugs, Therapy," *The Psychiatric Times* (July 1990): 16–17; M.E.P. Seligman, *What You Can Change and What You Can't* (New York: Ballantine, 1993); C. Tavris, "Anger Defused," *Psychology Today* (November 1982): 25–35; D.M. Wegner, "Try Not to Think of a White Bear," *Psychology Today* (June 1989): 64–66; R. Williams, "The Trusting Heart," *Psychology Today* (January–February 1989): 36–42; R.R. Wilson, *Don't Panic: Taking Control of Anxiety Attacks* (New York: Harper & Row, 1986).

Chapter 5

[1] S.L. Nickman, "Challenge of Adoption," *The Harvard Mental Health Letter* (January, 1996): 5–6.

[2] K. Fisher, "Sexual Abuse Victims Suffer Into Adulthood," *APA Monitor* (June 1987): 25.

See also: R.J. Ackerman, "Interview: Robert J. Ackerman: A New Perspective on Adult Children of Alcoholics," *EAP Digest* (January/February 1987): 25–29; "Bereavement and Grief—Part 1," *The Harvard Mental Health Letter* (March 1987): 1–4; "Children of Alcoholics: What Is the Problem?" *The Harvard Mental Health*

Letter (December 1993): 6; A. Kohn, "Shattered Innocence," *Psychology Today* (February 1987): 54–58; L. Kutner, "Parent and Child: The First Visit to a Child at College Can Be Confusing," *New York Times* (November 16, 1989): C8; J.S. Wallerstein, "Children after Divorce," *New York Times Magazine* (January 22, 1989): 19–44.

Chapter 7

[1]Leland Elliot and Cynthia Brantley, *Sex on Campus* (New York: Random House, 1997): 5.

[2]Statistics on the efficacy of birth control methods are from Elliot and Brantley, *Sex on Campus,* and "Contraception: The Choice Is Yours," (Raritan, NJ: Ortho Pharmaceutical Corp., 1996).

[3]N.E. Macdonald, et al., "High-Risk STD/HIV Behavior Among College Students," *Journal of the American Medical Association* 263 (June 20, 1990): 3155–59.

[4]K. Kanthal and K. Nye, "Students Know AIDS Facts but May Not Follow Safe Sex Rules," *Columbia University Spectator AIDS Supplement* (October 29, 1990): 5.

[5]Statistics on prevalence of STDs are from Elliot and Brantley, *Sex on Campus,* and C. Bietzke, "STD Scare: The Year of Living Dangerously," *Cosmo College* (Fall 1998): 26–28.

[6]M.E.P. Seligman, *What You Can Change and What You Can't* (New York: Ballantine, 1993): 154–55.

[7]T.H. Sauerman, *Coming Out to Your Parents* (Washington, D.C.: Federation of Parents and Friends of Lesbians and Gays, Inc., 1984). See also: T. Bodde, *Why Is My Child Gay?* (Washington, D.C.: Federation of Parents and Friends of Lesbians and Gays, Inc., n.d.); G. Cowley, "AIDS: The Next Ten Years," *Newsweek* (June 25, 1990): 20–27; Nancy Friday, *Men In Love* (New York: Delacorte Press, 1980); ———, *My Secret Garden* (New York: Pocket Books, 1973); H.D. Gayle, et al., "Prevalence of the Human Immunodeficiency Virus Among University Students," *New England Journal of Medicine* (November 29, 1990): 1538–41; "Gay Student Wins Bid to Revise Anti-bias Policy," *New York Times* (April 15, 1990): 33; G.C. Higgins, "Sexual Problems," in P.A. Grayson and K. Cauley (eds.), *College Psychotherapy* (New York: Guilford, 1989); S. Johanson, *Talk Sex* (New York: Penguin, 1988); E.W. Johnson, *Love and Sex in Plain Language* (Toronto: Bantam, 1988); J.E. Kaplan, M. Meyer and J. Navin, "Chlamydia Trachomatis Infection in a Male College Student Population," *Journal of American College Health* (January 1989): 159–61; Alfred Kinsey, et al., *Sexual Behavior in the Human Male* (Philadelphia: W.B. Saunders, 1949); ———, *Sexual*

Behavior in the Human Female (Philadelphia: W.B. Saunders, 1953); "Sexual Disorders—Part 2," *Harvard Medical School Mental Health Letter* (January 1990): 1–4.

Chapter 8

[1]D. Pace, "Acts of Intolerance on Campus: Focus on Date Rape" (Unpublished manuscript, Grand Valley State University, Allendale, Michigan).

See also: N. Biggs, "When Is It Rape?" *Time* (June 3, 1991): 48–55; J. Castelli, "Campus Crime 101," *New York Times* (November 4, 1990), Education Supplement: 34–36; W. Celis, "Students Trying to Draw Line Between Sex and an Assault," *New York Times* (January 2, 1991): A1, B8; M.P. Koss, "Date Rape: Victimization by Acquaintances," *The Harvard Mental Health Letter* (September 1992): 5–6; NYU Committee on Safety, *Rape: Awareness, Prevention, Crisis Intervention* (New York University, 1990).

Chapter 9

[1]H.W. Perkins, "College Student Misperceptions of Alcohol and Other Drug Norms Among Peers," *Designing Alcohol and Other Drug Prevention Programs in Higher Education* (Newton, Mass.: The Higher Education Center for Alcohol and Other Drug Prevention, 1997).

[2]P.W. Meilman, C.A. Presley and J.R. Cashin, "Average Weekly Alcohol Consumption," *Journal of American College Health* (March 1997): 201–4; C.A. Presley, P.W. Meilman, J.R. Cashin, *Alcohol and Drugs on American College Campuses*, vol. 4 (Carbondale, Ill.: Southern Illinois University, 1996): 16.

[3]H. Wechsler, G.W. Dowdall, G. Maenner, J. Gledhill-Hoyt and H. Lee, "Changes in Binge Drinking and Related Problems Among American College Students Between 1993 and 1997," *Journal of American College Health* (September 1998): 57.

[4]"Marijuana," *The Harvard Medical School Mental Health Letter* (November 1987): 1–4.

[5]"Pathological Gambling," *The Harvard Mental Health Letter* (January 1996): 1–5.

[6]American Psychiatric Association, *Diagnostic and Statistical Manual of Mental Disorders*, 4th ed. (Washington, D.C., 1994): 618.

See also: "Amphetamines," *The Harvard Medical School Mental Health Letter* (April 1990): 1–4; "Cocaine: Waking Up to a Nightmare," (Phoenix, Ariz.: DIN Publications, 1989); "Drug Abuse and Dependence—Part 1," *The Harvard Mental Health Letter*

(October 1989): 1–4; "Freedom from Smoking," *Regarding Women and Health Care* (New Brunswick, N.J.: Robert Wood Johnson University Hospital, Summer 1990): 1; D. Goleman, "Breaking Bad Habits: New Therapy Focuses on the Relapse," *New York Times* (December 27, 1988): C1, C11; "MDMA: Madness, not Ecstasy," *Psychology Today* (June 1986): 14; "Nicotine Dependence—Part I," *The Harvard Mental Health Letter* (January 1997); C.L. Otis and R. Goldingay, *Campus Health Guide* (New York: College Entrance Examination Board, 1989); S. Peele, *Diseasing of America* (Boston: Houghton-Mifflin, 1989); F.S. Stinson, B.D. Williams et al., "Demographic Trends, Alcohol Abuse and Alcoholism: 1985–1995" (Washington, D.C.: NIAAA. Division of Biometry and Epidemiology [Epidemiologic Bulletin No. 15], 1986); "Treatment of Alcoholism— Parts I and II," *The Harvard Mental Health Letter* (August–September 1996); "Why Men Can Outdrink Women," *Time* (January 22, 1990): 61; M. Paulus, Personal communication, August 1, 1990.

Chapter 10

[1]"Eating Disorders—Part I," *The Harvard Mental Health Letter* (October 1997): 2.

[2]Willard Gaylin, *Rediscovering Love* (New York: Penguin, 1986): 103.

[3]M.E.P. Seligman, *What You Can Change and What You Can't* (New York: Ballantine, 1993): 174–97.

[4]"Eating Disorders—Part I," *The Harvard Mental Health Letter* (October 1997): 3–4.

[5]M.C. Commerford, "Treating an Eating Disorder in 12 Sessions or Less," (New York: Unpublished manuscript, New York University, 1997).

[6]R.M. Lee, "Anorexia Nervosa and Bulimia Nervosa," in P.A. Grayson and K. Cauley, *College Psychotherapy* (New York: Guilford, 1989): 274–97.

[7]J.E. Brody, "Personal Health," *New York Times* (February 22, 1990): B9.

See also: American Psychiatric Association, *Diagnostic and Statistical Manual of Mental Disorders*, 4th ed. (Washington, D.C.: American Psychiatric Association, 1994); M. Bloom, "Running Supports the Work of a Diet," *New York Times* (June 18, 1990): C11; J.E. Brody, "Secret of Successful Dieting," *New York Times* (July 3, 1991): C9; K.D. Brownell, "When and How to Diet," *Psychology*

Today (June 1989): 40–46; H. Bruch, *The Golden Cage: The Enigma of Anorexia Nervosa* (New York: Vintage, 1979); S. Cunningham, "Bulimia's Cycle Shames Patient, Bests Therapists," *American Psychological Association Monitor* (January 1984): 16–17; "Eating Disorders—Part II," *The Harvard Mental Health Letter* (November 1997); J. Gurin, "Leaner not Lighter," *Psychology Today* (June 1989): 32–36; E. Hall, "PT Conversation—Judith Rodin: A Sense of Control," *Psychology Today* (December 1984): 38–45; C.L. Otis and R. Goldingay, *Campus Health Guide* (New York: College Entrance Examination Board, 1989); C. Simon, "The Triumphant Dieter," *Psychology Today* (June 1989): 48–52; H.M. Weinstein and A. Richman, "The Group Treatment of Bulimia," *Journal of the American College Health Association* (April 1984): 208–15.

INDEX

A

AA *See* Alcoholics Anonymous
abbreviations, note-taking 28
abortion 146, 147
abstinence
  alcohol 170
  sexual 127
abuse
  in relationship 120–121
  sexual, in childhood 103–104
acid (LSD) 174, 175
ACOAs *See* Adult Children of Alcoholics
acrophobia 73
ADD *See* attention deficit disorder
adjustment
  to adult status 210
  to college 1–5
  parental divorce and 96–97
adjustment disorder with depressed
    mood 48
adopted children, problems of 92–93
adoption, unwanted pregnancy and 147
Adult Children of Alcoholics (ACOAs)
    103, 173
adult status, adjustment to 210
advisors, academic 213
aggressiveness, counteracting 7
agoraphobia 73
AIDS
  false sense of invulnerability 142
  fear of 143–144
  protection against 139, 145–146
  sources of help 216, 219
  transmission of 144
Al-Anon 172
alcohol/alcohol abuse 164–173
  and date rape 158, 163
  and depression 48, 50
  effects of, gender differences in 165
  enabling of 172
  getting help for 169–170
  helping friends with problems 170–172
  mixing drugs with 176
  and panic symptoms 70

parental 102–103, 172–173
peer pressure and 175
prevalence of 166
setting limits 167, 168
and sexual performance 132
signs of problem 168–169
sources of help 217, 219
staying out of trouble with 167
and stress 85
and suicide 63
tolerance for 165–166
and unprotected sex 146, 165
Alcoholics Anonymous (AA) 170
alienation 11
all-or-nothing thinking 51, 182, 189
amphetamines 174
anabolic steroids 174
angel dust (PCP) 174
anger 78–80
  management of, sources of help 217
  at parents 104–105
anorexia 180, 190–191
  versus bulimia 190
  getting help for 191
  sources of help 217
antidepressants 59–60
  for obsessive-compulsive symptoms 75
  for panic attacks 71
  side effects of 61
  stopping 62
anxiety 68–77
  about dating 106–110
  math 33–34
  about pleasing 107–108
  about sex 126
  and sexual performance 132
  sources of help 218
  test-taking 31–32
appointment books 23
arguments
  with adoptive parents 92–93
  in relationships 115–116
assertiveness 79
  about birth control 143

228

with parents 87, 89, 99–100
with roommates 5–7
attention deficit disorder (ADD) 34–35
  sources of help 218

B

binge-eating disorder 180
  cause of 187–188
  getting help for 188–189
bipolar disorder 47–48
  family influences and 49
  medication for 60
biracial backgrounds 20–21
birth control
  assertiveness about 143
  methods of 139–141
  resistance to 141–143
  sources of help 216
bisexuality 148
body image 181–183
broken record technique 7
bulimia 180, 186–189
  versus anorexia 190
  cause of 187–188
  getting help for 188–189
  sources of help 217

C

caffeine, and anxiety 70
calendars 23
career(s)
  choosing 203–204, 206–207
  indecisiveness about 208–209
  information on 220
  switching 207
Career Development Office 207, 208,
    214
catastrophizing 51, 182
cervical cap (contraceptive) 140
cheating 40
chlamydia 144–145
class participation 30–31
claustrophobia 73
cleanliness 14
clergy, campus 214
cliques 10
clubs
  exclusionary 16–17
  minority student 20
cocaine 173–174
coded communication 114
cognitive approach
  to anxiety 71–72
  to body image 182
  to down periods 50–52
  to eating disorders 189
  to panic attacks 69
  to procrastination 25

to stress 83–84
to test anxiety 31
cognitive therapy 199
cold sores 145
communication
  about physical relations 158
  in groups 16
  and lovemaking 128, 130–131
  with parents 87, 89, 99–100
  in relationship 114, 115–116
  with roommates 6–7
  tips for success 14
commuting students, and friendships 15
compulsions 74–75
computer addiction 178–179
conceit, versus self-esteem 56
condoms 139
  assertiveness about use 143
  resistance to use 141–143
confidentiality, in counseling 197–198
conflicts, resolving 6
conformity 12
constructive thoughts 25, 31, 52, 69,
    72, 83
contraception See birth control
coping devices, healthy 123
counseling 193–202
  benefits of 194–195
  choice of counselor 199
  confidentiality in 197–198
  cost of 197
  decision to go into 196–197, 202
  for depression 58–59, 61–62
  ending 202
  for family issues 93, 95, 101, 102
  for gays and lesbians 151
  group therapy 198
  and medication 61–62
  for panic attacks 70–71
  procedures in 193–194
  for rape victims 160
  for relationship problems 116, 122
  relationship with counselor 200–201
  for sexual abuse 104
  for specific problems 76, 78, 79
  for suicidal urges 67
  theoretical approaches to 199
Counseling Center 213
crabs (pubic lice) 145
creams (contraceptive) 141
criticism
  from parents 100–101
  self- 30, 56–57
cults 17
culture
  foreign See international students
  and sex roles 135–136
cynophobia 73

D

date rape
　perpetrators of 162
　reporting 158–159
　risk of committing 129
　safety measures 157–158
dating, anxiety about 106–110
deans 214
death of parent 97–98
decision(s)
　academic 40–44
　to enter counseling 196–197, 202
　making 77–78
　parental interference in 99–100
deep muscle relaxation 84
denial of problems 171, 196
Depakote 60
dependency, in relationships 119
Depo-Provera 140
depression
　counseling for 58–59, 61–62
　drug abuse and 173–174
　family influences and 49
　kinds of 47–48
　medication for 59–61, 62
　versus sadness 46–48
　and sexual difficulties 131
　and smoking 176
　sources of help 218
　and suicide 63
　warning signs of 48–49
diaphragms (contraceptive) 140
dieting
　versus healthy eating 183–186
　irony of 188
diversity issues 18–21 *See also*
　international students; minorities
divorce, parental 93–97
down periods, fighting 50–54
dreams 76
drugs/drug abuse 173–176
　and depression 48
　enabling of 172
　mixing with alcohol 176
　peer pressure and 175
　and sexual performance 132
　sources of help 217
　and suicide 63
　and unprotected sex 146
dyslexia 34
dysthymia 47

E

eating habits/problems 180–192
　anorexia and food restriction 190–191
　bulimia and binge eating 186–189
　dieting versus healthy eating 183–186
　recognizing problems 180–181

relationship breakup and 123
　and sleep 4
　sources of help 217–218
　and stress 85
ecstasy (MDMA) 174
emotions, denying 80
enabling, of alcohol/drug abuse 172
envy 10–11
essay questions 33
essays, writing 29–30
exams
　final, time organization during 24
　studying for 32
exercise
　and health 185–186
　lack of, and stress 85
　and sleep 4
exhibitionism 138
exposure and response prevention 75
exposure therapy 71
extracurricular activities, and friendships 15

F

failing 40
family issues 86–105
　and eating disorders 187
　in "normal" families 86–93
　parental death 97–98
　parental divorce 93–97
　in troubled families 98–105
fantasies, sexual 137–138
fear *See also* anxiety
　of AIDS 143–144
　of rejection 108–109, 110–111
　of sexual intimacy 127
fear-fighting strategy 71–72
female condom 139
female students
　academic problems of 36–37
　sexual problems of 133–134
fertility awareness method 141
film (contraceptive) 141
final exam period 24
Financial Aid Office 214
financial issues, time off and 44
fitting in 9–15
flooding 73
foams (contraceptive) 141
foreign students *See* international students
fraternities 16–17
Freudian psychoanalysis 199
friendships
　breaking 15
　versus counseling 195
　diverse 20
　one versus many 9–10
　versus relationships 119
　and romance 110

starting 14
ups and downs in 9

G

gambling 177–178
gays, stereotypes about 149 *See also*
  homosexuality
genital warts 145
gestalt therapy 199
gonorrhea 145
grades 38–40
  test-taking strategies and 32–33
  worrying about 38
graduate schools 208
graduation anxiety 203–212
grooming 14
group therapy 198
groups, shyness in 15–16
guilt, parental divorce and 95–96

H

habits
  exercise 186
  and mood-swing prevention 54
  study 23
hallucinogens 174
harassment 112–113
  of gays and lesbians 154–155
  sexual 156–157
Health Service 214
heroin 174
herpes 145
heterosexuality 148
high school, versus college 22
HIV *See* AIDS
home
  return after graduation 209
  support from 3
  visits 86–87, 102
homesickness 2–3
homophobia 150, 152
homosexuality 148–155
  coming out 153–154
  sources of help 219

I

identity 57–58
  biracial 20–21
  confusion about 57–58
  formation of 58
  sexual 148
impotence 131–132
indecisiveness 77–78
  about career choice 208–209
infertility, STDs and 145
insecurity 10–11
  and jealousy 118
  parental influence and 102

insomnia 3–4
international students 21
  academic problems of 37
  and class participation 31
  and parental obedience 90–91
Internet 178–179
intrauterine devices (IUDs) 141
isolation, and depression 53
IUDs *See* intrauterine devices

J

jealousy 118
jellies (contraceptive) 141
job interviews 207–208
journal writing 12
  and identity formation 58

L

language barrier 37
laziness, versus lack of motivation 26
learning disabilities 34
  accommodations for 36
  assessment of 35
  sources of help 218
lesbians, stereotypes about 149 *See also*
  homosexuality
listening
  to group discussions 16
  nondefensively 6
  as social skill 14
lithium carbonate 60
love, uncertainties about 113–114 *See*
  also relationships
LSD (acid) 174, 175

M

major(s)
  and career choice 204
  choosing 40–41, 77
  parental interference in choice of 99
  switching 41
major depression 47
male students
  rape victims 162
  sexual problems of 131–133
manic-depressive disorder *See* bipolar
  disorder
marijuana (pot) 173
marriage 124–125
  pregnancy and 146
masturbation 136–137
  exercise 132–133
math anxiety 33–34
maturation
  process of 86–87
  and sex 126
MDMA (ecstasy) 174
mediation, in roommate relations 9

medical leave of absence 45
medication(s)
  and counseling 61–62
  for depression 59–61, 62
  information on 219
  for panic attacks 71
  for speech anxiety 72
meditation 84
memorizing 28–29, 32
men See male students
mescaline 174
minorities 18–21
  academic problems of 37
  interracial relationships 119–120
mnemonic devices 29
mood swings 46
  medication for 60
  parental 102
  preventing 53–54
motivation
  counseling and 195
  to-do list and 23
  lack of 26
mourning
  parental death 97
  relationship breakup 121
multiple-choice questions 33
mushrooms (drug) 174
mysophobia 73

N

Nar-Anon 172
narcotics 174
Narcotics Anonymous (NA) 170
negative thinking 51, 182
nightmares 75–76
noise 3–4
nonverbal behavior, evaluating 14
Norplant capsules 140
note taking 27–28

O

obsession(s) 73–74
  with body image 181
  treatment for 75
obsessive-compulsive disorder (OCD) 74–75
oral sex 135, 146
organizations 16–17
organizing time 22–24
orgasms, female 134, 135
overassuming 51, 52, 182
overgeneralizing 51, 52

P

panic attacks 68–71
  counseling for 70–71
  responses to 69–70
paradoxical techniques 74, 77

parent(s)
  cold and remote 101
  coming out to 154
  comparisons with 91–92
  death of 97–98
  disagreement with views of 89–91
  divorce of 93–97
  drinking problems 102–103, 172–173
  irrational and unpredictable 102
  keeping in touch with 87–88
  living with, after graduation 209
  lying to 88–89
  overcontrolling 99–100
  perceptions of 87
  relationship pressure by 119–120
  visits 89
partner(s)
  attracting 106–107
  choosiness about 108–109
  dependency on 119
  potential, approaching 109–110, 111
part-time student status 82
passive tactics 6
PCP (angel dust) 174
peer counseling 215
peer influences
  and drug/alcohol abuse 175
  keeping in perspective 12
perfectionism 38–39
performance anxiety 71–72
phobia 73
pill (contraceptive) 140
pornographic websites 178–179
pot (marijuana) 173
prayer meetings 17
pregnancy
  prevention of 139–141
  unwanted 146–147
prejudice 19
privacy, loss of 5
procrastination 24–26
  tips to break 25
propranolol 72
psychedelic drugs 174
psychiatrists 199
psychologists 199
pubic lice (crabs) 145

Q

questioning, and memorizing 29, 32

R

racial minorities See minorities
rape 157–163
  blame for 160
  helping victims of 161
  male victims of 162
  partners of victims of 161

perpetrators of 162
psychological aftereffects of 160–161
reporting 158–159
risk of committing 129, 162–163
safety measures 157–158
sources of help 219
reading 26–27
  deficits 34
  three-step system 27
reality-testing approach 77
rejection 110–113
  fear of 108–109, 110–111
  healing after 111–112
relationships 106–125
  arguments in 115–116
  breaking up 121–124
  communication in 114, 115–116
  couples' problems 113–121
  first steps in 106–110
  versus friendships 119
  game-playing in 129
  and identity formation 58
  interracial 119–120
  long-distance 119
  marriage 124–125
  rejection 110–113
  self-disclosure in 117
  skills 11–12
  violence in 120–121
relaxation exercises 84
  for panic attacks 70
  for test taking 32
Residence Life staff 214–215
rhythm method (birth control) 141
Rohypnol 158
roles
  in relationships 116
  sex 135–136
roommates 5–9
  animosity between 8–9
  annoying traits of 7–8
  assertive communication with 6–7
  with drinking problems 171
  gay/lesbian 153–154
  and stress 81
  suicide threats by 65–66

S
SAD See seasonal affective disorder
sadness
  versus depression 46–48
  overcoming 50–54
sarcastic roommate 8
schedule(s)
  balanced 83
  daily 24
seasonal affective disorder (SAD) 48
self-consciousness, reducing 13

self-criticism 56–57
  and writing problems 30
self-cutting 66–67
self-defeating patterns
  in eating disorders 189
  identifying and challenging 50–52
  in math anxiety 33
  in procrastination 25
self-disclosure, in relationships 117
self-esteem 54–57
  versus conceit 56
  factors influencing 54
  improving 54–57
  low 10–11
    and overstudying 40
    and procrastination 24–25
    and relationship problems 108
self-sufficiency, and attraction 108
sex 126–155
  alcohol and 146, 165
  casual 128–129
  couples' problems 130–136
  experimenting with 135
  fantasies 137–138
  gender differences in 135–136
  inability to enjoy 133–134
  inexperience with 126–128
  performance difficulties 131–133
  protection 139–146
  readiness for 130
  revulsion to, in rape victims 160–161
  setting limits 129–130, 157
sexual abuse, childhood 103–104
sexual assault See rape
sexual harassment 156–157
sexual orientation 147–155
sexually transmitted diseases (STDs)
    144–145
  protection against 139, 145–146
  sources of help 216, 219
shyness
  causes of 13
  in groups 15–16
  overcoming 13
siblings
  mentally ill 98–99
  sexual abuse by 103–104
  younger, problems of 91
sleep habits 3–4
  and stress 85
smoking 176–177
social skills
  developing 13
  in groups 16
  tips for success 14
social workers 199
sodium valproate (Depakote) 60
solitude, and depression 53

sororities 16–17
sources of help
  on campus 213–215
  national 216–220
speaking
  in class 30–31
  deficits in 34
speech anxiety 71–72
stage fright 71–72
STDs See sexually transmitted
  diseases
stepfamilies 96
steroids 174
stress 80–85
  graduation and 210
  management of 81–82, 83–84
  and sexual difficulties 131
  signs of 81
  and smoking 176
Student Affairs personnel 214
studies 22–45
  class participation 30–31
  excessive efforts 40
  high school versus college 22
  memorization 28–29
  procrastination 24–26
  reading 26–27
  and stress 83
  time organization 22–24
  writing 29–30
study abroad 43–44
Study Skills Center 213
suicide 62–67
  causes of 62–63
  incidence of 64
  intervention for 64–66
  myths about 64
  sources of help 220
  thoughts about 3, 66–67
  warning signals 63
summary sheets 28, 32
support groups
  for adult children of alcoholics 103
  for gays and lesbians 151
  for survivors of sexual abuse 104
suppression 74
symbols, note-taking 28

syphilis 145
systematic desensitization 73

T

television, addiction to 179
test anxiety 31–32
test-taking strategies 32–33
time budget 24
  in test taking 32–33
time chunks 25
time off 44–45
  parental illness and 98
  from relationship 113
time organization 22–24
to-do list 23
tobacco 176–177
tranquilizers 85
transferring 41–42, 166
transitions
  to college life 1–2
  to work 204–206, 209–210

V

vacations
  parental divorce and 94
  visits home during 86–87
violence, in relationship 120–121
visualization
  and recall 29
  and relaxation 84
voyeurism 138–139

W

weight loss 183–184
withdrawal (contraceptive method) 141
women See female students
work
  first job 205–206
  school See studies
  transition to 204–206, 209–210
work-and-study combinations 82–83
worry habit 76–77
writing 29–30
  deficits 34

Y

year off 44–45